"From the murder of Abel by his brother Cain to the dissension between Joseph and his brothers, Paul Borgman weaves together biblical stories, previously seen as remnants, into a richly textured and provocative Genesis tapestry. Here humans embody belief and unbelief, flounder and thrive, each accompanied from start to finish by a relational God who loves them toward individual wholeness that promises healing for the world at large. Listening to texts particularly troublesome for women, Paul responds with exegesis so engaging of readers that it encourages further questions and prompts one to reread Genesis."

NANCY LINTON, *The Oregon Extension*

"This book I shared right away with my rabbi, my Jewish friends and colleagues. It is at once creative, enlightening and psychologically sophisticated. Borgman's enjoyable commentary offers astonishingly compelling narrative truths to unlock the giant riddles of Genesis. No longer is God 'inscrutable,' being a 'chosen people' an entitlement of indelible righteousness, or God's 'plan' mere arbitrary triumphal tribalism. And so, it illuminates an intrinsic coherence between contemporary Christian theology and the ethical relational striving informed by precursor truths known to the historical Jew Jesus."

STEVE NISENBAUM, *Ph.D., J.D., Department of Psychiatry, Massachusetts General Hospital and Harvard Medical School*

"Borgman has read widely and is well rooted in the scholarly literature. His goal, however, is to make sense of the text by asking the kinds of questions that are raised by readers who have not been tamed away from the shock and puzzlement of the text. The book will interest those who have a literary sensitivity and face a literature that is theologically thick but unfamiliar. Borgman gives easy access but does not compromise the unfamiliarity and does not 'explain' the thickness in an easy way. Readers are invited to hear as for the first time."

WALTER BRUEGGEMANN, *Columbia Theological Seminary, author of* Genesis *and* Theology of the Old Testament

"In this book Borgman reminds us that God seeks real relationship and friendship with self-interested humanity. Such a relationship often involves change for both parties—indeed, this is one of the key points of *Genesis: The Story We Haven't Heard*. These thoughts are pointers for understanding God and our own journey with him. This is a book well worth reading."

RUTH ANNE REESE, *Asbury Theological Seminary*

"In a prefatory note Paul Borgman remarks that Genesis has proved to be the most difficult book with which he and his literature classes have struggled over the years. If this strikes you as anomalous, then you are the one to read this book on Genesis. Borgman is a vastly astute and massively well-read critic. I have never read a book like this—and I am deeply bothered by some of it. I don't like my suppositions haled up for remorseless scrutiny. But I do like Borgman's lucid English prose, and his assiduity as a biblical scholar."

THOMAS HOWARD, *author of* Christ the Tiger *and* The Novels of Charles Williams

"Paul Borgman is an exciting and experienced teacher, and this book on Genesis—not your standard biblical commentary—comes from many years of dialogue in the classroom. It is a work that will prove interesting and useful both to laypersons and to college students. I highly recommend it."

JAMES S. ACKERMAN, *Indiana University, editor of* Literary Interpretations of Biblical Narrative, *author of* Teaching the Bible as Literature

"The subtitle of Paul Borgman's book signals the nature of his achievement, namely, the ability to look closely at an ancient text that seems elusive to a modern reader. The virtues of this beautifully written book include its willingness to wrestle with the baffling aspects of Genesis, its unobtrusive but conscientious attention to scholarship on Genesis, its systematic coverage of the entire book of Genesis, its unfolding of the richness of human experience to be found in Genesis, and the fresh slant provided by a literary approach to the text. Paul Borgman has lived closely with Genesis for twenty-five years. This book is a mature and triumphant sharing of what he has discovered."

LELAND RYKEN, *Wheaton College, coeditor of* A Complete Literary Guide to the Bible *and* Dictionary of Biblical Imagery

GENESIS

The Story
We Haven't
Heard

PAUL
BORGMAN

InterVarsity Press
Downers Grove, Illinois

InterVarsity Press
P.O. Box 1400, Downers Grove, IL 60515-1426
World Wide Web: www.ivpress.com
E-mail: mail@ivpress.com

InterVarsity Press® is the book-publishing division of InterVarsity Christian Fellowship/USA®, a
student movement active on campus at hundreds of universities, colleges and schools of nursing in the
United States of America, and a member movement of the International Fellowship of Evangelical
Students. For information about local and regional activities, write Public Relations Dept., InterVarsity
Christian Fellowship/USA, 6400 Schroeder Rd., P.O. Box 7895, Madison, WI 53707-7895.

Unless otherwise indicated, all Scripture quotations are taken from Genesis: Translation and
Commentary by Robert Alter. Copyright ©1996 by Robert Alter. Used by permission of W. W. Norton
& Company, Inc.

Excerpts from "Little Gidding" in Four Quartets, copyright 1942 by T. S. Eliot and renewed 1970 by
Esme Valerie Eliot, reprinted by permission of Harcourt, Inc., and Faber and Faber Ltd.

Cover illustration: Tate Gallery, London/Art Resource, NY

ISBN 0-8308-2655-6

Printed in the United States of America ∞

Library of Congress Cataloging-in-Publication Data

Borgman, Paul Carlton, 1940-
   Genesis: the story we haven't heard / Paul Borgman.
     p. cm.
   Includes bibliographical references (p.).
   ISBN 0-8308-2655-6 (paper: alk. paper)
    1. Bible. O.T. Genesis—Criticism, interpretation, etc. I. Title.
   BS1235.2 .B584 2001
   222'.1106—dc21

                                            2001024411

23 22 21 20 19 18 17 16 15 14 13 12 11 10 9 8 7 6 5 4 3 2 1

20 19 18 17 16 15 14 13 12 11 10 09 08 07 06 05 04 03 02 01

CONTENTS

IV. JOSEPH & FAMILY; JUDAH & TAMAR

Preface

I grew up as one of six brothers. Our two sisters, who emerged last, had trouble emerging at all. My twin and I and two brothers were all bunched in the middle, within only two years of age. Our two older brothers tried to keep the rest of us in check. We had the normal sibling rivalries and simmering disputes, which evolved into dinner-table conversations. Involving both parents, our dialogue nevertheless often verged on argument. Religious education only stoked the fires and added to the fun. A story from Genesis like Jacob's taking advantage of his famished older twin, swapping soup for birthright, intrigued me. About this and all sorts of things we talked each evening around that dinner table, failing sometimes to leave for a good while after dessert. From out of such squabbling and pleasure has grown this book, for which I thank my family.

I had the good fortune to get my Ph.D. in the art of stories, and then to go and talk about stories with very good students. They and I have sat in a family-like circle and talked, as if around a dinner table. Our conversation has always been very focused, on this text or that. For twenty-five years I have been exploring Genesis, one of the great and most complex literary masterpieces of the world. I didn't always think so. It seemed more like a loose collection of a few interesting stories and a lot of dull stuff in between that was either bizarre or made very little sense. Then my students and I began applying the discipline of understanding literary texts to the exploration of Genesis. From out of these classes has grown this book, for which I thank my students.

In graduate school we would sit around a long and glossy table and talk. Such conversation was called a "seminar." Since then, I have never stopped tuning in to what other scholars and lay-readers think, engaging them in an inaudible but very real conversation. About this present book I have carried on a dialogue, written or oral, with three Genesis scholars. Their insights have proven especially helpful. From out of our conversation has come important fine-tuning, for which I thank them by name: James Ackerman, Walter Brueggemann and Terence Fretheim.

Several colleagues have given me hours of careful reading and comment, for which I thank just a few: Gian Sandri and Greg Laughery, Swiss L'Abri; Doug Frank, Oregon Extension; and Marv Wilson, Elaine Phillips and Harold Heie, Gordon College.

And then there are the casual conversations. Why would anyone chat, in everyday settings, about something so long ago and so far away as Genesis? With three close friends especially I have reflected on what has become, for me, so riveting and transforming. From out of such conversations, also, has come this book, for which I thank Kelly Clark, Tom Howard, and Marsha, my wife.

FOR TWENTY-FIVE YEARS, MY COLLEGE STUDENTS
and I have struggled to understand the Genesis story.
Initially the characters, including God, have seemed
arbitrary in their actions and inscrutable in their
motives. These students are mostly English majors,
and I, a professor of English. We do well enough with
everything from Homer to Hemingway, including the
most inaccessible narratives of a William Faulkner or
a Saul Bellow. Of all the world's great literature,
however, we find Genesis the most difficult to
understand. Why should this be? I wish to explore that
question in this introduction, along with two others:
How might we hear better? and What is the Genesis
story all about?

INTRODUCTION

Why Haven't We Heard?

L ET'S REPLICATE A TYPICAL COLLEGE CLASS OF MOSTLY ENGLISH majors. With only a vague notion of Abraham's whole story, my students are asked to respond to the text's most memorable scene:

> And it happened after these things that God tested Abraham. And He said to him, "Abraham!" and he said, "Here I am." And He said, "Take, pray, your son, your only one, whom you love, Isaac, and go forth to the land of Moriah and offer him up as a burnt offering on one of the mountains which I shall say to you." (22:1-2)[1]

This is usually the most familiar episode in Genesis. Some students may have heard about Jacob's deceitful one-upmanship with older brother Esau, or Joseph's special coat of favor that helps earn him the murderous resentment of his brothers, or Cain's murderous refusal to be number two by killing the divinely favored Abel. But it's this scene

---

[1]Robert Alter, *Genesis: Translation and Commentary* (New York: W. W. Norton, 1996). Of all the good translations now available, I consider Alter's translation the most sensitive to the literary nuances of the text and, at the same time, the most readable. Scripture citations, unless otherwise noted, are by chapter and verse in Genesis from Alter's translation, not by page in Alter's volume; quotations from his commentary are cited as Alter, *Genesis*.

of relinquishing a son that registers most clearly for most students. How could God ask it? they wonder aloud. And how could Abraham do it, taking the three-day journey, building the altar, binding his son, and placing him on the altar? And raising the knife?

And I'll respond, "What has this scene got to do with anything else in the story?" They'll look at me as if I had asked how this episode exposes the secret of atomic energy. For these otherwise good readers of literature, this very basic question doesn't register because they don't think Genesis qualifies as great literature. Though religiously trained and usually devout, they assume the opposite, that this is plodding stuff, bits and pieces with no overall pattern or meaning. My question about how this scene connects with anything else in Abraham and Sarah's story never gains an answer because it arises out of a possibility my students haven't considered, that this is a coherent and unified drama. Meanwhile, they assume God to be inscrutable and all the more majestic for being so. Of course, a bits-and-pieces approach will yield nothing else but inscrutable characters who act apparently on this whim or that. A God who is understood by the reader, a God who is *not* inscrutable, requires a story that has coherence. A jumbled plot yields jangled characters. In their chunk-by-chunk approach, no chunk connected with another, my students are like most other readers over the past two hundred years, including scholars, sermonizers, and religious educators.

A popular writer, Karen Armstrong, for example, takes a "bits and pieces" approach, and concludes that "[God] is omnipotent but powerless to control humanity; omniscient but ignorant of human yearning; creative but a destroyer; benevolent but a killer; wise but arbitrary; just but partial and unfair."[2]

A brilliant literary scholar, in a well-known exploration of the sacrifice scene that we began with, makes the same essential mistake as my students and Armstrong. Erich Auerbach quotes the beginning of the episode, as I have done above, and asks, "Where are the two speakers [God and Abraham]? We are not told. The reader, however,

---

[2]Karen Armstrong, *In the Beginning: A New Interpretation of Genesis* (New York: Alfred A. Knopf, 1996), p. 117.

knows that they are not normally to be found together in one place on earth."[3]

But Abraham and God *have* been found together, speaking—if one is reading attentively and with the expectation of connectedness. There have been six prior visits between these two, Abraham and God. These six visits are, in key respects, very much like this seventh one. (We will explore these seven visits in chapters three through six.) Without noting the pattern of these prior visits between "the two speakers," we will be lost when approaching God's request for the letting go of a son. It will seem bizarre, an archaic voice out of the blue asking for the ridiculous. In fact, there is something wonderful in this last test for Abraham, as there is for God. These visits are like a dance between two partners, a dance that becomes more and more complex each time out on the floor. "All [is] fitted together in an almost symmetrically articulated architectonic structure," as Martin Buber notes about Genesis in general and the seven-visit structure of the Abraham-Sarah story in particular.[4] Overlooking such patterns of repetition that run through Genesis contributes to its being a story we haven't heard, a story whose God gets shaped by our own projections and biases rather than by the text.

Auerbach's image of God, for example, is a common projection. This God is inscrutably majestic and mysterious, a God who hasn't "told anything of his reasons for tempting Abraham so terribly." The reader, for Auerbach, is as clueless as Abraham: "nor have the deliberations in [God's] own heart been presented to us; unexpected and mysterious, [God] enters the scene."[5] If we fail to understand the request to relinquish a beloved son in its story-long context, the God who emerges is, indeed, an inscrutable God who keeps the divine counsel hidden from poor mortals who can only grovel in awe and with blind

---

[3]Erich Auerbach, *Mimesis: The Representation of Reality in Western Literature* (New York: Doubleday/Anchor, 1942), p. 7. Auerbach's comparison of this episode with a scene from Homer is wonderful, for all my misgivings, and I must credit his treatment as a major factor in awakening my interest in the serious exploration of biblical narrative.

[4]Martin Buber, "Abraham the Seer," in *On the Bible* (New York: Schocken, 1968), p. 25. Buber calls these seven visits the seven revelations of God, and discusses how common it is to overlook biblical narrative's artful design.

[5]Auerbach, *Mimesis*, p. 6.

obedience. It is completely misleading to insist as Auerbach does that
in this sacrifice scene "God . . . leaves his motives and his purpose
unexpressed."[6] An attentive reader will have come to understand quite
a bit about how God sees things and wants things, and most especially
in this seventh visit, the climax of the entire story.

   Along with almost all readers over the last two hundred years, my
students have approached this seemingly bizarre scene of requested
sacrifice as if it were an isolated episode. They assume that any possible ordering of these bits and pieces reflects only the demands of a
rigid chronology: now this happened, and after a few days or months
or years, that happened—as in the opening words of the story: *"And it
happened after these things* that God tested Abraham." The promise of
this guide is to help with finding the connections that provide theme
and character for Genesis—including the character of God. These connections are almost always by way of repeated elements: word plays
(*adam* is created from *adamah* in a creation account); or doubled episodes (Abraham risks his wife's chastity twice); or very large and complicated patterns of repeated features, like the seven visits. In
addition, there is a complicated parallelism, reversed in its repetitive
order. Called a "chiasm," this mirror-like repetitive device is used frequently throughout Genesis and in subsequent biblical narrative. *Webster's New World Dictionary* offers this example: "She went to Paris; to
New York went he." The fourth element parallels the first; the third
parallels the second. Even the seven visits have their chiastic aspect:
the seventh and last test parallels the first test (just as, above, "went
he" parallels "She went"); the sixth test parallels the second; the fifth
parallels the third; this leaves the fourth test by itself, at the chiasm's
"heart." Is this just surface glitter, aesthetic delight? No. Rather, the
most profound meanings of the narrative are disclosed in such repetitions, as we will see in chapter six. At the chiastic heart of the visits,
for example, Abraham is challenged not to fear. And that turns out to
be his underlying and most troubling problem, a normal but devastating response to primal fear, the original anxiety. Such fear, and the
normal human response to such insecurity, informs all of the stories

---

[6]Ibid., p. 8.

of Genesis. We haven't heard this story very well.

Pick up Genesis, and you'll probably experience what my students do—and what I felt for so long: a bump-along affair, bits and pieces. Contributing to this impression has been the work of biblical scholars. Their valuable efforts have focused on the textual history and the religious setting behind this or that chunk of the story. With little exception, the dynamics of the story as a whole have been sacrificed in favor of a quest for textual and religious origins. This huge enterprise of the past two hundred years has resulted in what one author has described as "the eclipse of biblical narrative."[7] Until very recently, most commentaries on the Bible have been influenced by this bits-and-pieces approach. Even Erich Auerbach, the literary critic already cited, starts from the biblical scholar's premise. He calls the sacrifice scene "a homogenous narrative produced by the so-called Elohist."[8] That is, the episode stands by itself as an isolated chunk, with its own author, the Elohist; it is essentially unconnected to the fabric of the whole. No clear picture of character can emerge without a continuous and connected action.

The eclipse or loss of the biblical narratives as whole stories has also come about for reasons only vaguely connected with biblical scholarship. Persons of faith often use bits of text as devotional prompts. This may work to some extent with a psalm or proverb, though even these have contexts and internal dynamics worth exploring. But such a dip-in-here, dip-in-there approach fails miserably with biblical narratives, systematically distorting their meaning—as is the case with any great literary text. In a similar manner, religious leaders use pieces of a story for sermons, homilies, or lessons. Often based on commentaries, such teaching or preaching can lead to a high degree of subjectivity. Bible study groups, similarly, often examine this or that chunk, missing the forest for the trees.

---

[7]Hans Frei, *The Eclipse of Biblical Narrative: A Study in Eighteenth and Nineteenth Century Hermeneutics* (New Haven: Yale University Press, 1974). For Frei, the "eclipse"—the hiding of the narratives in their realistic and history-like wholeness—resulted from the honest and remarkable efforts of historians to ferret out the actual literary sources of the text and the histories of the cults responsible for those sources.

[8]Auerbach, *Mimesis,* p. 5.

Each of these uses of Scripture may be of value in its own way, but all ignore the sophisticated and subtle ways in which this ancient Hebrew narrative weaves strands of story together into a coherent tapestry. We miss out, then, not only on the pleasure of truly great literature but also in our understanding of the work as genuinely sacred, as Scripture. Revelatory power is in the story. The text claims that its God is a God working things out historically in partnership with human beings. Humankind, as Abraham Joshua Heschel understands, "was given a share in His wisdom [and] is called to responsible living and to be a partner of God in the redemption of the world."[9] Genesis introduces us to this fundamental biblical insight about being "a partner of God in the redemption of the world." Genesis, as so much that follows in both Hebrew and Christian Scripture, is story, because only story can capture the dynamic interaction between humans learning to be partners and a God who calls and prods humankind toward partnership. By failing to understand a narrative like Genesis as a dramatic whole, we fail to get a full portrait of the biblical God and of the drama of relationship between God and these troubled mortals. When we view it as a unified drama, however, we find a dynamism of change—both human and divine.

Let's suppose, then, that we can move beyond these limited approaches to Genesis, reading it as a whole and letting the text present itself to us on its own terms. We still have the problem, however, of personal biases and points of view that cloud the text. Biases and presuppositions we have always with us, and they are a problem in getting a clear view of any text, just as preconceptions about a person can keep us from understanding that person's real story. With a sacred text like that of the Bible, the problem of predisposition and bias looms very large indeed. We orient our lives around our beliefs, after all, and so we may want to "fit" the biblical story to our prior beliefs (often given to us by our parents and mentors). My students—and I!—have a much smaller problem getting an accurate grasp of Homer's *Odyssey* partly because we have much less at stake person-

---

[9]Abraham Joshua Heschel, *God in Search of Man: A Philosophy of Judaism* (Northvale, N.J.: Jason Aronson, 1987), p. 66.

ally. Homer's view of the gods is interesting, but not unsettling; this is mostly just a wonderful tale of a hero adventuring home to wife and hearth. But with a text considered sacred to so many, the problem of being objective is much greater. Can we ever come to any text, or to another person, without ways of seeing already in place? The answer is *no*. But as I say to students, we need to work with our biases and our interpretive "lenses" by learning to recognize them. Only then can we understand whether our approach is adequate. Perhaps that text or other person can suggest, not only a reality other than our own, but a more appropriate way for us to see that reality in the first place. And why this effort to pay such careful attention to the other? The answer lies in the hope that the other—person, place, or text—may inform us, help us, shape us, sharpen us, stretch us.

In my approach to the Genesis story, then, I try to be as *objective* as possible, "not influenced by personal feelings or prejudice," as the dictionary has it. I wish to be "unbiased" and to present "an objective opinion."[10] Is this a hopelessly naive goal, as many of my contemporaries think? We can strain to hear well, surely. At best, we will end up with what the dictionary suggests as "an objective opinion." That is, objectivity always results in opinion, however well-founded. No one person or tradition can lay claim to Absolute Truth. Only God has access to such clear sight, such perfect hearing.

In trying to hear this Genesis story in its organic unity, I have also tried to take into account my own biases and predispositions. I cite two. Theologically, I trust in the reality of God as One. I think that I have discovered that God in Genesis. My sense that God is One, however, may have influenced my view that the Genesis story presents a unified portrait of God. You, the reader, must judge. Methodologically, I trust in the potential coherence of a given literary text. Perhaps I have foisted on Genesis my presupposition that a great text can be understood as many different parts, all connected and related to a whole. Maybe Genesis is not so unified as I have found it to be. On the other hand, maybe it is. What I offer, then, is "an objective opinion" that

---

[10]*Webster's New World Dictionary*, second college edition, 1970; fourth meaning offered for "objective."

must be examined by the reader with my book in one hand and Genesis in the other.

I am suggesting a humility before the text, an openness. Buber suggests that we haven't yet learned how to be truly open because we fail to understand the text on its own terms. We have failed to be objective, to recognize its unified "subtlety of design" and its texture as story:

> Scripture does not state its doctrine as doctrine but by telling a story, and without exceeding the limits set by the nature of a story. It uses the methods of story-telling to a degree, however, that world literature has not yet learned to use; and its cross references and interconnections, while noticeable, are so unobtrusive that a perfect attention is needed to grasp its intent—an attentiveness so perfect that it has not yet been fully achieved. Hence, it remains for us latecomers to point out the significance of what has hitherto been overlooked, neglected, insufficiently valued.[11]

Reading with what Buber calls perfect attention to the text's interconnections, we can get closer to the text and closer to a portrait of the Genesis God.

Without at least an honest stab at such objectivity, we will make what we want of this little episode or we will bend that little bit of narrative to fit our own agenda. We easily end up using the text, just as we can use persons, to bolster our own way of seeing the world and fitting comfortably into it. I am recommending humility before the text, as before another person. To the extent that I am objective in viewing another person, a colleague for example, to that extent I will see her and hear her for who she is, rather than understand her according to my own idealizations or demonizations of her. This is the true humility without which the text, or another person, can never touch us or shape us.

How Then Might We Hear?

Such attention as I am recommending is pleasurable, and profitable as well. Genesis is a narrative that relies on ancient story-telling techniques of repetition. Miss the repetition, miss the story—and any chance of objectivity. From echoing word sounds to parallelisms and doubled episodes, Genesis plays very seriously with the possibilities

---

[11]Buber, "Abraham the Seer," p. 30.

of repetition. Herein lies a buried treasure of meaning and disclosure of character, including God's.

A Chinese proverb can help us understand the genius of how this narrative works, and how we might get into it:

Tell me and I will forget.
Show me and I will remember.
Involve me and I will understand.

I want to involve the reader by helping to sort out the text's clues. This is how the story itself proceeds, by way of clues and silences. The biblical writer "will leave gaps for the reader to puzzle over—nonsequiturs, discontinuities, indeterminacies, multiple versions."[12] In trying to get at the genius of biblical narrative, Meir Sternberg uses the phrase "the drama of reading" in his subtitle. My students invariably come to experience their reading as drama: they get involved with the text, in putting it together. We will find no kindly Aesop telling fables with a moral punch line. Genesis refuses to *tell* us much—maybe because we would forget. There is almost never any narrator in the story to point things out, to hold our hand. It's the Genesis way of getting the reader involved, which makes perfect sense given the text's goal of getting the hearer involved with nothing less than the divine, with nothing shy of personal transformation.

Beyond engagement with the text, the second kind of involvement hits close to home. For many of my students through the years, involvement has to do with the story finally "grabbing them." They, and I, often come to experience a confirmation of what we have always longed for but had no words to express.

What, Then, Is the Story All About?

There is repetition, and there is change. Things stay the same, but then there are twists. What stays the same sets up the possibility for change. The Genesis story is about what repeats itself in human experience, but also about what can change, what needs to change.

---

[12]Meir Sternberg, *The Poetics of Biblical Narrative: Ideological Literature and the Drama of Reading* (Bloomington: Indiana University Press, 1987), p. 42.

God visits Abraham seven times, for example: the same thing, over and over, God challenging and promising, and Abraham responding. But this repetition makes change possible. What is never the same can't change, since there's nothing to change from. The challenges in each successive visit, for example, become more difficult, and at one point, in fact, become interior, presenting monumental challenges for change to the inner spirit. Of course, what this change suggests is a change in Abraham, a spirit-change that must inform external action but is not itself that action, and that's what the Genesis story is all about. How does Abraham change, and why must he change? What has God to do with that change, and for what ultimate purpose?

In Jacob's story, there are two pairs of wrestling scenes. These four episodes encompass the plot, just as the seven visits do in the story of Abraham, Sarah and Hagar. Jacob wrestles with God the first time, not literally, but by holding God to certain divine promises while holding God off with a conditional promise of his own. In the second struggle with God, Jacob literally wrestles with the divine, once again holding God to certain blessings. And he wins! But God wins, too—a "draw" of the highest order. Meanwhile, and intersecting with these repeated struggles with God, Jacob wrestles his brother Esau. The first time, he wrestles his elder twin out of birthright and blessing; the second time, he wrestles Esau into an acceptance of himself, Jacob, and into an acceptance of blessing that Jacob seems anxious to return. Both pairs of repeated wrestling scenes set things up for dramatic change—a profound change in Jacob's spirit that leads to an unthinkable but realistic resolution. Jacob's final successful wrestling with Esau is of one narrative piece with his successful striving with God. The meaning that emerges from this sophisticated plot intertwining proves crucial for the Genesis story as a whole.

Finally, in Joseph's story we find many examples of crucial repetitions, among them three descents. Three times Joseph goes down into a pit or pit-like place. As we would anticipate from the prior two narratives, this concluding story of Genesis reveals a repetitiveness that is all about change. Joseph must change, from the normal self-promoting way of being in the world to a superior way of providing for others.

Repetition and change, then, are a major narrative technique of the Genesis story, but in the technique is buried meaning about the very nature of human experience. What will emerge in this exploration of Genesis looks something like this:

☐ Changing divine direction and even decisions, God chooses would-be-partners to help implement the divine desire, which is blessing to all nations.

☐ These partners are ordinary human beings with normal dispositions toward self-aggrandizing choices.

☐ God works with the chosen ones, short of ever forcing their will, or hand, toward change.

☐ The chosen ones learn to choose better, and to work with God's will for blessing.

☐ This divine-human synergy brings blessing to otherwise troubled individuals, families and foreign peoples.

We begin now at the beginning, with the Genesis prologue. This introductory material concludes with the Babel builders, whose desire to make a name for themselves sums up all that is wrong about the human condition: our normal way of being in the world is a striving to be number one—or at least better than someone else! The prologue prepares us for the righting of what invariably goes so wrong within individuals, families, and the global community.

*IN THE BEGINNING, GOD CREATED HUMANS WHO
would choose freely, in the image of a God who
chooses freely. In the beginning, the self-promoting
choices of Adam and Eve are chief among the normal
and destructive ways of being in the world. The episode has little to do with conventional notions of forbidden fruit. Along with their son Cain, then Lamech
and the builders at Babel, our "First Couple" succumb
to the normal but insidious whisperings of the heart.
Pssst, goes the serpent. Wouldn't you like to be noticed
more? To be like that someone over there who is
greater? Like God, in fact? God doesn't force humans
to choose better. God so regrets the destructiveness of
human choice that nearly the entire race is erased.
But the new human race, beginning with Noah, also
fails. The failure of each "race" emphasizes what once
was. Where humans had been at ease with God, now
there is hiding. Where the human couple had enjoyed
a marriage in which neither partner was in authority
over the other, now the wife and husband reap the
whirlwind of their desire by experiencing the curse of
having the husband rule over the wife. What the prologue of Genesis points to is the need for something
new from both God and humankind if the individual
is to be made whole, marriages recovered, and peoples
of the earth blessed. Only with radical change of
what's normal will companionability be recovered
between human and human, and between human
and God.*

1

I WANT A NAME
FOR MYSELF
Genesis 1–11

MY LITERATURE STUDENTS HAVE NO PROBLEM GOING THROUGH the account of creation given in the opening chapter of Genesis, but they falter badly when they find a second creation account in the very next chapter, one that seems to contradict aspects of the first, and has its own peculiarities. The first creation story is familiar to them. It's clear and orderly, a prose poem with a wonderful refrain. Here's how it begins:

> When God began to create heaven and earth,
> and the earth then was welter and waste
> and darkness over the deep
> and God's breath hovering over the waters,
> God said, "Let there be light."
> And there was light. And God saw the light, that it was good. . . .
> And God called the light Day, and the darkness He called Night.
> And it was evening and it was morning, first day.
> (1:1-5, my line arrangement)

Everything is completely harmonious in this first creation account. Its poetry of phrasing comes through even in translation. Furthermore, each of the six days is like a separate stanza with a similar formula: God said, Let there be . . . and so it was . . . and God saw that it was good. God's six days of activity culminate in the human being.

And God created the human in his image,
    in the image of God He created him,
        male and female He created them. (1:27)

God blesses the humans, challenging them to procreate, and assigning to them a stewardship role over creation (no violence, of course—their diet, in fact, is to be vegetarian). Then we find a superlative added to the refrain: "And God saw all that He had done, and look, it was *very good*" (1:28-31, emphasis mine).

This far into the text, my students have no problem. They notice fairly easily—these are very good readers—that the first three days are paralleled with the second three days (such parallelism is a hallmark of Hebrew poetry). On the first day, Night is separated from Day; the fourth day, Night and Day reappear with Night receiving moon and stars, Day getting the sun. The second day is echoed by the fifth day: the sea-water and rain-water of day two get appropriate inhabitants on the fifth day, sea-life for the sea waters and rain-life, the birds, for the rain waters. Similarly, vegetable-life for land in day three gets its counterpart in day six—"crawling things and wild beasts" (1:25).

One Creation Account—and Then Another: Why?

Then comes a radically different perspective. My students wonder about the confusing order of events in a second version of creation, and what it all can mean:

On the day the LORD God made earth and heavens, no shrub of the field being yet on the earth and no plant of the field . . . then the LORD God fashioned the human, *[earthling from earth,]* and blew into his nostrils the breath of life, and the human became a living creature. . . . And the LORD God said, "It is not good for the human to be alone, I shall make him a sustainer beside him." And the LORD God fashioned from the soil each beast of the field and each fowl of the heavens and brought each to the human. (2:5, 7, 18-19)[1]

---

[1]Italicized portion suggested by W. G. Plaut. As Plaut points out, the Hebrew is a play on words, *adam* from *adamah*—the human being from earth (W. G. Plaut, ed., *The Torah: A Modern Commentary* [New York: Jewish Publication Society, 1981], p. 29).

How can it be, my students ask—as I still do!—that animals come on stage in this account only *after* the human has been fashioned and given life? And how can it be that we hear God saying, "it is *not* good"? This is God, some will insist, so how can it be "not good"?

I encourage the questions, suggesting that the biblical writer wants our engagement, our own "co-creating" efforts in having the story make sense. We have heard the refrain, for example, "It is good, it is good, it is very good," yet now we hear God's words, "It is not good." Tuned ears, as those of the original audience certainly would have been, could not have missed the importance of the "not good." And the text is clear enough: God steps back and views the scene, and decides that it is not good because the human creature is alone. This is fundamental, then, about human nature. Being alone: not good. So what, I ask, does God do about the companion problem? With only rare exception, the answer comes back, God makes Eve.

Wrong, I urge; look at the text again, and don't flinch. Let yourself be bothered. "And the LORD God said, 'It is not good for the human to be alone, I shall make him a sustainer beside him.' And the LORD God fashioned from the soil each beast of the field and each fowl of the heavens and brought each to the human" (2:18-19).

In puzzling over this animal business, my students become involved and excited. For a suitable companion, a sustainer beside him, God comes up with animals. The biblical text involves us by inviting us to consider the obvious dilemma. Yes, a dog can be a very good and loyal friend. But no, there's a reason why a dog—or a bear—*can't* be a true companion, a "best friend." It's right there in the Hebrew, which our translation captures: *ezer kenegdo*, sustainer-beside-him ("partner," NRSV). I always wait until one of my students, almost always timidly, wonders if maybe the animals-as-partners idea isn't intended—by God and the writer—to show that, well, a human can't "rule over" someone and at the same time be that someone's best and most ideal friend. That is, no matter how close a relationship is formed between hunter in pick-up truck and black lab beside him, the dog will ultimately be unsuitable as the man's *ezer kenegdo*, "sustainer-beside-him."[2]

God sees the problem, of course: "But for the human no sustainer beside him was found." Perhaps, argues Terence Fretheim, the human "does not accept what God presents [the animals]; God accepts the human decision and goes back to the drawing board."[3] In any case, "the LORD God cast a deep slumber on the human," and only then does the solitary and lonely human creature—up until now ambiguous in gender—become two separate and emphatically sexual creatures, male and female *(ish* and *ishah,* 2:21-23).[4] The most delicate and reciprocal friendship is created: husband and wife. They become "one flesh," so excellent is the fit. How better to express the meaning of *ezer kenegdo,* a power suitable or equal to, than to have animals be the first and delightful but finally inadequate companion for the lonely human? Human being for human being, a friendship based on reciprocity and complete mutuality. This dramatic focus of the second creation account is its "point"—a focus on what it means to be most fully human. Such a focus couldn't possibly have registered with such power if included within one comprehensive creation account. What does it mean to be human, then, to be created "in God's image?" The second account gets to the fundamentals: to be human, in God's image, is to not be alone. To be most fully human is

---

[2]After tales of marriage disappointments, stemming mostly from rivalry in "who rules," the late medievalist Geoffrey Chaucer concludes with a portrait of perfect marriage in which the husband vows to his wife "that never in all his life, by day or night, / would he take authoritarian role over her" because, as the generous and ideal host the Franklin argues, "There is one thing, sirs, I can safely say: / that those bound by love must obey each other / if they are to keep company long. / Love will not be constrained by mastery; / when mastery comes, the god of love at once beats his wings, and farewell—he is gone" (Geoffrey Chaucer, "The Franklin's Tale," in *The Canterbury Tales* [New York: Bantam, 1964], p. 297).

[3]Terence Fretheim, *Genesis,* in *The New Interpreter's Bible,* Vol. 1 (Nashville: Abingdon, 1994), p. 352.

[4]The Midrash (collected Jewish commentaries from the exile period to about 1200 C.E.) goes so far as to suggest that "Man and woman were originally undivided, i.e., Adam [translated "the human being"] was at first created bisexual, a hermaphrodite" (Plaut, *Torah,* p. 33). The biblical writer waits until the rib scene to unveil the gender terms for female and male *(ishah* and *ish,* 2:21-23). *"Ha adam,"* which usually denotes "the human" (or *adam,* "human"), acquires an exclusively male reference after the rib scene in 2:23. The proper name "Adam" does not appear until much later, perhaps as late as chapter 5.

to find as mutual a companion-spirit as possible.

Woman's curse, which follows almost immediately, reinforces the ideal of reciprocity and mutuality: "And for your man shall be your longing," God says, "[yet] he shall rule over you" (3:16). That no sort of one-way submission could be part of the Ideal Marriage is underscored by what is lost. The wife, now, must submit to the ruling husband. This is part of the "curse."

The focus of the second creation account is on the human condition, and on God's intimate connection with what the human most fundamentally needs. In the first creation account, the dramatic energy hovers around God, and on God's majestic control—speaking all into existence with poetic precision. This is *Elohim*, God of gods. The God of the second account has a different name and wears a different face. This is *Yahweh Elohim*—a more personal God. Yahweh comes down from on high to fashion the human and animals from mud, and then finds ways to accommodate human need. The one God in two aspects couldn't have been dramatized any more succinctly and powerfully than by having these two accounts of creation side by side.

Every once in a while, a perceptive student will note that the first account of creation ends in blessing—"And God blessed the seventh day and hallowed it, for on it He had ceased from all His work that He had done" (2:3)—while the second ends with human wrong-doing and curse. We look next at the dynamics of wrong-doing: What does it mean to be normal, and so wrong in that normalcy? The story of Eve's and Adam's wrong and destructive choice-making is the story of Everyman and Everywoman.[5]

Fear and Needing a Name (2:5−3:24)

Eve has everything survival requires, and then some. She is pictured by the biblical writer as inhabiting an environment so ecologically ideal that in no instance does life feed off the taking of life. Animals eat grass, not each other. Best of all possible harmonized worlds, life sus-

---

[5]From the beginning of this second account, as Michael Fishbane sees it, "'Man' here is 'everyman' " (Michael Fishbane, *Text and Texture: Close Readings of Selected Biblical Texts* [New York: Schocken, 1979], p. 18).

tains itself by furthering life: in the pruning of fruit trees and other vegetation, for example, our first parents are nourished. It is all so lovely. Work and play are one and the same thing, a tending to animals who are friends—certainly not for eating!—and to a garden habitat yielding occupation, nutrition and pleasure simultaneously. Woman and man enjoy each other as perfectly matched companions; theirs is a reciprocity of relationship reflecting the perfection of a God who said, "Let us make them in our image." There is, in such a world, no death. In the breezy time of day God comes for a walk in the garden (3:8). Here, God and the couple are apparently accustomed to visiting together in a state of easy harmony.

Somehow, into this world of no-fear and all-joy a very wise serpent has insinuated himself. The serpent discovers, and works to advantage, the most subtle and sophisticated anxiety known to the human species. This is the fear that, no matter how well endowed I am with all manner of personal and environmental good, it is not enough. Someone else has it better, or *is* better, an uneasiness that gnaws like an aching tooth.

The serpent wonders aloud, in front of Eve, about God's injunction against eating fruit from *any* tree in the garden (3:2). No, Eve answers, that's not what God forbids—just not to touch the *one* tree "in the midst of the garden" (3:3). Eve is clever in correcting the serpent—or so the serpent lets her think. Well, the serpent goes on, surely there is great and glorious possibility in that tree, the furthest thing from death! You shall live as a god! *That's* what God wishes to withhold from you, god-likeness (3:4-5). Perhaps Eve is already assured of her own cleverness by correcting the serpent's wily rhetorical "mistake" about *any* tree: might she now presume to correct God? Or perhaps it's more complicated, a matter of pride compensating for insecurity. Maybe she is not so assured, after all. She would have to be anxious about her state as just plain old Eve to be so tempted, to go beyond her creaturely limits as the woman God created her to be. Is Eve simply wanting greater knowledge, perhaps a knowing that is, in part, sexual? The text seems fairly clear: "The promise 'to be like God,'" as Claus Westermann understands, "is not something over and above knowledge, but describes it and all that it is capable of. *It is concerned with a divine and unbridled ability to master one's existence.*"[6] In her fear of being less than that someone over there—someone divine in mastering one's own exist-ence—she is just like any of us.

Take the fruit, the serpent urges in its last word, and "become as gods knowing good and evil." (3:5) Eve's yes to the serpent's deadly tease is a no to who she was created to be. Adam is led to the same choice by Eve. As happens later with Cain, and still later with the Babel-builders, Eve and Adam are exiled, cast out from their comfort zones. Attempting to secure significance of name and place, they end up diminished as human beings, and without a place of their own. And this first couple is "exiled" from each other, insofar as Eve and Adam experience a new gulf between them. "Your yearning shall be for your husband," God laments, "yet he will lord it over you" (3:16 JB). Does saying "God laments" stretch the point? I think not. This is a curse, a sad result of the prior human choice to be greedy, to go beyond the boundaries of who I am created to be, at my fullest potential—to be like that someone else I deem greater, to be like God. God wants blessing, and created us for the blessing of male and female, one flesh, companions with nothing of the rule-over implicit in human-animal relationships. God's curse is not God's ideal. The further question, of course, is, What are the characters who fill out the pages of Genesis to make of this ideal-turned-curse? Do they sim-ply live with the curse?

What God had wanted was a good world in which humans would find their highest good in a balanced partnership with one another, as in marriage, and also in partnership with God—taking care of the gar-den in which God delighted. In fact, God could be found "walking about in the garden in the evening breeze" (3:8), but after the disas-trous choice of Eve and Adam there is great loss. At the tranquil gar-den-hour when "the LORD God called to the human 'Where are you?'" there comes only the frightened voice of the human, "I was afraid . . . and I hid" (3:9-10). And now, the husband rules over the wife. What God had wanted for this most ideal of friendships between humans, an

---

[6]Claus Westermann, *Genesis 1-11: A Commentary*, trans. John J. Scullion, S.J. (Min-neapolis: Augsburg, 1984), p. 248, emphasis mine.

intimacy based on reciprocity, is severely diminished. *Where are you?* The textual point here is that of loss and fear, of hiding and being shut out from closeness with God. And between the married couple there can be no longer an easy and equal exchange of spirit. Companionability becomes problematic not only between human and God, but between human and human as well.

Free to choose, the humans choose to ignore God by trying to become like the gods—to be like that someone over there who is greater. Still, God is gracious, giving humans a responsibility "to till the soil from which he had been taken" (3:23)—just as before, when "the LORD God took the human and set him down in the garden of Eden to till it and watch it" (2:15). But now there will be "thorn and thistle," and "with pangs shall you eat from it all the days of your life" (3:17, 18). Eve and Adam have chosen what will be forever the normal choice of self-aggrandizement, and so bring curse upon themselves.

And from where do such normal choices arise? Is it not fear? Again: this is an anxiety that no matter how well endowed I am with all manner of personal and environmental good, it is not enough. A perceptive friend reflected, here, on this matter of fear:

> Sometimes we think there's an evil seed (usually labeled pride or rebelliousness) down deep in every person—that we're just unaccountably bad. It's not simply pride, but fear, felt helplessness, vulnerability. We humans are scared, underneath it all. We're not merely bad, prideful beings, but scared, cowering beings doing what we think we have to do to survive.[7]

Yes. I want a name for myself, but not for anything frivolous: it's a matter often of life over against death—the fear of death, of not counting, of no name, no significance.

From their fear-based choice to be more than they were created to be, Adam and Eve are exiled from the Ideal State, just as the later people of God, the Israelites, will experience their own exile from the Land of Promise, where they will rehearse the details of this first loss, this first exile. Is exile forever? Is there never to be a return to the ideal intimacies and pleasures of Eden, and to the land of promise?

---

[7]Doug Frank, in a letter of response to this chapter and later chapters, April 25, 2000.

I Refuse to Be Number Two (4:1-22)

Adam and Eve have two sons, but one kills the other, sounding a note we have heard ringing ever since. Cain does lethal mischief to Abel because the younger brother has taken over as "number one." Cain has been reduced, he thinks, to number two standing, since God has favored younger brother Abel. Being displaced proves intolerable for Cain.

The universality and seriousness of the mischief and its occurrence so early in the Bible's first book have given this very short tale a prominent place among the best known classics of literature. However little my students may know about biblical or world literature, hardly any haven't heard about Cain's murder of Abel. Even after a careful reading, however, most students remain hazy about its dramatic focus. The story is not about God's obvious favoritism or what was wrong with Cain's gift.

Immediately after being given notice of their birth, we read that "Abel became a herder of sheep while Cain was a tiller of the soil" (4:1). Neither vocation is stated as superior to the other. Cain the farmer brings a gift of farm goods to his heavenly parent. Similarly, Abel the younger brother, a herdsman, brings a gift from the herd to God. The heavenly parent likes Abel's gift, but not Cain's. We don't know why this is so, except possibly for a detail not dwelt on by the story, that Abel brought "from the choice firstlings of his flock," while Cain "brought from the fruit of the soil" (4:3-4). Was there old fruit or not-yet-ripened vegetable in Cain's cornucopia? Passing over any possible interest in why God favors Abel's offering, the story moves on quickly, as the reader should.[8] The dramatic focus emerges: an exploration of Cain's response to rejection, and God's response to the depressed Cain.

---

[8]Claus Westermann has it right: "The point of departure is equality; both have the means of subsistence in the division of labor. Both recognize the giver in their gifts and therefore both are linked with the power which is the source of blessing. Now inequality enters in; it has its origin in the regard of God. Blessing or its absence depends on the regard of God. It is a misunderstanding of the real meaning to look for the reason for the inequality of God's regard. The narrator wants to say that in the last analysis there is something inexplicable in the origin of this inequality. It does not consist in application, in attitude or in any circumstance that one can control. When such inequality between equals arises, it rests on a decision that is beyond human manipulation. The reason why God regards Abel's sacrifice and not Cain's must remain without explanation. And the narrator wants to make clear that this is one of the decisive motifs for conflict wherever there are brothers" (Westermann, *Genesis 1-11*, p. 297).

Cain was very incensed, and his face fell. And the LORD said to Cain,

"Why are you incensed,
   and why is your face fallen?
For whether you offer well,
   or whether you do not,
at the tent flap sin crouches
and for you is its longing
      but you will rule over it." (4:5-7)

The question is rhetorical. In effect, God is asking, "Why do you let the past affect your present?" What follows is a bit of reality therapy: "Live in the present; do well, and you will be OK—guaranteed, because I God promise it." What could be more clear, more reassuring? But God senses the depth of Cain's hurt, and his need for affirmation: "If you dwell in the past and do not do well, be on your guard—there lurks a horror that you must control, lest it consume you." That is, Cain has choices. He is not doomed to be second rate in God's eyes nor in his own. To be declared OK by God is to be OK, period. But the ball is in his court. What will he do? He's had nothing less than a divine coach. This encouragement from God, and the responsibility given Cain to choose right or wrong, are the heart of the little drama, its focus.

"Cain's reaction is normal and justified," as Claus Westermann understands; "without reason he is disadvantaged and rejected. His outburst and his sullenness are the corresponding reactions." Alter translates God's words here as "For whether you offer well, / or whether you do not," but Westermann's translation fits the context better: "if you conduct yourself correctly (if you do well), then there is 'lifting up' (of the countenance)."[9] That is, all depends on Cain's attitude. He can lift up his face (again) if he does well. The note of warning will therefore make clear to Cain that it depends on him. The warning points to the alternative: "If you do not do well . . ."

Cain's need is the universal and normal desire to be accepted, which so often translates into being better than at least one other person—in order to be noticed. In Cain's eyes, Abel seems to have been viewed as better than he by no less a one than God. Solution? Destroy

---

[9]Ibid., pp. 298-99.

number one, and move up. Abel is killed by Cain. Such a need is vora-
cious, all-consuming, the "beast" at Cain's tent door—just as it became
for Eve in her grasping after the promised superiority. Eve has no one
better than she, except God. Be, then, like God! As in Eve's case, Cain
is presented with a choice. We choose, most of us and almost always,
from that deep need to be accepted, to be OK, to be, at least in our little corner, the Best.

How far will this freedom be allowed to go? Will God allow Cain's
choice to murder Abel? Will Adam and Eve then need to live out their
days with the untimely death of their son hanging over them? Do they
not have the right, or at least the reason, to ask, "Can't God *do* something?" God does what God can do: before the deed, God comes to Cain
with whispers of good counsel and comfort.

Eve, Adam and their son Cain share a radical need to be noticed
that leads to arrogance and defiant action. Wrongdoing becomes a
violation of their own beings, and they are cursed with the logical
consequences of their own preening. Far from being like a god, Eve
labors in giving birth; from being the reciprocal female counterpart
to male, created in God's image (1:27), Eve now suffers her husband's
rule. Now Cain loses his farmland and any comfort he could have
enjoyed in his family relationships. Now he will be everyone's
stranger, not noticed by anyone except as a possible object for harm.
"Now that You have driven me this day from the soil," Cain com-
plains to God, "and I must hide from Your presence, I shall be a restless wanderer on the earth and whoever finds me will kill me" (4:14).
God puts a mark on Cain to prevent anyone's killing him (4:15), but
Cain will suffer that which he brought on himself. Demanding to be
noticed by God, he will have to hide from the divine presence; insisting on being accepted to the point of killing, he will wander without
any acceptance at all, an alien.

We all want to be accepted, and perhaps there's nothing wrong with
that. It seems innocuous enough. But the need for acceptance is on a spec-
trum that includes the desire to be noticed, to be thanked, to be approved
of, to be considered really important, to be thought of as better than
another . . . and so forth. Rather than being at peace with thinking and
doing the right thing for its own sake, for its own intrinsic goodness, we

flounder in thinking and doing those things which others will credit us for, starting with simple acceptance and ending with the lust to be number one. And exactly here is where we run into Lamech, a far worse case of the same emotional-spiritual disease suffered by Eve, Adam, and Cain. He serves as an exclamation point to the plight of Eve and Cain in his foolish and murderous need to be number one, king of the hill.

King of the Hill—Right, My Queens? (4:23-24)

Lamech's tale is a tiny one, powerful in its brevity.

> Adah and Zillah, O hearken [to] my voice,
> You wives of Lamech, give ear to my speech.
> For a man have I slain for my wound,
> a boy for my bruising.
> For sevenfold Cain is avenged,
> and Lamech seventy and seven. (4:23-24)

Here's a grown man calling to his wives in order to announce that he is a very superior being. Lamech thinks to enhance his standing, somehow, by refining his boast—not just has he slain a man in revenge for a wound, but a "mere boy" for only a bruise. Even his speech is grand, another example of poetic parallelism.[10]

Cain killed to regain standing, perversely, with God: he alone of the two brothers is left to be noticed by the Gift-Receiver. Revenge for any who would murder Cain is established by no less than God, who warns folks off by providing Cain a mark. Revenge will be sevenfold. Things are deteriorating precipitously since the expulsion from Eden. Lamech kills to reinforce standing with his wives, not God; he himself establishes guidelines for revenge should he ever come to harm. The exaggerated brutality of his threat—seventy and seven times as a revenge factor—comports with the brutishness of his self-acclaimed actions and the buffoonery of his chest-pounding.

---

[10]Robert Alter notes that "this poem follows the parallelistic pattern of biblical verse with exemplary rigor. . . . [T]here is a pronounced tendency in the poetry to intensify semantic material as it is repeated in approximate synonymity. Perhaps, then, what Lamech is saying (quite barbarically) is that not only has he killed a man for wounding him, he has not hesitated to kill a mere boy for hurting him" (Genesis: Translation and Commentary [New York: W. W. Norton, 1996], p. 20).

God Regrets—Then Starts Afresh

What could God have expected, giving humans their will? It seems the results couldn't have been much worse. In fact, "the LORD regretted having made the human on earth and was grieved to the heart." (6:6). The solution is drastic: "I will wipe out the human race I created from the face of the earth," says the Lord, "for I regret that I have made them" (6:7). So God changes the divine mind about the whole thing. All will be destroyed, back to square one. But wait: God notices that Noah is righteous, and changes direction once again, deciding to start over with another human race and all life itself (6:8-13). A flood wipes the slate clean, except for Noah's family and selected animal specimens.

From the start of this second creation there is new promise but new despair. Once again we hear the same basic blessing given to the original humans:

> Be fruitful and multiply and fill the earth. And the dread and fear of you shall be upon all the beasts of the field and all the fowl of the heavens, in all that crawls on the ground and in all the fish of the sea. In your hand they are given. All stirring things that are alive, yours shall be for food, like the green plants. . . . As for you, be fruitful and multiply, swarm through the earth, and hold sway over it. (9:1-7)

So it once was, with nearly the same words and phrasing: "Be fruitful and multiply and fill the earth and conquer it, and hold sway over the fish of the sea and the fowl of the heavens and every beast that crawls upon the earth" (1:28). But the differences between the first and second blessings are momentous. In the first, only plant life was for eating; in the second—a divine concession?—flesh can be eaten as well. In the first blessing as in the second, humans are to hold sway over all animal life, which similarity only accentuates the dismaying difference, that after Noah there will be "the dread and fear of you" upon all animals.

If it is the case that God makes a concession to humankind, granting that yes, now humans will eat and terrorize those who have been their animal friends, what might explain such a divine "caving in" to human frailty? Perhaps God's accompanying new promise can help to explain a promise repeated a bit later as a covenant with the rainbow

as sign: "I will not again damn the soil on humankind's score," says
God. "For the devisings of the human heart are evil from youth. And I
will not again strike down all living things as I did" (8:21; 9:12-17). God
understands the normal impulses and choices that dominate everyday
life—that "the devisings of the human heart are evil from youth." But
what changes about God, starting with Abraham and Sarah, is God's
refusal to accept such a normal state of human affairs. God will work
with humankind to reverse both "normal" and its disastrous consequences, consequences that we recognize as curses.

Noah promptly gets drunk "and expose[s] himself within his tent"
which leads to further curse, rather than blessing (9:20-25). Such a bad
start to a second human race does not bode well, and after a second
genealogy of the new nations that "branched out on the earth after the
Flood" (10:32), we find a tale at the end of the prologue that indicates
that companionability between human and human is utterly lost,
along with the ease of communion between human and God.

Let Us Make a Name for Ourselves!

> Come, let us build us a city and a tower with its top in the heavens, that
> we may make us a name, lest we be scattered over all the earth. (11:4)

The nations that "branched out on the earth after the Flood" have one
language (10:32, 11:1). They all migrate east to a plain where they
make bricks and build a city in order, as they themselves put it, "that
we may make us a name" (11:1-4). They are afraid. What is their fear of
being "scattered over all the earth"? It is said that in numbers there is
safety. The bigger your own tribe, the better the athletes in your high
school—*voilà*, the less threat from another tribe, another high school.
Babel is a neighborhood like any, full of Cains and Lamechs, Eves and
Adams—a grouping together of essentially anxious individuals. The
final solution? Build the biggest, the something-really-tall, "a tower
with its top in the heavens." The name of their city would become
great, surely, and their security assured. But as it was with Eve, Adam,
Cain and Lamech, the chaos resulting from Babel's presumptuous
choice is precisely the chaos feared in the first place, only greater.
Afraid of being scattered and vulnerable? Well then, says God, be

scattered indeed, worldwide—and alienated as well by garbled language. "Therefore [the city] was called Babel, because there the LORD confused the language of all the earth" (11:9).

This little story concludes the descent from Edenic paradise begun with the disastrous choice of Eve and Adam to change places with someone greater than they. By the time of Babel, humankind is in an earthly hell. It is all, indeed, a "paradise lost."

God had shown an intimate side with *ha adam*, the human being, in remedying the aloneness, and later in trying to speak the greatly depressed Cain out of his anger and deep funk. But this God has progressively retreated from any warm regard for the human scene—or so it seems. First, divine regret that anything was created in the first place, followed by world-wide devastation (6:6-7). And now, divine compassion is replaced by divine sarcasm and dispatch. "Come, let us," say the Babel folks, "let us build us a city and a tower with its top in the heavens, *that we may make us a name*, lest we be scattered over all the earth." "Come, let us . . ." mimics a displeased God, then zap, the people can't understand each other, and are scattered all over the earth. So much for a name—and so much for challenging God's command.

Within a short time, for these Babel folks, their fearful scrambling after a name has led to the utter frustration of their efforts: "And the LORD said, 'As one people with one language for all, if this is what they have begun to do, nothing they plot will elude them. Come, let us go down and baffle their language there so that they will not understand each other's language'" (11:6-7). And that's that. No visit, no conversation, no effort on God's part other than an ironic and overwhelming tit-for-tat. You want a name? You'll not even understand each other's words. You want to gather in a city and be a powerful tribe? Be scattered, lost. It sounds harsh, with no chance for interaction with the human, nor divine hope for or encouragement of human transformation.

The Babel story is the last of four snapshots in the prologue of those who sought in some way to achieve significance rather than usefulness, self-promotion rather than stewardly service. Each desired a name: Eve and Adam; Cain; Lamech; the Babel builders. The implicit fear or insecurity behind Babel's arrogance is present in all four. It will be up to God, beginning with Abraham and Sarah, to change direction in establishing partnership with the human. And it will be up to the human—with God's mentoring help—to say yes to change that takes years and years. In the Genesis prologue, God acted unilaterally in promising Noah and his seed that never again would the earth and inhabitants be destroyed by flood (9:11). But starting with Abraham, such covenant-making changes drastically, right from the start. God challenges Abraham to leave home, following with promises that appear contingent on Abraham's actually leaving home! What is implicitly a mutual responsibility—with God always initiating and helping and waiting, of course—becomes explicit by the end of Abraham and Sarah's story. Now, God won't change things without human cooperation, and humans can't change without divine assistance. Only when choosing to grow in partnership with God will the human recover lost companionability with both God and fellow human. That is God's fervent wish.

Noah was born nearly blameless, for all we know. Abraham, the main protagonist of the first major narrative, has to work toward blamelessness through a difficult twenty-five years. "Be blameless," God has to challenge Abraham, in the fifth of their seven visits together (17:1). Noah and Abraham are very much the same: the biblical writer distinguishes each by paralleled terms, "righteousness," "wholeness," and "walking with God." The similarity accentuates their striking difference.

Noah is the prologue's odd man out—as unnatural in his goodness as the others are normal in their self-destructiveness. We'll never know about Noah, about how he came to be so good. God simply finds him that way, noticing him at the eleventh hour as a possibility for starting the human race all over again (6:6-8). But in Abraham, God finds an ordinary man who needs to be taught a better than normal way of going about business. As Martin Buber points out, "God seems to command Abraham to become that which Noah was by nature!" What the biblical writer emphasizes, as Buber points out, is this: "with Abraham what matters is not his character as God finds it, so to speak, but what he does, and what he becomes."[11]

---

[11]Martin Buber, "Abraham the Seer," in *On the Bible* (New York: Schocken, 1968), p. 33.

   Genesis is a story that discloses everyday matters of the heart we would
rather not see. We are adept at keeping these secrets hidden, even from our-
selves. This is the dark reality of Genesis, the heart of Eve and Adam, Cain,
Lamech, the Babel builders; of Abraham, Sarah, Hagar, Jacob, Rachel,
Leah, Judah and Joseph. For each of these, there is striving for position in
the world, rather than for usefulness. However subtly, each seeks to pro-
mote his or her own name, though at the expense of others' well-being.
Families nearly self-destruct with subtle or shocking rivalries and one-
upmanship. Such darkness is always threatening a fragile hope, based on
the longing of God for blessing. Fragile, yes: for God's will turns out to rest
in large measure on the transformation of human will, and on a resulting
partnership between God and human. The darkness and the hope come
into full view with Abraham and Sarah, in the Bible's first major narrative.
At times, their story reads a bit like the evening news with all its sugges-
tions of real life and disjointed sorrow. But it's also a story of change: how
much Abraham must change and does change, and how things change for
Sarah, and even how God changes. We look next at the earthy trials that
Abraham and Sarah fail. They are ordinary persons making normal
choices. In subsequent chapters, we will explore the interweaving of divine
trials, and how it is that Abraham and Sarah mature toward the ultimate
goal of bringing blessing to all peoples.

A FEW SHORT LINES INTO THE STORY, AND HUN-
dreds of miles south of his homeland, Abram hazards
his wife's sexual chastity. Late in the story, it happens
again. Both times, Abram has proposed to Sarai that
she pass as his "sister." That way, the supposedly
rapacious and murderous foreigners can possess her
sexually without having to kill Abram first (there's no
curse for sleeping with a brother's sister as there is for
sleeping with a husband's wife). Both times, the ruse
works—the men get Sarai, and Abram lives and pros-
pers. What Abram does in these paralleled episodes
reflects normal human attitude and action, the desire
for self-preservation and self-promotion—a "name"—at
another's expense. Sarai is no better. Between the paralleled incidents of her husband's abuse, Sarai herself
terrorizes a slavegirl, Hagar. A similar episode comes
later. The first time, Hagar returns Sarai's one-upmanship by belittling her mistress, while Abram washes
his hands of Sarai's brutish actions and their disastrous consequences. Something changes for the good,
however, in the second episode of Sarai's harshness, as
is the case in the second instance of Abram's abuse of
Sarai. All the time these everyday trials have been
going on, God has been testing Abram—and making
promises to him, and finally to his wife. In following
chapters we will explore the weaving together of divine
and earthly trials, and how God's change of demeanor
connects with human transformation. Right now, we
take a look at two sets of repeated episodes, in which
everyday folks make ordinary choices of the worst
sort.

2

ORDINARY CHOICES
OF THE WORST SORT

F ROM THE VERY START, GOD HAS PROMISED ABRAM A LIFE AND NAME.
His offspring will become a great nation:

> And the LORD said to Abram, "Go forth from your land and your birth-
> place and your father's house to the land I will show you. And I will
> make you a great nation and I will bless you and *make your name great*,
> and you shall be a blessing. And I will bless those who bless you, and
> those who damn you I will curse, and all the clans of the earth through
> you shall be blessed." (12:1-3, emphasis mine)

Abram proves to be so anxious about this promised name that he
immediately chooses to protect it and promote it at his wife's expense.
With his father and family, Abram had left his homeland in Ur—his
"birthplace" (Persian Gulf area)—and traveled to Haran (Syria), where
his father died; now he leaves Haran, his father's new homeland, and
stops in "the land of Canaan" (Palestine). This land, says God, will
belong to Abram's offspring (12:5, 7).

So far, so good. Abram has responded well to God's challenge: relinquish land and birthplace and father's house. Almost immediately,
however—ten verses into the story—there is famine, and Abram, on
his own initiative, moves down to Egypt with his family and holdings.

Hazarding Sarai's Chastity: The First Time (12:10-20)

In Egypt, Abram approaches Sarai with a proposition my students and I find nearly beyond thought:

> "Look, I know you are a beautiful woman, and so when the Egyptians see you and say, 'She's his wife,' they will kill me while you they will let live. Say, please, that you are my sister, so that it will go well with me on your account and I shall stay alive because of you." (12:11-13)

This is the plot's single greatest complication, the most serious threat to God's intentions of making Abram and Sarai a blessing to all nations through offspring and land. The outcome is just as Abram, apparently, had imagined:

> And it happened, when Abram came into Egypt that the Egyptians saw the woman was very beautiful. And Pharaoh's courtiers saw her and praised her to Pharaoh, and the woman was taken into Pharaoh's house. (12:14-15)

As Abram had hoped, he is not only saved, but it "goes well" with him. He is given the gifts appropriate for yielding such a lovely sister for sexual purposes. My students, many of whom have at least heard of Abram, are astonished. A biblical scholar phrases the obvious question for all of us: "What's going on here? Abram, with a mastery of understatement, requests that Sarai avail herself sexually to the male population of Egypt 'that it may go well with me because of you.'"[1]

Another good reader, Walter Brueggemann, comments: "This episode in Egypt presents Abram as an anxious man, a man of unfaith. He is ready to secure his own survival because at this point he does not trust exclusively in the promise."[2] Abram's wife becomes another man's wife. Becoming a wife, in these narratives, always implies sexual relations. The curse for sexual relations, in fact, comes true: "And the LORD afflicted Pharaoh and his household with terrible plagues because of Sarai, the wife of Abram." Instead of bringing blessing to all nations, Abram has brought curse. "What is this you have done to me?" the wronged monarch fulminates: "Why did you not tell me she was

---

[1]Dana Nolan Fewell, "Divine Calls, Human Responses: Another Look at Abram and Sarai," *Perkins Journal* 41 (1988): 14-15.

[2]Walter Brueggemann, *Genesis* (Atlanta: John Knox Press, 1982), p. 126.

your wife? Why did you say, 'She's *my sister,*' so that I took her to me as *wife?* Now, here is *your wife.* Take her and get out!" (12:17-19, emphasis mine). In Pharaoh's sputtering, Abram is hit in staccato fashion regarding his deceitful confusion between wife and sister. (Later, Abram will claim that Sarai is a half-sister.)

Perhaps Abram was counting on God to intervene on Sarai's behalf. If so, he conveniently found it easier to trust God for his wife's fate rather than for his own. It certainly seems that Abram knew what he was doing. "To say that she is his sister is to invite [sexual] overtures or more from those who hear," as George Coats puts it.[3] Among the excuses made on Abram's behalf is that he is crazed by fear, and simply overlooks the obvious implications regarding Sarai's certain fate. "He does not raise the possibility with her that one of the Egyptians will take her as wife," Victor Hamilton notes. "Maybe that possibility never entered his mind, if for no other reason than that his concern is with his own fate, not Sarai's."[4] The possibility never entered his mind? To my students and me, this seems quite a stretch.

What do we know of Sarai, of how she felt? There is nothing in the text for a long while. Does this suggest her silent acquiescence? Is Sarai living out the shattered ideal of marriage predicted for Eve: "Your yearning shall be for your husband, yet he will lord it over you" (3:16 JB)? As we see next, when Sarai finally speaks, she thunders.

Sarai, Hagar and Trouble: The First Time (16:1-16)

God has promised Abram seed, which the reader might assume is to come through both Abram *and* Sarai, though we have no record so far of Sarai being named as the mother. She herself could have wondered, and so she takes action. "Look, pray," Sarai says to her husband, "the LORD has kept me from bearing children. Pray, come to bed with my slavegirl. Perhaps I shall be built up through her" (16:2). Better to "be built up" by means of a slavegirl, Sarai figures, than not to count at all

---

[3]George W. Coats, *Genesis, with an Introduction to Narrative Literature* (Grand Rapids, Mich.: Eerdmans, 1983), p. 111.
[4]Victor P. Hamilton, *The Book of Genesis 1-17* (Grand Rapids, Mich.: Eerdmans, 1990), pp. 380–81.

in anybody's eyes.[5] For a wife in Sarai's day, being barren was a terrible fate, a loss of any significance—as this story and all the stories of Genesis bear out. Concubines were a common cure. Never mind that the slavegirl Hagar will have to forfeit her child to her master and mistress. Sarai knows that it's all perfectly legal. So Abram sleeps with Hagar, who becomes pregnant. But Sarai "saw that [Hagar] had conceived and her mistress seemed slight in her eyes" (16:4). Sarai, who wanted to be built up by way of having offspring, feels torn down. "Her mistress seemed slight in her eyes," or, as other translations have it, Sarai is treated with contempt (NRSV); she is despised by Hagar (NIV). What Abram did to Sarai in Egypt, what Cain did to Abel, what Lamech did to the little boy—the sad tale is repeated here, as it will be again and again in Genesis: "Hagar somehow diminishes Sarai's status," as Terence Fretheim observes.[6] Sarai is furious: "This outrage against me is because of you!" she exclaims to Abram. "I became slight in her eyes. Let the LORD judge between you and me!" (16:5).

The dramatic spotlight shifts for an important moment to the berated husband. How will Abram respond to these seemingly outrageous charges, and to the implicit threat against the future mother of his child? "Look," Abram says, "your slavegirl is in your hands. Do to her whatever you think right" (16:6). Was it easiest for Abram, of all the choices open to him, to wash his hands of the mess, preserving the peace at whatever cost? Has he stopped to consider that the "slavegirl" is bearing his child? He must know the reasonable consequences: Sarai "harassed [Hagar] and she fled from her."

To Sarai, Hagar counts for nothing. In fact, Hagar is not even deserving of being named by Sarai—or by Abram for that matter. The exchange between wife and husband about the "slavegirl" is framed by Hagar's being named, first by the narrator ("And Sarai Abram's wife took Hagar . . . and she gave her to Abram her husband as wife," 16:3) and afterward by God ("And the LORD's messenger found her. . . . And

---

[5]Everett Fox translates the verb "built-up-with-sons" with this explanation: "Heb[rew] *Ibbane,* a play on *bano* (build) and *ben* (son)" (*The Five Books of Moses* [New York: Schocken, 1995], p. 68).
[6]Terence Fretheim, *Genesis,* in *The New Interpreter's Bible,* Vol. 1 (Nashville: Abingdon, 1994), p. 452.

he said, 'Hagar,'" 16:7-8). Belittling the one by whom she felt belittled, Sarai succeeds in ridding herself of the threat. Passively, Abram pursues for himself the path of least resistance and personal distress.

But God will not tolerate Hagar's being forced out into the wilderness to die. Always, from creation on through to the end of Genesis, God is emphatically for life over death, and blessing over oppression. "And the LORD's messenger found her by a spring of water in the wilderness. . . . And he said, 'Hagar, slavegirl of Sarai! Where have you come from and where are you going?' " (16:7-8). As with Cain, God is the great reality therapist: God seems to be giving Hagar the chance to reflect, to think it through and come up with her own ideal solution, under the circumstances. The God of Genesis will not provide Hagar with a magic-carpet ride from this death-dealing wilderness back home to Egypt. So Hagar faces the realistic options. Where she has come from may be intolerable, but where she is going—out into this wilderness alone, pregnant—is certain death. "Return to your mistress," says God, "and suffer harassment at her hand" (16:9). God won't force Sarai to be nice to Hagar: Sarai must choose, with God's help, to do the right thing. It's in her hands. While God won't, or by divine fiat can't, snap a divine finger and change the home environment from which Hagar has fled, God does answer the second question—"where are you going?"—by promising Hagar a future. Bear the present, God says, for you will walk into a promising future:

> Look, you have conceived and will bear a son
>   and you will call his name Ishmael,
>   for the LORD has heeded your suffering.
> And he will be a wild ass of a man—
>   his hand against all, the hand of all against him,
>   he will encamp in despite of all his kin. (16:11-12)

Return, says God, but know that you will be blessed by me with seed— "for the LORD has heeded your suffering." In these Genesis narratives, God is willing to wait, to help in working things out for the best. Hagar is sent back, for now, to where there will be physical safety—though not without more emotional bludgeoning.

"And she called the name of the LORD who had addressed her, 'El-roi' "—*The-God-Who-Sees-Me* (16:13). Hagar names God, who has called her by name. For Hagar, it is enough. She has had an encounter with God that even her mistress Sarai hasn't had. She gets to name God, which neither her mistress nor her master have been privileged to do. God has done well by Hagar, and Hagar returns the favor by addressing God with a new name. By contrast, we understand that Sarai and Abram have done poorly. Neither Sarai nor Abram have "seen" this one who, to them, is a nameless slavegirl. But God has seen her, and named her. It all seems quite sad, and quite normal.

In the repeated instance of this messy domestic triangle, to be taken up in a moment, glimmers of change begin to appear. The same suggestion of hopeful change is present in the paralleled episode of Abram's scheming at Sarai's expense, which we look at next. By noting the similarities, differences emerge in striking fashion. The differences indicate change within characters, and change in characters' circumstances.

Hazarding Sarah's Chastity: The Second Time (20:1-18)

Hagar has returned and given birth to Ishmael; God has changed the names of Abram and Sarai where we—and presumably Sarah—hear the first explicit news that Sarah's womb will bear the child (chap. 17). Whatever inner change the outer name change symbolizes—if any—Abraham once again jeopardizes his wife's womb. Once again Sarah becomes a sexual pawn in her husband's gambit to preserve himself, and to prosper at the same time. Was God's action of name-change merely a formality, a magic move from on high, compensating for intractable human nature? At first glance, it may seem so:

> And Abraham journeyed onward from there to the Negeb region and dwelt between Kadesh and Shur, and he sojourned in Gerar. And Abraham said of Sarah his wife, "She is my sister." And Abimelech the king of Gerar sent and took Sarah. And God came to Abimelech in a night-dream and said to him, "You are a dead man because of the woman you took, as she is another's wife." But Abimelech had not come near her, and he said, "My Lord, will you slay a nation even if innocent? Did not he say to me, 'She is my sister'? and she, she, too, said, 'He is my brother.' With a pure heart and with clean hands I have done this." (20:1-5)

God accepts Abimelech's protestations, acknowledging the king's integrity but insisting that "I on My part have kept you from offending against Me." This time, there will be no sexual relations between Sarah and a man other than her husband; this time, God won't stand for it. "Now, send back the man's wife," God continues, "for he is a prophet, and he will intercede for you, and you may live" (20:7). This is perhaps the most significant difference of all between Abram's betrayal of Sarai in Egypt, and here as Abraham in Gerar. Initially, Abraham looks worse this second time around, simply for repeating the ruse. But in Gerar, Abraham has somehow—and we need to think back over the story—grown to the status of "prophet," one who intercedes on behalf of another. "The slightest strategic variations in the pattern of repetitions," as Robert Alter notes about biblical narratives in general, "[can] serve the purposes of commentary, analysis, foreshadowing, thematic assertion, with a powerful combination of subtle understatement and dramatic force."[7] That Abraham can be called upon by God, in Gerar but not in Egypt, to pray for the victim of his own making, indicates God's growing confidence in Abraham's reorientation of the normal sad choices reflecting self-protection and self-aggrandizement. Just before this scene, Abraham has interceded on behalf of the people of Sodom and Gomorrah. He has done so brilliantly, passionately, bravely—as we will see in a later chapter. Having proven himself as an able intercessor, Abraham can now be trusted by God as "prophet." Confident at last in Abraham's compassion, God advises Abimelech to have the prophet Abraham intercede.

"And Abimelech called to Abraham and said to him, 'What have you done to us, and how have I offended you, that you should bring upon me and my kingdom so great an offense? Things that should not be done you have done to me. . . . What did you imagine when you did this thing?'" (20:9-10). In effect, Abimelech is asking the obvious question, *What's going on here?* The supposedly lustful foreigner is the one who fears God. Abraham won't demonstrate such a "fear of God" to God's own satisfaction until the story's climax (22:12). God's partner-in-the-making acts profoundly fearful all his life. Would the "fear of God" exhibited by Abimelech prove an anti-

---

[7]Robert Alter, *The Art of Biblical Narrative* (New York: Basic Books, 1981), p. 91.

dote against Abraham's normal human anxieties?

Abraham talks with the king—something he didn't do, or get a chance to do, with Egypt's monarch.

> And Abraham said, "For I thought, there is surely no fear of God in this place and they will kill me because of my wife. And, in point of fact, she is my sister, my father's daughter, though not my mother's daughter, and she became my wife. And it happened, when the gods made me a wanderer from my father's house, that I told her, 'This is the kindness you can do for me: in every place to which we come, say of me, he is my brother.' " (20:11-13)

"In every place to which we come!" All story long, the couple has been coming to different places. In each place the ruse was practiced, confesses Abraham. Is this the first time in all the couple's travels that God has intervened to stop a repeat of what happened in Egypt, where Sarah actually became another man's wife? Abimelech restores the misplaced wife to her husband, and, echoing in reverse the first story where Pharaoh had expelled Abraham, the king here invites the couple to stay in his land.

Abimelech's largesse is at the opposite extreme from Pharaoh's angry and understandable expulsion of the couple. But another difference is even more striking, indicating a change in Sarah's circumstance. The king addresses Sarah personally. "Look, I have given a thousand pieces of silver to your brother. Let it hereby serve you as a shield against censorious eyes for everyone who is with you, and you are now publicly vindicated" (20:16). In referring to Abraham here as Sarah's "brother," we gather that the king's tone is soft, or gently sardonic—unlike the blasting away by Pharaoh, "Why did you not tell me she was *your wife*? Why did you say, 'She's *my sister*,' so that I took her to me as *wife*? Now, here is *your wife*. Take her and get out!" More significantly, Sarah here is noticed, and given significance—though she will not be truly significant in this culture's eyes and her own until she bears a child. But Abimelech does what he can, naming Sarah as one to be vindicated. Sarah now can "lift up her face"—a more literal reading of "vindicated." Things begin to change for Sarah. And what, now, of Abraham? What change?

Here, the biblical writer saves for last some information that could have come before, but works brilliantly to tie several ends together. It's literary sleight of hand—a "flashback":

> And Abraham interceded with God, and God healed Abimelech and his wife and his slave-women and they gave birth. For the LORD *had shut fast* every womb in the house of Abimelech because of Sarah, Abraham's wife. And the LORD singled out Sarah as He had said, and the LORD did for Sarah as He had spoken. And Sarah conceived and bore a son to Abraham.[8] (Gen. 20:17—21:2, emphasis mine)

We learn now what happened earlier: the Lord had shut fast every womb. This flashback emphasizes two points, that Sarah is honored "all at once" by both earthly and heavenly potentate, and that Sarah's infertile and finally fruitful womb is linked to the infertility and then fruitful wombs of Abimelech's women.

The text is careful to point out that Abimelech's women have suffered because of Sarah: "For the LORD had shut fast every womb in the house of Abimelech because of Sarah." Sarah's womb, too, has been shut—a blessing under the circumstances of her being shunted between her husband's bed and the houses of Pharaoh and Abimelech and who knows how many others. God's intervention with Abimelech regarding Sarah underscores the lack of that intervention back with Pharaoh, when Sarah actually became Pharaoh's wife. The cause of barrenness for Abimelech's women, and in all likelihood for Sarah as well,[9] is the scheming of Abraham—just as the cure for all these dormant wombs, including his wife's, is "triggered" by Abraham's prayer of intercession. Are we to imagine that this newly designated "prophet" intercedes not just for the one victim, Abimelech, but the other notable victim as well, his wife? Miraculous change for Sarah, in any case, is linked by the writer with this most significant change

---

[8]The original scroll for this story had no chapter or verse markings, and if we read the episode in its entirety, it becomes clear that the flashback leads to the true conclusion: Sarah's pregnancy!

[9]In 11:30, just before the story proper begins, we read, "And Sarai was barren, she had no child." My reading of the story suggests the possibility that God keeps Sarai barren because of the jeopardy to her womb that God either knows about (her status in Egypt as another man's wife is not necessarily the first instance of womb jeopardy), or God anticipates the probability of Abram's risking his wife's womb, knowing, as only God can, Abram's fear and subsequent habit of choosing.

within Abraham: he has become fully what he has not been always, a "prophet." In the case of his pleading with God against the destruction of evil Sodom and Gomorrah, Abraham's compassion was exemplary but disinterested. That is, he had no personal investment, outside of a lingering loyalty to his nephew Lot and Lot's family (19:29). But here, with Abimelech, Abraham has had to stretch the prophetic role to include compassion for one whom he himself has wronged. Abraham lives up to the designation of "prophet" conferred by God in upholding the interests even of those he has victimized.

That Abraham risks his wife's chastity a second time, after seeing the devastating curse brought on the Egyptians because of Sarah's having become another man's wife, makes him more culpable than even the first time around. He should know better, by now. He seems to have learned nothing, riddled by the normal fear for self-preservation and self-promotion.[10] On the other hand, Abraham himself comes out of this sordid scene a changed man. In the end, he's achieved something conspicuously missing from his character in the first episode in Egypt. To plead the interests of someone you have harmed greatly is to reverse field from the normal impulse to defend yourself. It's natural to blame the victim. In upholding Abimelech's best interests before

---

[10]John Ronning explores the two episodes and concludes that Abraham goes from bad to worse: "Though outwardly the offense [passing off his sister] appears the same in both cases, several considerations indicate that the second lapse was much more blameworthy than the first. It was suggested earlier that in A [first episode] the promise of the heir could have been considered as being fulfilled through Lot, so that it did not depend on Abraham's continued existence. Likewise no mention had been made of Sarah's involvement in the promise. These factors mitigate Abraham's actions somewhat; he failed to do what is right no matter the consequences, which could have been death. In B [second episode], however, the same error indicates flat unbelief in God's explicit promise; he had by now received the promise that he would die "in peace" (15:15), yet he fears that he will be murdered. And God had just told him that in a year's time Sarah will bear him a son. Finally, the experience of God's intervention in plaguing Pharaoh's house on his behalf in a similar situation gives him even less excuse for unbelief. Even if he just proceeded in the same way because he knew God would rescue him again, then he was guilty of testing God. These considerations make very dubious Polzin's view [see next footnote] that the situation in B is transformed into a morally better situation than A' ("The Naming of Isaac: The Role of the Wife/Sister Episodes in the Redaction of Genesis," *Westminster Theological Journal* 53, no 1 [1991]: 18).

God, how could Abraham not have entertained his own role as victimizer? God's timing in granting a child to Abraham and Sarah at this point, after the promised year has expired, seems warranted.[11]

We do not read of any further subterfuge on Abraham's part. But does the fear linger? Can God be sure yet about Abraham's capacity to trust God as a shield and protector, as one who can provide Abraham with the promised name, and life? In fact, the narrative moves on from Gerar to God's seventh and final test of Abraham, the plot's final resolve and the focus of the following chapters.

By the conclusion of this repeated subterfuge, Abraham has become, fully, a prophet,[12] and Sarah's fortunes change from very bad to very good. Her shame is eased by Abimelech, who restores her to honor through his gracious understanding and gifts. Dishonor is erased, immediately following, by God, who brings fruitfulness out of barrenness. God didn't do this alone: Abraham had to pray. Abraham couldn't do this alone, either: God has been visiting Abraham with challenges and promises—six times by this point, with one visit left.

Sarah, Hagar and Trouble: The Second Time (21:9-21)

Sarah's conception leads to a son named Isaac, which means "laugh-

---

[11]In this view, God's growing confidence in Abraham's maturing capacity to finally stop risking his wife's womb—with the help of divine intervention (warning Abimelech)—could have led to the promise, back in the fifth visit, that one year hence Sarah would bear Abraham's child. Robert Polzin ("The Ancestress of Israel in Danger," *Semeia* 3 [Missoula, Mont.: Scholars Press, 1975]) notes the similarities and differences between the two accounts of subterfuge and points to the appropriateness of actual progeny for Abraham and Sarah as a couple: "With no information to the contrary we can assume that this [first] version of the story involves what might be termed 'actual adultery' " (p. 83), comparing this to the intervention of God and the intercessory prayer of Abraham and the explicit saving of Sarah's chastity in the second instance. He concludes that "God's blessing is seen as a *process* and the process is essentially complete when wealth and progeny are obtained under certain conditions" (p. 88), conditions which, when met by Abraham, suggest a reorientation toward increased generosity of spirit.

[12]John Van Seters, whose critical approach denies or ignores any significant unity in Abraham's story, nonetheless notes in a comparison of the subterfuge in Egypt ("story *A*") and in Gerar, the improved moral standing of Abraham: "The whole relationship between Abraham and the king is reversed from that of story *A* in order to give great moral stature to the patriarch" (*Abraham in History and Tradition* [New Haven, Conn.: Yale University Press, 1975], p. 175).

ter." But bitterness comes quickly in this paralleled scene of domestic trouble among Sarah, Hagar and Abraham.

Sarah perceives something amiss between Ishmael (child of Abraham and Hagar) and Isaac (child of Abraham and Sarah). Is it sibling rivalry? On the surface, the problem seems fairly harmless, a perfectly normal dynamic. "Sarah saw the son of Hagar the Egyptian, whom she had born to Abraham, laughing" (21:9). The Hebrew for "laughing" is *metsaheq*: it can mean sexual dalliance, play, or mocking laughter.[13] It's not to Sarah's liking, whatever it is. The Hebrew text plays on the root for "laughter" by placing Ishmael's laughter close to the laughter which defines "Isaac":

> And Abraham was a hundred years old when Isaac his son was born to him. And Sarah said,
>> "*Laughter* has God made me,
>> Whoever hears will *laugh* at me."
> And she said,
>> "Who would have uttered to Abraham—
>> 'Sarah is suckling sons!'
>> For I have born a son in his old age."
> And the child grew and was weaned, and Abraham made a great feast on the day Isaac was weaned. And Sarah saw the son of Hagar the Egyptian, whom she had born to Abraham, *laughing*. (21:5-9, emphasis mine)

Perhaps Ishmael's laughter mimics—mocks, even—the "laughter" lying at the core of Isaac's name, his identity. Ishmael could well be exercising one-upmanship—"Isaac-ing-it," as Robert Alter suggests.

In the first instance of this domestic triangle, Hagar is harassed by Sarai, who has been belittled by the pregnant slavegirl. Abram has allowed Sarai free rein to her rage. In the second episode of this same domestic triangle, Sarah, a mother at last, fixes her energies and possible ego-needs on Isaac. Sarah doesn't like what she sees between her child by Abraham and Hagar's child by Abraham. Sarah is a normal sort of mother. "Drive out this slavegirl and her son," she demands of Abraham, "for the slavegirl's son shall not inherit with my son, with Isaac" (21:10). Perhaps Sarah is thinking, *Today, the mocking laughter*,

---

[13]*Metsaheq*: this transliteration, and all others, are from the Alter translation or commentary notes.

tomorrow the inheritance. She has confronted Abraham once again, challenging him as in the first episode to *do* something: *Drive out this slavegirl and her son!* How will Abraham respond this second time?

It's different for Abraham, now. "And the thing seemed evil in Abraham's eyes" (21:11). Perhaps the suspected change within the "prophet" Abraham in the preceding episode in Gerar is playing out in positive ways. The dramatic focus of the narrative as a whole, from Haran to Sarah's burial plot, is on the eyes and the will of Abraham. How do things seem to him, how do they *look*? Will he see only as humans normally do, or will he be acquiring the vision of God, who saw Hagar when no one else did? This time, the thing seems evil "because of his son." Only his son? As God understands, Abraham's distress is on account of Hagar as well as Ishmael—or perhaps God is nudging Abraham into a concern for Hagar that is very nearly at his conscious level, but not quite:

> And God said to Abraham, "Let it not seem evil in your eyes on account of the lad *and on account of your slavegirl*. Whatever Sarah says to you, listen to her voice, for through Isaac shall your seed be acclaimed. But the slavegirl's son, too, I will make a nation, for he is your seed." (21:11-13, emphasis mine)

Without being instructed to do so, Abraham rouses himself early to send them off. He must let go of this son, but he provides what he can: "And Abraham rose early in the morning and took bread and a skin of water and gave them to Hagar, placing them on her shoulder, and he gave her the child, and sent her away, and she went wandering through the wilderness of Beersheba" (21:14). In the very next chapter, Abraham will have to relinquish another son, Isaac, whom he loves even more than Ishmael. In each case, he must trust in God's capacity and willingness to provide.

Once again, God takes notice of Hagar by opening her eyes to provision, and by promising future blessing:

> And when the water in the skin was gone, [Hagar] flung the child under one of the bushes and went off and sat down at a distance, a bowshot away, for she thought, "Let me not see when the child dies." And she sat at a distance and raised her voice and wept. And God heard the voice of the lad and God's messenger called out from the heavens and said to her,

"What troubles you, Hagar? Fear not, for God has heard the lad's voice where he is.
> Rise, lift up the lad
>> and hold him by the hand,
>>> for a great nation will I make him."

And God opened her eyes and she saw a well of water, and she went and filled the skin with water and gave to the lad to drink. And God was with the lad, and he grew up and dwelled in the wilderness, and he became a seasoned bowman. (21:15-20)

"Hold him by the hand," says God. What has God to do with such ordinary human gestures of affection and regard? It's a gentle suggestion: "Hold him by the hand."

Abraham must let go of both his son Ishmael and the boy's mother. It will go well enough with them, God assures Abraham. Abraham lets go. All turns out better than anything he could have provided by clutching: God opens Hagar's eyes to see water in the wilderness—and Ishmael "became a seasoned bowman." And what lies beyond is even brighter, as God repeats the promise yet again: "for a great nation will I make him."[14]

This second instance of triangle trouble helps us to understand the implications of the first. In the first episode, Abraham avoids confrontation with a miffed wife by letting Sarah do with Hagar whatever she wishes. This is wrong, as suggested not only by God's attentions to Hagar the first time but also by Abraham's goodly attentions the second time, mirroring God's. In the paralleled instance, Abraham does not give the angry Sarah leave to do whatever she deems appropriate. Driving the slavegirl once again out into the wilderness? "It seemed an evil thing to him." God honors Abraham's compassion by speaking with

---

[14]Other interpretations are possible. "God supports, even orders, [Hagar's] departure to the wilderness," claims Phyllis Trible, "not to free her from bondage but to protect the inheritance of her oppressors." That God has Hagar's best interests in view is denied by Trible, who wants to maintain that Hagar belongs "to a narrative that rejects her" (p. 27); she ignores, from my perspective, the many pointers and clues I have cited that demonstrate quite the opposite—and she ignores the fact that the Abraham narrative concludes with the genealogy of Hagar's son Ishmael, as is fitting in a Genesis story that emphasizes the foundational promise of blessing to all nations (*Texts of Terror: Literary-Feminist Readings of Biblical Narratives* [Philadelphia: Fortress, 1984], pp. 25, 27).

him, and assuring him in regard to the mother and son. What can seem evil—this thrusting out of mother and child—becomes, ironically and providentially, the opportunity for Ishmael's line to distinguish itself and thrive, as the story's ending demonstrates. The story of Abraham and Sarah ends, as we will see, with the lineage of Ishmael! (25:12-18).

Abraham is coming to see things as God sees things: each are deeply concerned for Hagar and her son. God has been the best sort of teacher, waiting to see human compassion, in this second instance, before intervening with divine compassion. God's will waits on human willingness.

What has plagued Abraham is fear for his life and zeal for his own interests ("that it may go well with me," Abraham says, rather baldly, in getting Sarah to prevaricate on his behalf). What lies at the root of his wrong choices is an improper but perfectly normal response to fear. Abraham experiences a radical insecurity regarding life and name. As we see next, this entire mess involving Abraham, Sarah and Hagar is part of a bigger story in which God visits Abraham as mentor, as one who challenges and promises. Seven times God visits, over twenty-five years, from the couple's mid-seventies to their late nineties. At the heart of the plot—in the central of these seven visits—God tells Abraham not to fear. In our next chapter, we explore the first four of the progressively difficult challenges put to Abraham by God. These divine trials intersect with the earthly trials we have just been witnessing. The biblical writer has alternated the two dimensions of challenge, the everyday and the divine, so that the reader can understand the growing partnership—and the need for such partnership—between God and Abraham.

ALL THE TIME THAT EVERYDAY TRIALS HAVE
plagued Abram and Sarai, Abram has been having
visits with God that include trials along with promises. The successive trials increase in difficulty, but
they are not a matter of God's raising the bar to see
what heights of rarified "spirituality" Abram can
attain. God tests Abram in practical ways toward
results that will affect the real world, making it a better place. Abram's responses prove transformational,
and not for himself alone. In seven visits that encompass the entire drama, God teaches and encourages—
and waits. In the first four visits, we find Abram
changing from silent respondent to a partner who
speaks up. In fact, by visit four Abram is offering God
demurrals and interesting alternatives. And in visit
four, at the literal and figurative center of all seven visits, Abram is challenged to live without fear. Fear lies
at the heart of what has plagued Abram, leading to
the subterfuge that has, presumably, plagued his wife.
Meanwhile and all the while, God and Abram are
working on a divine-human partnership in which God
challenges Abram toward a more generous way of
envisioning the world and living in it.

3

LET GO,
DON'T BE AFRAID
Visits 1-4

And the LORD *said to Abram, "Go forth from your land and your birthplace and your father's house to the land I will show you. And I will make you a great nation and I will bless you and make your name great, and you shall be a blessing. And I will bless those who bless you, and those who damn you I will curse, and all the clans of the earth through you shall be blessed." And Abram went forth as the* LORD *had spoken to him and Lot went forth with him. (12:1-3).*

Visit One: Let Go (12:1-3)

The story proper—the narrative plot—begins with this first visit between Abram and God, and God's first challenge. Abram responds positively: "And Abram went forth as the LORD had spoken to him." He could have said no, of course. From the very first of seven visits, Abram is called upon as a potential partner in God's designs. He has a part to play, a role that will expand with each successive visit.[1] You do

---

[1]Commenting on this, God's first call to Abram for a partnership role, Derek Kidner points to the partnership itself and the conspicuously larger role played by God: "Abram's part is expressed in a single though searching command, while the heaped up *I will's* reveal how much greater is the Lord's part. At the same time their futurity emphasizes the bare faith [and action!] that was required" (*Genesis, An Introduction and Commentary* [Downers Grove, Ill.: InterVarsity Press, 1967], p. 114).

this ("go forth") and I'll do so-and-so ("make you a great nation"). What Abram is being challenged to do, specifically, is to change the knee-jerk way that all human beings have in making self-preserving choices. True, God follows challenge with promise of good things to Abram—a "carrot," as it appears, to reinforce the self-interested choice-making of Abram. But the ultimate promise, the point of all promises, is the blessing to all nations, a decidedly non-parochial interest that Abram must take a lifetime to understand and embrace. Meanwhile, the challenges "school" him in how to reverse the clutching to life and name and family that characterizes all normal human behavior. Abram must learn something better than being normal. His ordinary way of being in the world must change. And God is changing course as well, challenging and promising in a preventative and curative way, rather than reacting quickly and punitively as in the case of the Babel builders. Whereas the Babel folk sought to make a name for themselves, God promises Abram a name; whereas the people of Babel were cursed by becoming alienated nations unable to understand each other, God promises that "all the clans of the earth through you shall be blessed."

From the time of our first couple, through Cain and Lamech, human choices had become so self-destructive that God determined to wipe out everything, as we recall. At the eleventh hour, God found righteous Noah, and relented. So: a second race, a second try. But this failed miserably, also. Humans went on being normal. God's recourse, starting with Abram and Sarai, is to change divine course by working with human beings, within their ordinary world of poor choices. Instead of fiats from on high, there will be familiarity made possible by successive visits. The partnership between Abram and God doesn't happen overnight. Starting with this first visit, it's always the same: God challenges and God promises—and Abram responds. These visits are woven into the fabric of ordinary human existence and into the drama of change within Abram and change of direction for God. They circumscribe the plot, from its beginning complication up to and including its dramatic resolve (I, 12:1-3; II, 12:7; III, 13:14-17; IV, 15:1-21; V, 17:1-22; VI, 18:1-33; VII,

22:1-18).[2] Each visit is a back-and-forth affair with similar choreography, like a dance: you do this, says God; I'll do that. In later visits, the dance step stays essentially the same but with interesting variations and "side-steps." For example, by the time we come to visit four, at the end of this chapter, Abram has found his voice with God for the first time.

With this first visit and challenge, Abram seems wonderfully compliant. Without a word or a moment's delay, he leaves home, relatives and native land. Maybe Abram's response to God's first challenge isn't that difficult. Some years ago, Abram's father had picked up stakes and traveled north with the family from Mesopotamian Ur (11:31-32). When Abram hears what he thinks is a god's voice telling him to leave his land and his family, we may not think of his doing so as anything particularly noble and fine. Leave the homeland? Well, Dad's already done that.[3] Leave family? Well, Dad has died; why not?

Could it be that wanderlust runs in the family? Like father, like son, perhaps. Abram's father and family, including Abram and Sarai, had lived on the world's major trade route, where merchants came and went all the time. The family originally had moved from the trade route's eastern end, Ur, near the port cities of the Persian Gulf. They followed the trade route up to its northernmost point, Haran, near what is today the Turkey-Syrian border. Haran was roughly halfway to the trade route's westernmost point, Egypt. Haran, a lesser light compared to the bright center of civilization back at Ur, could have given Abram itchy feet—especially with Egypt, the other center of known civilization, awaiting him at the trade route's other end.

On the other hand, maybe Abram is courageous and full of faith in

---

[2]God's intervention in the domestic strife involving Hagar and Ishmael in chapter 21 is a possible eighth visit. Alone, this appearance of God to Abram involves a specific issue in which God intervenes, as opposed to the seven visits in which specific challenges and promises are given to Abraham and to Sarah. Martin Buber finds the same seven unified visits—or revelations, as he calls them (Martin Buber, "Abraham the Seer," in *On the Bible* [New York: Schocken, 1968], p. 25).

[3]Though in 15:7 God says to Abram, "I am the LORD who brought you out of Ur of the Chaldees." Perhaps Abram shared with his father the original call in Ur, a call that apparently gets repeated in Haran, where God clearly speaks to Abram in 12:1.

obeying the "voice." We can't be absolutely sure until we've gotten into the story. A strange thing about this narrative is that it keeps circling back on itself even while it moves forward. If we read it moving only forward, without hearing the echoes that keep taking us back, we'll miss the fullness and central meanings of the story. Whether or not Abram has done anything praiseworthy by leaving Haran can't be decided, for example, until we run across a similar "leave-taking" at the story's end, when he relinquishes not only his father's house but his only son.

There's at least one important detail that suggests immediately the difficulty of letting go of homeland—that this is no simple case of wanderlust. "I will bless you and make your name great," God says. It's a promise that contains a challenge. Leave homeland and family—and the quest for a name, God says; leave it to me. Abram can relinquish home and the normal Babel-like quest for "name"—or not. The two stories, Babel's and Abram's, are linked by the name game and what lies at the heart of all human ill, this fear-filled urge to count for something, to have a place in the sun. At an appropriate point in their journey, halfway through the story, God literally gives new names to both Abram and Sarai: *Abraham* and *Sarah*. The name-giving indicates a process of interior change as we will see, a journeying away from the dynamics of Babel.

What seems to be the point of this leave-taking, this unnatural letting go? As God puts it, saving the ultimate promise for last: global happiness. You leave, says God, and I'll give you something better—but it's not about you, alone, or even primarily. It's that "all the clans of the earth through you shall be blessed." These are the terms of their partnership, never altered through the next six visits: You do this, and I'll do that.

What Abram is asked to do is not normal. What the world had seen of "normal" both within the biblical record and outside it, up to this turn-around point, has been the ordinary clutching to what's mine and ours at the expense of yours. Us against them. It's all very familiar; it's our normal way of being "family" in the world. Abram and Sarai begin by leaving behind all that is familiar and familial. They head out for an unknown destination, which proves as much a journey of the soul as a matter of geography. It's not easy: that's what the story goes on immediately to demonstrate. There is the promise, yes, of seed and land. But Sarai is barren, and the land God has in mind will prove problematic. In the next visit, with only the briefest of promises in the absence of any expressed challenge, Abram nonetheless takes initiative toward God.

Visit Two: Taking Initiative with God (12:7-8)

> And the Lord appeared to Abram and said, "To your seed I will give this land." (12:7)

They have left their homeland in Haran. After traveling several hundred miles south, along the trade route toward Egypt, "The LORD appeared to Abram" or, more literally, "The LORD was seen by Abram." God, always taking the initiative, allows the divine self to be seen! The text moves quickly, from the first visit's leaving to this second visit's arriving.

There was only a voice in visit one. Here, the voice says very little, but "the LORD was seen." What is the appropriate response to such a promise, to seeing the Lord? Is any response called for at all? What is Abram to make of this spot designated by God as a new home? And why here? There's a fertile region with some small cities in the valley, and wild bush and scrub grass on the hills from which he looks. The only distinguishing geographical feature noted by the writer is "the terebinth of the Oracle" (12:6)—the "oak of Moreh"—a sacred "teaching-tree"—in other translations.[4] The only other detail concerning the place is that "the Canaanite [traditional enemies of Israel] was in the land" (12:6). What will Abram make of all this? How will he respond, if at all, to the promise of this land as destination, and to this particular spot, this religious marker of the Canaanites?

The unstated challenge of this visit may be more troubling for Abram and Sarai than that of visit one, to leave home. One can always leave, as difficult as it might be emotionally. Leaving is definite, a

---

[4]J. Gerald Janzen, for example: "*Moreh* is the hiphil form of *yarah*, which means to point out, show, direct, teach" (*Abraham and All the Families of the Earth: A Commentary on the Book of Genesis 12-50* [Grand Rapids, Mich.: Eerdmans, 1993], pp. 23-24).

thing that's not hard to figure out. But what of arriving at an uncertain or unlikely destination—a designated spot but with no explicit instructions on what to do, having arrived? Abram can say to himself, or perhaps to Sarai, "It's all a mistake. We'll go on down to Egypt, trade some livestock, then head back for Haran—maybe go all the way back to Ur."

As always, God is taking a chance with Abram. Abram can choose to accept the land and its promising God, or not. He can invoke the Canaanite deity of this Oracle tree, or not. What Abram does, without being told, is good: "And he built there an altar to the LORD who had appeared to him" (12:7). The physicality of an altar corresponds to the visual seeing—repeated here by the narrator—rather than just a voice heard, as in the first visit. In the next verse we read that Abram takes his family and flocks a short distance away, to Bethel. The writer calls attention to a second and significant initiative. Not only does Abram again build an altar, but this time he "invoked the name of the LORD" (12:8). God has promised Abram a great name, and now Abram invokes the name of the Lord, after embracing this God by building the altar. These initiatives may not indicate much of any change from the natural instinct to secure his own name, but invoking God's name is surely an important first step in relinquishing the effort to establish one's own. If I think there is only the cosmic void, and I am all there is, then scrambling for all the marbles and making them mine is the reasonable or at least normal way to go about life. To the extent that I give God a place in my consciousness of things—building an altar to and invoking the name of this God, for example—my own natural drive for self-aggrandizement is subject at the very least to challenge by this God. Abram chooses to open up within himself a significant space for the God of what-is-to-come, the God who is promising. Clearly the promise works to plant in Abram's consciousness new possibilities, but just as surely Abram responds to the implicit challenge of the promise very well.

In this second visit, so brief in external details, there is great movement forward for both God and Abram. Abram is given the psychic room to take initiative, since God's challenge is not directly spoken. Will I say yes to this offer of desolate land, an offer I can always refuse? If yes, in what form shall I offer my agreement? God the parent backs off a bit from the growing child, watching, waiting. The wait is rewarded by Abram's choice to celebrate this God of future possibilities.

But immediately we read of the fiasco in Egypt. When it comes to everyday challenges, Abram's initiative to preserve and promote himself, even at his wife's expense, proves disastrous. These divine visits appear all the more necessary when viewed in the light of Abram's very normal way of being in the world.

Visit Three: Stake Out Land You'll Never Live to Own (13:14-18)

> And the LORD had said to Abram after Lot parted from him, "Raise your eyes and look out from the place where you are to the north and the south and the east and the west, for all the land you see, to you I will give it and to your seed forever. . . . Rise, walk about the land through its length and its breadth, for to you I will give it." (13:14-17)

Just after the back-to-back visits by God with which the story began, the promises of land and seed have already been threatened. As we have seen, Abram chose to cling to his life and name—and well-being—at the expense of Sarai's chastity. As wife to Pharaoh, Sarai's womb had been endangered, to say the least. Returning from Egypt, the land was threatened because of squabbles between shepherds of Abram and nephew Lot (13:1-13). It was the familiar struggle for territory, in this case, grazing rights. Abram offered Lot first choice of land, and Lot did the normal thing. He took the fertile land, the apparently good land. Maybe Abram was being heroic and good, or maybe he was just washing his hands of a problem. In either case, Abram got the inferior portion. It's at this point that we read of God's challenge and promise in visit three—look up, and walk around. It's all yours for the looking and the walking.

As in the prior two visits, God makes promises that include or go on to offer challenges. Abram's tent is pitched high up in the hill country, between Bethel and Ai. He can see great distances. So this is a promise of much land, assuming good eye-sight—but he must walk the great distances seen, and under most peculiar circumstances. The original audience would have understood what God wanted: to walk around a land's perimeter was to confirm it as personal property. But there can be no legal purpose to Abram's walking, since there are no witnesses. And we find out that it will be four hundred years down the road before his children come to "own" the land. So for the most part this is a symbolic walking—a promissory sort of stroll. It would appear crazy to any outside observer—to Sarai, for example. Or to a stray herdsman up in the hills, seeing this old man tramping about with no herd and no apparent business of any sort. It's a walk beyond what seems normal and shy of what, in fact, is legally binding in this case.

The first visit had concreteness and drama to the "test": leave home, pack up and go. The second visit was much more ambiguous in its test: this land I give to you and your seed, says God. And what does one say to that? Or do with it? But in this third visit, the ambiguous becomes downright strange. Lift your eyes from the everyday concerns in front of your nose and see how far you can see, and then walk it—a few days, a week or two? Walk through scrub brush, with no immediate import of any sort. As the challenges or tests become progressively more difficult, God's trust in Abram grows, just as Abram's trust in God grows. Abram appears to be learning partnership. And, at the very least, God is making changes in accommodating Abram's growth.

But shouldn't partners be able to talk things over with each other? In three visits, Abram has yet to say a word. Ah, but all good things take time. It appears that God participates in time as we humans experience it. God pursues. God's initiative involves waiting on Abram, waiting for the time it takes him to make up his mind, to finally make fundamental changes of mind-set and to talk—to speak up.

Visit Four: Don't Be Afraid (15:1-21)

> After these things the word of the LORD came to Abram in a vision, saying, "Fear not, Abram, I am your shield. Your reward shall be very great." (15:1)

As always, promise follows challenge. Fear not, and good will follow. You do this, and I'll do that. The explicit use of the word "reward" reinforces what has been implicit all along. There is to be shared responsibility in this game plan for personal fulfillment and global happiness. The reward "shall be very great"—no less than that "all the clans of the earth through you shall be blessed" (12:3). But of course Abram may not have come to embrace that reward, or to understand its greatness. Who of us does? It's more normal to think of reward as personal, familial.

If the idea of what exactly constitutes the greatness of reward is left hanging for Abram, how much more so is the challenge to fear not? It's the least concrete and the most demanding of challenges to date. "Fear not." Rid yourself of anxiety. E. A. Speiser points out that Abram "had cause for personal anxiety," though he locates that anxiety in the absence of any son.[5] Or, perhaps as in other theophanies of the Bible, God is simply reassuring Abram in the light of this vision, even though Abram has been privileged three times already in hearing God's voice, and once in seeing God. Do these possibilities of being terrorized by a divine vision, or by his son-less state, go to the heart of Abram's fear? In any case, the voice comes out of the blue, dramatically. We can't be sure what Abram understands about the challenge "Fear not." In fact, Abram and his retinue have just rescued nephew Lot and five local kings from four powerful kings of international infamy. It's "after these things"—after Abram's heroics—that God decides to utter the challenge, "Fear not." What sense are we to make of this strange narrative timing, given the just-demonstrated courage, and lack of any apparent concern for reprisal on Abram's part? As usual, the narrator won't help us with the answer. So we must make something of the puzzle: Where's the fear? And for what does Abram need God as shield?

For the first time in his visiting with God, Abram speaks out, but he doesn't speak to the challenge of "Fear not," nor does he address anything to do with a need for God as shield. Rather, he picks up on God's mention of *reward*.

> And Abram said, "O my Master, Lord, what can You give me when I am going to my end childless, and the steward of my household is Dammesek Eliezer?" And Abram said, "Look, to me you have given no seed, and here a member of my household is to be my heir." (15:2-3)

Is there a touch of bitterness or complaint in the first question? "What can You give me," asks Abram, "when I am going to my end

---

[5]E. A. Speiser, *Genesis*, Anchor Bible (New York: Doubleday, 1964), p. 115.

childless, and the steward of my household is Dammesek Eliezer?"
There is no obvious fear in the question, "What can you give me?"
Rather, one might detect a touch of possible whining: Really, God,
what's the use, given my childlessness? Besides, he goes on, I've taken
care of things. It's too late for anything better. I've got my steward
Dammesek Eliezer. Rather than fear, this sounds like an effort to reassure God, to keep the status quo that Abram himself has managed.

The writer separates this expression of possibly unhappy resigna-
tion from a second "Look, God," which follows immediately: "And
Abram said, 'Look, to me you have given no seed, and here a member
of my household is to be my heir.' " Abram twice seems to be saying,
"Look, God, let's leave well enough alone. I've got it all figured out. It's
OK." Abram has legal precedent in considering his steward an heir.

There may be petulance in Abram's proposals to God, but there is
no evidence of fear, just as there had not been any sign of fear in the
immediately preceding rescue of Lot. His obvious concern regarding
an heir from his own seed surfaces here as a bit of whining and bra-
vado—You've given me no child, God, so I've taken care of the matter—but not of fear. So, again, what fear is God referring to in the
initial challenge? And what is the possible relevance of the shield
promised by God? The writer seems to be asking that we keep the
story as a whole drama in mind. The only fear we know about is
Abram's overwhelming fear in the story's beginning, made explicit by
Abram himself when he asked Sarai to say she is sister and not wife—
since, as husband, "they will kill me while you they will let live." If this
is the fear being referred to, then perhaps it's not so easily gotten rid
of. Fear of death is basic, as is the fear of not "having enough,"
reflected in Abram's postscript to Sarai that she lie "so that it may go
well with me"—that is, that he might prosper, which he does. So it
becomes a strong possibility for the reader that God is referring to this
original fear, and that God knows, even though the reader doesn't, that
the fear still lurks. This fear for life and name and "doing well" had
indeed dogged Abram's steps "everywhere we wandered" as Abram
pleads before Abimelech many years later, toward the end of the story.
A shrewdly observant student notes that the later Abimelech episode
"demonstrates that [Abraham] doesn't just fear the Egyptians, but men

in general; he generally doesn't trust the security of his marriage, self, or wife to God."[6] God's promise to be a shield, midway between the two explicit episodes of fear-based unfaithfulness, makes sense: If Abram can count on God's provision for a shield against the presumably rapacious and murderous men desiring his wife all the days of his traveling life, then there will be no room for fear. That such trust works as an antidote to such fear becomes more convincing as the story progresses, and as Abram continues changing.

The challenge not to fear, particularly at the level of survival, is the challenge of anyone's lifetime. We are anxious about our place in the world, about being significant in others' eyes, if in fact we are not in daily fear for our life. Of the four challenges up to this point, "Fear not" is the least manageable. What can one *do* about anxiety and fear? In what he says to God, Abram has slid past the fear challenge and the shield offer. His sardonically confident responses have focused on the promise of reward, as if to say, "Why bother, God?—I've got the heir thing all figured out." On the other hand, Abram talks with God for the first time. This is progress. This is good. If the visits have been viewed in relation to each other, Abraham's maturation becomes clear.

After listening to the two separate responses from Abram, "the word of the LORD came to him, saying, 'This one [Eliezer] will not be your heir, but he who issues from your loins will be your heir' "(15:4). What is expected of Abram now? How is he to proceed, with this promise of a future—an heir from his aging loins—that overturns what he presents to God as a present security, the steward Eliezer? The answer lies in the heart. "Fear not" is interior, a challenge for the deepest psyche. Abram's response is appropriately interior: "And [Abram] trusted in the LORD, and He reckoned it to his merit" (15:6). Perhaps Abram is on his way toward mastering the fear problem, after all. This is another step forward. In walking the land (visit three), Abram presumably gave some evidence of such trust, since the land could not become his just by the walking. Now, in visit four, that trust becomes explicit. And praiseworthy. God likes it. God considers such trust a tribute to Abram's goodness of person, his righteousness, his merit. God

---

[6]Danielle Tate, class journal, January 17, 2000.

considers Abram's trust as true righteousness, as being upright. Abram is learning "to take [God] as reliable, and to rely upon that [God]" and this is what God is looking for in a partner: such reliance is to Abram's "credit" or "merit."[7] Such reliance will have everything to do with everyday life. That's the promise of this story, which is confirmed in the end.

The fourth visit now breaks into a second phase. The challenges and promises and responses in these visits have been getting more complex, and now the texture of the visits themselves will become more complicated. Such are the ways of a growing friendship.

"And He said to him, I am the LORD who brought you out of Ur of the Chaldees to give you this land to inherit" (15:7). Just as the seed shall come from *your* loins, God says, it's *this* land that is yours to inherit. But Abram, once again, speaks out. "And he said, 'O my Master, LORD, how shall I know that I shall inherit it?' " (15:8).

God responds favorably to Abram's pressing questions, laying out the requirements of a partnership ritual. Abram must act. Animals are to be killed and cut open. It's all a bit mysterious, though the custom of two partners confirming an agreement by walking between split carcasses was practiced in the surrounding cultures. Here, it appears that God takes the major initiative and responsibility. It's as if God swears by the divine self to be cut in two if failing to uphold the divine end of the bargain.[8] Even though God is the major player in this ritual, Abram must do the cutting and must ward off carrion birds that would like to eat the carcasses before the ritual has been completed. Abram says yes as willing partner, though he must embrace a future for his offspring that will not be available for another four hundred years (15:13).

From silent response in the first three visits, Abram progresses in visit four by speaking up. And in visit four God, for the first time, responds both in the exchange of dialogue with Abram and in agreeing

---

[7]See J. Gerald Janzen's exploration of differing interpretive possibilities here—for example, that Abram may have credited God with righteousness or merit, rather than the other way around (*Abraham and All the Families of the Earth*, pp. 37-39). Grammatically, both are possible; in context, I think Alter's translation is correct, that "He [God] reckoned it to his [Abram's] merit."

[8]See NIV Study Bible note on this verse.

to Abram's desire for a more solid assurance. The implicit partnership is here made explicit in the agreement pact proposed by God, though not without Abram's request for something a bit more definite between them.

The partnership is again ratified in the next visit, visit five. As we may have come to expect, it will be Abram this time, rather than God, who must take the lion's share in enacting the covenantal rite, the terms of agreement. But something must still be amiss, since God's first challenge to Abram in this fifth visit is to be blameless, to walk with God. Where has Abram been blameworthy? We think, perhaps, of Sarai's dishonor. Sarai, for the first time, happens to be an explicit part of this fifth visit, her womb cited by God for the first time as the womb of promise. At this point God deems it time to grant the name change. Why now?

IN VISIT FOUR, GOD'S TESTING TURNED FROM THE external world to the heart: do not fear. What not to harbor in the recesses of one's psyche is followed in visit five by something more positive: be blameless; walk before me. What can "blameless" mean? And such walking: this is even more difficult than "walk the land" of visit three. While in visit four, animals are cut for the agreement ritual, in visit five, male foreskins must be cut, and for the same purpose, that of ratifying partnership. Abraham takes a more active role in the repeated instance of cutting. And he encounters a less familiar and more global God than ever before. Then, in visit six comes the most leisurely and delightful of all seven visits. For the first time, Abraham rather than God initiates conversation, and God responds to Sarah's voice. For the first time, Abraham and Sarah, rather than God, play host. There is dinner, followed by after-dinner conversation of the most serious sort. Here is a picture of partnership's give-and-take, a portrait of perfected friendship.

4

WALK WITH ME— AND SPEAK UP!

Visits 5 & 6

And Abram was ninety-nine years old [twenty-four years since the first visit!] and the LORD appeared to Abram and said to him, "I am El Shaddai. Walk with Me and be blameless." (17:1)

Visit Five: Walk with Me (17:1-27)

What can be more challenging for any of us than to let go of all anxiety? Letting go of his homeland and father's house following visit one was surely a significant achievement for Abram. Even better, in visit two, to embrace the God who asked for this leaving, and who then indicated a desolate land as destination. Then, having turned your back on past securities, to walk this land for an unknown future, as in the third visit. Surely this is remarkable. In visit four, however, "do not fear" appeared the most challenging of all the tests. What next? What is more difficult? In this visit, we hear the challenge and may shake our heads. "Be blameless." Perfection?

And "walk with Me"? The Hebrew for "walk" in this visit is the same verb as in the challenge to "walk the land" in visit three. Abram passed the test to go out and walk land-boundaries that would be no boundaries, in reality, for hundreds of years. One might feel foolish on such a walk, but one knows what to do, and in a few days or weeks it's over, done with. But walk with God? For all walking, for all the time? Some translations have the more literally accurate "walk *before* me," or, in God's favor.[1] Perhaps Abram is being asked to walk in such a path that God would take, if on earth. Abram has to walk with God's challenges in mind, "before" his every step. Whether "walk with me" or "walk before me," the challenge assumes increasing human responsibility.[2] There are only two more visits left after this fifth one, so Abram must get used to walking with God (there will still be momentous events in his life) even when God is not around.

As always, God follows the challenge with a promise: "Walk with Me and be blameless, and I will grant My covenant between Me and you and I will multiply you very greatly" (17:2). Abram flings himself on his face, and God speaks to him, saying:

> *As for Me*, this is My covenant with you: you shall be father to a multi-tude of nations. And no longer shall your name be called Abram but your name shall be Abraham, for I have made you father to a multitude of nations. (17:3-5, emphasis mine)

Before, Abram has been responding to God's challenges. Now, God is responding to Abram's response, the apparently reverential flinging of himself on his face before God. God goes on to emphasize the mutual-ity of the partnership. "As for Me, . . . " God says, I will do this and this. But it goes two ways:

> *As for you*, you shall keep My commandment, you and your seed after you through their generations. This My covenant which you shall keep, between Me and you and your seed after you: every male among you must be circumcised. You shall circumcise the flesh of your foreskin and it shall be the sign of the covenant between Me and you. (17:9-11, emphasis mine)

"As for Me, . . . as for you, . . .": Such shared responsibility has been clear from visit one but is here made explicit. The implicit connection

---

[1] "Would that Ishmael might live in Your favor!" exclaims Abraham to God, later in this scene (17:18). The preposition is the same: "Walk *before* Me," and may Ishmael live "before" you.

[2] Later generations, living in exile, will hear this challenge as a reminder to walk in the way of Torah.

of human doing and God's doing is present in the prior lines, "Walk with Me and be blameless, and I will grant My covenant between Me and you." (17:1-2) The reader may have missed the necessary connection between "You do this, and I'll do that" way back from the first visit on, but here the writer focuses on God's actual words—"As for Me" and "As for you"—which reinforce the growing mutuality of partnership responsibility, though God's initiative will always be paramount in this partnership.

Among the things God will do for Abram, if Abram chooses well, is to make his name great, one of the promises in the first visit. Here it begins to happen. God changes Abram's name to *Abraham*. The meanings of *Abram* and *Abraham* are similar—"exalted father"—but, as Robert Alter points out in his note on this verse, the change of name indicates a change of status. And what is this new status? Perhaps it's what the text here emphasizes. With God's visiting help, Abraham has been growing into partner status with God, demonstrated in the language of reciprocity. As for me, says God, I will do so-and-so. As for you, you must do so-and-so. Such partnership will lead to an "everlasting covenant" (17:7).

Before this covenant will be finalized, however, this man with a new name will come to trust in a God with a different name, a less immediately personal God than the Yahweh who has been appearing to him and speaking to him. "I am El Shaddai," says God, here, to Abram. "Walk with Me and be blameless, and I will grant My covenant between Me and you" (17:1-2). The meaning of *Shaddai* is uncertain; *El* is the singular form of *Elohim*, the same *Elohim* who, from an apparently great distance and initiating all creation activity with speech, made cosmic order out of chaos. There is no question of God being multiple; God is one. Why does the writer emphasize, then, the differing names? It was *Elohim* who brought into being all distinctions and forms of creation in an orderly and poetic six days.[3] *Yahweh Elohim*, on the other hand, was the God of the second creation account who came down to earth, focusing personally and compassionately on fashioning the first human couple and providing for their companionability.

---

[3] *El*, "God," is also the Canaanite sky god.

Abraham knows at least something of these two faces of God. After his rescue of Lot and the five kings, a foreign priest and king, Melchizedek, has blessed Abraham with these words, "Blessed be Abram to El Elyon . . . and blessed be El Elyon." Elyon may be a deity distinct from El; in the Hebrew, the meaning of *El Elyon* is "God Most High." Abraham responds to the priest's blessing by bringing God's two names together: "I raise my hand in oath to the LORD [Yahweh], the Most High God [El], (14:19, 22). Even that far back in his journey, then, between the third and fourth visits, Abraham had been able to incorporate, cleverly and reverentially, the personal God Yahweh with the foreigner's God, El Elyon.[4] But Elohim has not been making an appearance or speaking in any of the visits with Abraham up to this point, and even here it's Yahweh who has made the initial appearance. Appropriately, then, Abraham "flung himself on his face" before this less familiar and more remote aspect of God, Elohim. God is one, but God appears in differing divine aspects for specific persons in specific circumstances for specific reasons, all of which can be understood only within the fuller context of the story.

The possible meaning for *Elohim*, "God of all peoples,"[5] is reinforced by the immediate context here: Abraham's being renamed by Elohim is done so with repeated emphasis on his role for a "multitude of nations." God explains Abraham's new name to him: "And no longer shall your name be called Abram but your name shall be Abraham, for I have made you father to a multitude of nations. And I will make you most abundantly fruitful and turn you into nations, and kings shall come forth from you" (17:5-6). Just prior, "[Elohim] spoke to him, saying, 'As for Me, this is My covenant with you: you shall be father to a multitude of nation'" (17:3-4).

This linkage of Elohim with a multitude of nations is extended to Sarai's name change, also. "And [Elohim] said to Abraham, 'Sarai your

---

[4]"Whatever Melchizedek's theology, Abram elegantly co-opts him for monotheism by using *El Elyon* in its orthodox Israelite sense (verse 22) when he addresses the king of Sodom" (Robert Alter, *Genesis: Translation and Commentary* [New York: W. W. Norton, 1996], note on 14:19-20).

[5]*Elohim* is a name for God that "is appropriate to cosmic and world-wide relationships" (G. T. Manley, "Names of God," in *New Bible Dictionary*, ed. J. D. Douglas [Grand Rapids, Mich.: Eerdmans, 1962], p. 478).

wife shall no longer call her name Sarai, for Sarah is her name. And I will bless her and I will also give you from her a son and I will bless him, and she shall become nations, kings of peoples shall issue from her' " (17:15-16). Elohim exhibits an interest that includes but extends far beyond Abraham and Sarah. The possibility that a child and nations might yet issue from post-menopausal Sarah, ninety years old, and himself, one hundred years old, strikes Abraham as very funny. Once again, but in laughter, he flings himself to the ground in front of Elohim. Is he unable to control this spasm of hilarity when faced suddenly with the disparity between Elohim's global vision and the couple's own enfeebled state?

Yahweh has initiated God's appearance, as is customary in these visits, but Elohim has taken over for the momentous changing of names and spelling out of responsibilities. But does the text actually suggest such a dependence of God on the human partner? Does the God who desires blessing for all nations require a partner, a partner who will sire and be a blessing to many nations? The last two visits will answer that question even more emphatically in the affirmative. As for Abraham, God says here, there must be a keeping of the commandments. What commandments? So far, all we have are the five challenges of the five visits, each a commandment of sorts. Specifically, for example, and most immediately at hand, there must be a second cutting of flesh for a second ratification of their agreement: a challenge; a commandment. No mere rule-keeping, these challenges involve the human partner in action that will include initiative.

This time, Abraham is to be more personally involved. The prior cutting was external to Abraham. It didn't hurt him, at least physically, to cut the animals in half. But now in visit five God proposes that Abraham cut his own flesh—the foreskin of his penis—and that of all male members in his family. Abraham might have heard of circumcision back in Egypt where it functioned as a puberty rite. For Abraham and all his children, however, it is to be done as a sign of God's covenant and Abraham's willingness to participate in that covenant, not, as in Egypt, as a sign of entering adulthood. Forever, in daily and in procreative practice, Abraham and his family will be reminded that they walk with God, and that God walks with them.

This all seems like a very male thing, this partnership. But Sarah, as we have seen, has received a new name. Abraham may not have suspected that Sarah was critical to the whole enterprise, that in fact "she [would] become nations." Abraham has allowed Sarah, in fact, to become another man's wife to protect himself. Have some of his patriarchal biases been challenged? What we know for sure is that Abraham initially finds God's promise to Sarah of blessing, and of a son, a bit preposterous. After the laughter, Abraham gains control of himself and suggests that God be reasonable about this heir business, just as he had argued with God in the prior visit. "And Abraham said to God, 'Would that Ishmael might live in Your favor!' " (17:18). God had already rejected Abraham's suggestion, legally proper, that the household steward, Dammesek Eliezer, serve as heir. Now Abraham has, in his son by Hagar, an even better prospect for an heir. All of this builds to what the reader has suspected all along, that Sarah is central to the action here. She is vital to the plot.

> And God said, "Yet Sarah your wife is to bear you a son and you shall call his name Isaac and I will establish My covenant with him as an everlasting covenant, for his seed after him." (17:19)

Sarah's womb will become fruitful, but we might be wondering by now just how much this fertility depends on a change in Abraham, however sure we are that conception depends ultimately on God's promise and ability to bring life to a barren womb—to overturn, finally, the laws of post-menopausal nature.

Possibly Abraham is concerned not only for what is reasonable—Ishmael would do very nicely as an heir—but also for his son's well being. We find out later, when Sarah wants to cast out Hagar and Ishmael, that Abraham does indeed care for Ishmael very much. So does God. We are reminded that though Ishmael may not be part of the covenant being established here, he exists as the covenant's point. That is, Ishmael is one of the clans of all the earth that is to be blessed—the ultimate promise—through the partnership being forged between God and Abraham and Sarah. Ishmael counts for God as well as for Abraham:

> "As for Ishmael, I have heard you. Look, I will bless him and make him fruitful and will multiply him most abundantly, twelve chieftains he

shall beget, and I will make him a great nation. But My covenant I will establish with Isaac whom Sarah will bear you by this season next year." And He finished speaking with him, and God ascended from Abraham. (17:20-22)

The writer calls attention to the fact that God has been visiting Abraham close at hand by noting that "God ascended from Abraham." And how will Abraham do in holding up his end of the pact making? He does the unthinkable, painful thing immediately, starting with Ishmael:

And Abraham took Ishmael his son and all the slaves born in his household and those purchased with silver, every male among the people of Abraham's household, and he circumcised the flesh of their foreskin on that very day as God had spoken to him. (17:23)

Abraham could have turned back, even at this late date. He could have said, Enough. In this case, the covenant would have been off. And there's still more to come before God announces the fulfillment to the promise. There are still greater challenges for Abraham to meet before God can finally trust in Abraham's readiness to be a blessing for all peoples.

Visit Six: Talk with Me (18:1-33)

And the LORD appeared to him in the terebinths of Mamre when he was sitting by the tent flap in the heat of the day. And he raised his eyes and saw, and, look, three men were standing before him. He saw, and he ran toward them from the tent flap and bowed to the ground. And he said, "My lord, if I have found favor in your eyes, please do not go on past your servant. Let a little water be fetched and bathe your feet and stretch out under the tree, and let me fetch a morsel of bread, and refresh yourselves. Then you may go on, for have you not come by your servant?" And they said, "Do as you have spoken." And Abraham hurried to the tent to Sarah and he said, "Hurry! Knead three *seah*s of choice flour and make loaves." And to the herd Abraham ran and fetched a tender and goodly calf and gave it to the lad, who hurried to prepare it. And he fetched curds and milk and the calf that had been prepared and he set these before them, he standing over them under the tree, and they ate. (18:1-8)

Even though the partnership between God and Abraham—and finally

Sarah—has grown by stages in the first five visits, we may not be prepared for the willingness of God to show up, unannounced and in disguise—and silent. What will Abraham and Sarah do to accommodate their unknown guests? This time, for the first time, both Abraham and Sarah are visited. And for the first time Abraham is greeting God instead of God greeting Abraham—though of course God has taken the initiative in making this visit, as he did for earlier aspects of the developing relationship with Abraham.

The narrator spares no detail of delight in laying out the scene. So it comes to pass that Abraham and Sarah entertain God. And with such dash, such culinary effort! How pleased God must be at the attentive gusto of the couple! After dinner, Sarah hears for herself the promise of God for her long-infertile womb. "Where is Sarah your wife?" asks God of Abraham. "There, in the tent," Abraham responds. God calls attention to Sarah, while the writer notes the position of God and Sarah—they are separated by only a tent flap. Now it's time for God's word about Sarah within Sarah's hearing:

> And he said, "I will surely return to you at this very season and, look, a son shall Sarah your wife have," and Sarah was listening at the tent flap, which was behind him. And Abraham and Sarah were old, advanced in years, Sarah no longer had her woman's flow. And Sarah laughed inwardly, saying, "After being shriveled, shall I have pleasure, and my husband is old?" And the LORD said to Abraham, "Why is it that Sarah laughed, saying, 'Shall I really give birth, old as I am?' Is anything beyond the LORD? In due time I will return to you, at this very season, and Sarah shall have a son." And Sarah dissembled, saying, "I did not laugh," for she was afraid. And He said, "Yes, you did laugh." (18:10-15)

Nothing bad happens to Sarah for her laughing—just a recording of the fact by God, to her, personally. Maybe that's part of the narrative point: you can laugh at God's proposing, even in God's presence—as Abraham had done about the same news in the prior visit—without negative repercussions. And happiest of endings, their child will be called *Laughter*.

In hearing the promise for herself, and laughing, and then having God call her on the laughing, Sarah is challenged in ways that would be hard to express. Abraham along with Sarah is being challenged as responsible host. Both are being challenged toward an exquisite attentiveness and human initiative. God's test here—will Abraham play adequate host to God, incognito?—has come without divine trappings, making it all the more challenging.

Abraham serves the God who has been serving him. The serving is elaborate. Meals take time, especially this kind of feast, and without appliances. God is slowing down for Abraham, who is catching up with God. And such catching-up! The writer, usually sparing of detail, lavishes manic attention. Sitting Abraham is roused. Effusive offerings for foot washing and clean bedding are made. Abraham hurries, then requests that others hurry, and then hurries some more himself. He takes, he gives, and then he hurries once again—taking, preparing and laying out. Finally, the man who was sitting stands at attention, while the heavenly visitors who were standing sit at their ease. The scene manages to say much about Abraham's growing initiative on behalf of God. Maybe the parent wants to know how the nearly matured children will handle things if the parent isn't looming authoritatively.

By eating a meal prepared by Abraham and Sarah, God is bringing the divine self down to the level of communion at a human table. And of course by eating in their "home," God is blessing the neighborhood. This scruffy land of promise gets the divine seal of approval.

But there is another purpose to this visit. God wants to talk something over with Abraham. Or rather—as it turns out—God waits for Abraham to begin the conversation and to sustain it. And no idle after-dinner talk is this. God has seen the gross wrongdoing of an adjoining neighborhood, the cities of Sodom and Gomorrah. After their meal, Abraham and the three heavenly beings walk away from the tent area a bit. They gaze toward Sodom, where nephew Lot and his family reside. At this point the narrator records what appears to be a flashback—what God had been thinking. We are provided a glimpse into the mind of God at work.

"And the LORD had thought, 'Shall I conceal from Abraham what I am about to do?' " (18:18). God has promised blessing to all the tribes on earth and now intends to destroy two of them—but not without good cause. "The God who will not decide the fate of the wicked cities apart from their treatment of the two strangers," J. Gerald Janzen observes, "also will not decide apart from the agency of this called per-

son [Abraham]."⁶ How can God *not* confide in this partner? "For I have
embraced him," God goes on, reflectively, "so that he will charge his
sons and his household after him to keep the way of the LORD to do
righteousness and justice, that the LORD may bring upon Abraham all
that He has spoken concerning him" (18:19). "The community of faith
can continue only if children receive instruction,"⁷ toward the ultimate
goal of blessing to all nations. Yet here a nation is going to experience a
complete destruction toward which they have been headed on their
own. God wants to make things perfectly clear to Abraham. The language reinforces the growing reciprocity of the relationship: I have
embraced him, *so that* "he will charge his sons and his household after
him."

The two companions of God set out for Sodom, leaving God and
Abraham alone. However prepared we are for the growing reciprocity
between God and Abraham, the next two narrative details might well
astonish us. God stands before Abraham, rather than Abraham standing in God's presence. And then, the word of Abraham comes to God,
rather than the word of God coming to Abraham.

> And the men [the other two divine beings] turned from there and went
> on toward Sodom while the LORD was still standing before Abraham.
> And Abraham stepped forward and said, "Will you really wipe out the
> innocent with the guilty? Perhaps there may be fifty innocent within the
> city. Will you really wipe out the place and not spare it for the sake of
> the fifty innocent within it? Far be it from You to do such a thing, to put
> to death the innocent with the guilty, making innocent and guilty the
> same. Far be it from You! Will not the Judge of all the earth do justice?"
> (18:22-25)

So outrageous is this notion that "the LORD was still standing before
Abraham" that many translations obscure the matter.⁸ The word of

---

⁶J. Gerald Janzen, *Abraham and All the Families of the Earth: A Commentary on the
Book of Genesis 12-50* (Grand Rapids, Mich.: Eerdmans, 1993), p. 60.
⁷Terence Fretheim, *Genesis,* in *The New Interpreter's Bible,* Vol. 1, ed. Leander E.
Keck et al. (Nashville: Abingdon, 1994), p. 468.
⁸Even the ancient Masoretic text, as Robert Alter points out in his note here, "has
Abraham standing before the LORD." Alter adds, "but this reading is avowedly a
scribal euphemism" intended to circumvent the presumed lessening of God's magisterial presence.

Abraham that comes to God—for which God waits—is no mumbled piety. He concludes, "Will not the Judge of all the earth do justice?" The word is strong, and clear, and challenging—the best sort of word to offer this God. Abraham appears "up to it" in his growing partnership with God, just as God, in waiting before Abraham, displays growing divine confidence in the capacity of the chosen partner to choose well.

"Will not the Judge of all the earth do justice?" Abraham asks. Astonishing. If God were an autocratic bully, or were merely interested in throwing a bit of God-weight around, surely this would be the occasion. After all, Abraham along with his wife has already laughed at proposals of God. But God accepts Abraham's impassioned concern on behalf of other peoples, even if that concern is expressed as a possible indictment of the divine judgment actually being carried out with fairness.

"Far be it from You to do such a thing," adds Abraham. God respectfully listens. The writer relishes the detail of just how far this man has journeyed toward a partnership with God and in sharing the ultimate divine agenda of blessing to all the clans of earth. "Far be it from You to do such a thing, to put to death the innocent with the guilty, making innocent and guilty the same." And then a second time, "Far be it from You!" with the punch-line, "Will not the Judge of all the earth do justice?"

God listens patiently to the laborious spelling-out of Abraham's concern. If there are fifty righteous in Sodom, asks Abraham, will you destroy the city?

The bartering goes on to the end of the chapter, 18:26-33: Yes, says God. Yes, for fifty I will accept your idea of justice tempered with mercy.

Well, Abraham goes on, "perhaps the fifty innocent will lack five." Who does Abraham think he's talking to? By now the writer has made it clear that Abraham knows to whom he is speaking. And the story's truth, apparently, is that God encourages such forwardness, on behalf of others, from the human partner.

Yes, says God. For forty-five, yes.

Forty?

Yes, for forty. Spared.

Thirty?

Yes.

"Here," he says to God, "pray, I have presumed to speak to my Lord. Perhaps there will be found twenty?"

"I will not destroy for the sake of the twenty."

"Please, let not my Lord be incensed and let me speak just this time. Perhaps there will be found ten."

"And He said, 'I will not destroy for the sake of the ten.' And the LORD went off when He finished speaking with Abraham, and Abraham returned to his place."

With all of Abraham's haggling, albeit on behalf of mercy, God not only listens, but agrees! The partners see eye to eye. They have been face to face, friends of the noblest order. Abraham is learning to see more and more like God sees, to walk with God, to walk before God. In fact, he is challenging God to see things as he, Abraham, sees them. Surely God is pleased, this One who has stood silent before Abraham, waiting for Abraham's word. By responding with so much of himself in visit six, as a friend to God, Abraham discovers that the scales of mercy and justice are tilted toward a mercy as generous as is humanly possible to conceive. Abraham is learning about God's will, and growing in his accommodation of that will. God's ultimate expression of the divine will, as it affects Abraham, is blessing to all the tribes of earth.

Abraham's growth resembles the progress of child to adult, discussing politics with the parent. Or, more apropos to this particular narrative, Abraham's maturation traces a progress from vassal to partner.[9] Abraham comes to initiate conversation, honest-to-God opinion and doubt. What to do about this city, and that, for example? The question hinges on a fine-tuned exploration of the tension between justice and mercy. Abraham leads the way, holding his own—a quite satisfactorily grown-up child. The partnership between Abraham and God becomes more and more reciprocal. It's what friendship requires, this increasingly equal meeting of spirits. That's what a later prophet was to see in

---

[9]Suggested to me by Walter Brueggemann, who also stressed the political nature of this partnership—that the partnership is being forged on behalf of a nation that is intended to bring blessing to all peoples.

the text when he has God calling Abraham his "friend" (Is 41:8). It takes a while, the length of this story, for Abraham to catch up to God and for God to slow down for Abraham—and for the two to trust each other completely. From the very first visit, however, the terms of partnership and its goal—in part a political goal of blessing to a nation and through that nation to all peoples—are clear.

Destruction for Sodom and Gomorrah has been God's last and sorrowful resort, a consequence that follows logically from the magnitude of wrongdoing in Sodom. Catastrophe is always the natural consequence of great wrongdoing. Ruin's raging fire is an extension of the rapaciousness of Sodom's inhospitality. Abraham did what he could in responding to the implicit challenge of this sixth visit. He and Sarah have played proper hosts to God. Abraham has learned to care enough for others to plead on their behalf before God, with whom he takes the initiative.

But there is still more for Abraham, one last challenge. Even after the intimacy of this sixth visit, Abraham does very poorly as God's partner in the everyday world. For the second time, he risks his wife's chastity. But having learned to intercede for Sodom and Gomorrah, Abraham is ready now for a more difficult intercession. He pleads for Abimelech and the barren women, victims of his own doing. Then, just before the seventh visit, Abraham has to relinquish Ishmael, his son by Hagar. Abraham seems to be learning. God seems to be pleased. The partnership seems to be growing. But we can't be sure about any of it—nor can God, apparently—not until the plot's last episode, the seventh visit.

IN VISIT SEVEN, GOD TESTS ABRAHAM AT HIS
Achilles' heel. He has been an anxious man. Every-
where, he has feared for his own life and name. As a
result, Sarah has suffered dishonor. Now, in the plot's
climax, Abraham is asked to give evidence that he has
finally overcome this fear; he is asked to let go of one
dearer than his own life could ever have been. Will he
relinquish Isaac, the beloved son of his old age, his life
and the hope of any name beyond the grave? There is
a dynamic to God's character as well, a clear willing-
ness to wait, to find out if Abraham is ready for full-
time partnership. It's hard to miss the distinct pleasure
of what God concludes, when he is finally able to say,
Now I know about you, Abraham. Yes, now I can be
sure. Because you have done this thing, I will indeed
make good on the promise.

5

COMING TO TRUST IN EACH OTHER
Visit 7

And it happened after these things that God tested Abraham. And He said to him, "Abraham!" and he said, "Here I am." And He said, "Take, pray, your son, your only one, whom you love, Isaac, and go forth to the land of Moriah and offer him up as a burnt offering on one of the mountains which I shall say to you." (22:1-2)

Visit 7 (22:1-19)

As read initially by my students, this scene along with most scenes from Genesis can mean almost anything they want it to mean, because everything is viewed as disconnected from anything else. So it was with me, once upon a time. A twentieth-century rabbi (Steven Saltzman) and two notable nineteenth-century thinkers (philosopher Søren Kierkegaard and poet Emily Dickinson) are examples of such disconnected reading and arbitrary interpretation. Each of the three views fails to note the resonances between visit seven and any of the other visits and the larger story in general. Each of the three readers seriously distorts the character of God and misses the ever-increasing complexity of the dance-like relationship between God and Abraham.

Emily Dickinson, always able to give words to our deepest suspi-
cions, concludes from this episode what many already think, especially in reference to this Genesis God, that God is an arbitrary tyrant.
She recoils in horror, though playfully, suggesting that Abraham's com-
pliance pleased God. "Flattered by Obeisance / [God's] Tyranny
demurred," and, when told to his children by Isaac, the "moral" is
clear: "with a Mastiff / Manners may prevail."¹ In other words, be
properly wary and on your best behavior before an unpredictable pit
bull. Behind the poet's tongue-in-cheek response can be detected a
serious though misguided encounter with the text. In this view, God is
extremely jealous, a God who loves power and craves our bowing and
scraping. Dickinson has struck a common nerve about something we'd
rather not look at—here, our conventional notions of God as bully.

A recent reader, Rabbi Steven Saltzman, expresses our possible revul-
sion more directly. "It's the story of a man who failed the last and most
important test of his life: the test of being a father."² So God was only setting Abraham up to act the fool in responding to the test—or to act the
hero by defying God. In either case, we are to assume that God couldn't
seriously be testing Abraham's willingness to relinquish his son.

Like Emily Dickinson and Steven Saltzman, Søren Kierkegaard
also reacts to this scene out of context. The Danish philosopher
constructs a pious but misleading view of God as largely inscrutable
and mysterious—much as in Auerbach's view. Our response before
such mystery is "fear and trembling," the title of his philosophical
musings on the scene. Kierkegaard imagines the response of an
average anyone—himself, Emily Dickinson, you or me. "Anyone"—
and many of my students certainly qualify—thinks of Abraham's
supreme test as an instance of an arbitrary God. To pass the test,
Abraham must take a leap of faith in response to a call that "comes
out of the blue." It's a faith-leap, a leap into the dark.³

¹Emily Dickinson, poem #1317, in *The Complete Poems of Emily Dickinson*, ed. Thomas H. Johnson (Boston: Little, Brown and Company, 1890, 1960), pp. 571-72.
²Steven Saltzman, *A Small Glimmer of Light: Reflections on the Book of Genesis* (Hoboken, N.J.: KTAV, 1966), p. 57.
³For Søren Kierkegaard, Abraham's faith gets tested by God in what appears
humanly as "sport"—so exceptional as to have no precedent. The alert reader under-

But the God of Abraham, far from being arbitrary, capricious or simply mysterious, is an accommodating God who visits Abraham—and Sarah—again and again. The entire story is orchestrated around these seven personal visits between God and Abraham. In each of the visits, God nudges, prods, encourages, and, when the relationship has ripened, talks things over. The relationship changes; it matures. Abraham finally takes his cue and begins talking with, and sometimes talking back to God. His silent obedience to the test of God regarding the relinquishment of his beloved son, here in the final visit, can mean that Abraham has become, as for Kierkegaard, a religious hero, or, as for Rabbi Saltzman, a moral failure. Or, as for Dickinson, perhaps Abraham has been browbeaten by a tyrannical God into meek submission. Or, finally, maybe Abraham has come so fully on board with God—after all, that has been the tendency of the developing plot—as to be able to put God to the test, just as God is putting Abraham to the test. God will come through: this might be Abraham's confidence—just as God might be thinking, Abraham will come through. When God finally halts the test and speaks to Abraham, the divine words suggest just this: that now God can be absolutely sure of what God suspected would be the case, that Abraham would let go in order to move forward, son and all.

In visit seven there are genuine and critical surprises, final flourishes on the standard dance steps of the prior six visits. These surprises suggest something brand new and yet not entirely unexpected. They are twists on patterns established by the writer. Surprise, so apparent especially in this last visit, suggests a world of possibility, a chance of something genuinely new coming to be in a world shared and shaped by God and human.

First Surprise: Where's Yahweh, the Lord?

The first surprise occurs immediately, as the last visit opens: "And it hap-

---

stands God's final test of Abraham as appropriate, the opposite of "sport" (Søren Kierkegaard, *Fear and Trembling: The Sickness unto Death*, trans. Walter Lowrie [Princeton, N.J.: Princeton University Press, 1941, 1954], pp. 33-34).

pened after these things that Elohim tested Abraham" (22:1). The one
who has greeted Abraham in each of the prior six visits has been Yahweh,
"the LORD." But here the name of the greeter changes to Elohim, "God." In
the first visit, "And the LORD [Yahweh] said to Abram, 'Go forth . . . ! '" (12:1);
second, "And [Yahweh] appeared to Abram and said . . ." (12:7); third, "And
[Yahweh] had said . . ." (13:14); fourth, "[Yahweh] came to Abram in a
vision, saying . . ." (15:1); fifth, "and [Yahweh] appeared to Abram . . ."
(17:1); sixth, "And [Yahweh] appeared to him . . ." (18:1). But here, in the
seventh and last visit, "God [Elohim] tested Abraham. And He said . . . 'Go
forth . . . ! '" (22:1-2). Patterns of repetition count for so much in all biblical
narrative. Surely ancient ears, tuned to how each of these visits has
begun, would have been intrigued and perhaps bothered by this shift in
greeting from Yahweh to Elohim in the last visit only. Furthermore, the
language of this last visit closely resembles that of the first. Listen again:
"And [Yahweh] said to Abram, 'Go forth . . . ! '" in the first visit; in this last
visit, "[Elohim] tested Abraham. And He said. . . . 'Go forth . . . ! '" (22:1-2).
The first and last visits open with a challenge to leave (and to "let go"),
and to leave for an unknown destination. The shift from *Yahweh* to *Elohim*, then, might be the writer's way of nudging us toward closer reflection of just how difficult—how in a league by itself—this final challenge
actually is. *Elohim* is associated, as we saw in the prior chapter, with the
more remote and magisterial God of the first creation account, who, as
Michael Fishbane understands it, "worded forth" a world, from on high.[4]
Yahweh Elohim, on the other hand, takes over for the second creation
account as a consummate and compassionate artist; Yahweh Elohim
cares about the human form—its life and its quality of life: the original
audience would have recognized Yahweh as Israel's personal God, their
"LORD" (the most common translation of *Yahweh*). Compared to Yahweh,
Elohim is more mysterious and hidden, as Martin Buber observes.[5] In that

---

[4]Michael Fishbane, *Text and Texture: Close Readings of Selected Biblical Texts* (New York: Schocken, 1979), p. 4.
[5]"The active surrender of Abraham, which begins to be evident after the fourth reve-
lation . . . here [visit seven] reaches its apex. On the other hand, God does not here
allow Himself to be seen at the beginning as He did at the beginning of the two preceding revelations, and here for the first time He is called not YHWH but Elohim: it
is the hidden God who will reveal Himself only then" (Martin Buber, "Abraham the
Seer," in *On the Bible* [New York: Schocken, 1968], pp. 40-41).

aspect "appropriate to cosmic and world-wide relationships,"[6] God-as-Elohim initiates this last visit—a first!—and asks for the relinquishment of the means toward the ultimate end that "all the clans of the earth through you shall be blessed" (12:3; 22:18).

Second Surprise: No Promise!

From the prior visits, we are used to the Lord's appearing or speaking to Abraham with a challenge, followed immediately by a promise. Then Abraham responds, the promise presumably encouraging his meeting of the challenge. But this time, the last time, the only time, and the most difficult time, there is no promise accompanying the test.

Does the shift in name from *Yahweh* to *Elohim*—God of all peoples and of the heavens and the earth—create in Abraham a certain sense of distance between himself and God? Such distance would be compatible with the stark words of challenge from Elohim, followed by silence where we would expect promise. For the first time in any of the visits, God offers the challenge but without any follow-up promise! Now it's just "do it." There are no further words of reward, no reassuring promise. God seems to be saying, "you're all grown up—do this because I ask, without any promise. Period." We can appreciate the irony of this most heart-wrenching challenge of all—hitting so close to home in the letting go of one's only son—coming, not from the close-to-home Yahweh who offers reassuring promises, but from Elohim of the heavens and the earth, Elohim of all peoples. Elohim asks the seemingly impossible, and with no reassurance. Abraham is being challenged by the God of all families to look beyond the altogether normal loyalties to family.

Third Surprise: The Extent of Abraham's Letting Go

Abraham's neighbors sacrificed children to Elohim, so perhaps Abraham isn't taken completely off guard: They do it for Elohim, why

---

[6]G. T. Manley, "Names of God," in *New Bible Dictionary*, ed. J. D. Douglas (Grand Rapids, Mich.: Eerdmans, 1962), p. 478

shouldn't I?[7] But in the context of all seven visits, God is asking of Abraham something much more difficult than one specific act of relinquishment. God is asking Abraham throughout the story to give up a way of being in the world. Abraham is being challenged to move beyond parochialism in order to become a blessing to all families beyond his own family, to forfeit the desire to make his own name great—for the sake of the common good. If Elohim is going to make good on the promise for *all* families, then somehow Elohim will have to make good on the promise for *his* family. But has Abraham come to trust in this kind of see-to-it God, this husband who has failed so miserably to trust for life and name with his own wife's honor on the line? Will he let go of this son who is dearer than his own life could ever have been, this son who represents all that old Abraham's life and name can now be? Has Abraham progressed this far? God will find out.

After three days of traveling to a spot shown him by God, Abraham prepares the altar and binds Isaac. The firewood is ready, the knife is raised. Then a messenger of Yahweh interrupts the procedure: "Do not reach out your hand against the lad" (22:12). *Lad* is a term of tenderness in keeping with the switch here to *Yahweh*.[8] In this seventh visit

---

[7]*Elohim* may also have signaled to the ancient audience "the gods" or *elohim* of neighboring peoples who demanded child sacrifice. "In the framework of his time and experience," as W. Gunther Plaut points out, "Abraham could have considered the command to sacrifice his son entirely legitimate. . . . [I]n the beginning of the test the command is issued by Elohim—the generic term for God or gods—and the command is one that other elohim could and did make. But when the sacrifice is about to be performed it is Abraham's God, Adonai [Yahweh, or "the Lord"], who stays his hand. Elohim might ask him to proceed, but Adonai says 'No'. Whereas the fear of Elohim had led to child sacrifice, the 'fear' of Elohim for which Abraham is specifically commended (22:12) entails a rejection, once and for all, of any such sacrifice." This understanding of Elohim's appearance in visit seven is possible. It would be compatible with what I take to be the more central function of the Elohim-Yahweh usage here, that the cosmic God Elohim, whose goal is blessing for all peoples, wishes a final test of his chosen partner's willingness to share that worldwide goal. Abraham assures his son about that sacrifice, that Elohim will provide (22:8), suggesting his trust in the Elohim face of God. But it's an angel of Yahweh who speaks with Abraham as to a friend, "Now I know that you fear God [Elohim]" (W. Gunther Plaut, ed., *The Torah: A Modern Commentary* [New York: Jewish Publication Society, Union of American Hebrew Congregations, 1981], p. 149).
[8]This is the same word used for the two servants in 22:3—all three, lads, on such a journey!

we have, then, two complementary perspectives on the God who is One. Elohim and Yahweh are brought together masterfully by the writer in this one episode. Does Abraham recognize the two complementary faces of this God who is One, as does the reader? Elohim, God of worldwide relationships, asks for a radical move beyond parochialism for the sake of blessings to all people: *let go of your son, your only son, the son whom you love, Isaac.* The surprising shift from the familiar *Yahweh* to the global *Elohim* would seem to indicate that Abraham is ready to accommodate deep within his psyche a larger conception of God, the God of all peoples and indeed of all creation. In offering the challenge, God exhibits a profound trust in the human partner to act radically on behalf of more than just his own name and family, and that Abraham will trust in Elohim both for his own name and for the ultimate promise, blessing to all peoples. Such blessing begins, after all, with one family. The son is restored to the father. Yahweh is assured of Abraham's fear of Elohim.

The journey of Abraham's life has come to a focus in the three-day journey of relinquishing his son, at the request of Elohim. For three days Abraham has proceeded to a mountain Elohim will show him, with no promise. Again: for the first time, in this last visit the challenge comes unaccompanied by any reassurance or reward.[9] What a silence this is, this absence of God's reassuring word of promise. Never has this text moved more quickly with greater dramatic effect: "'Go forth . . . to the mountains which I shall say to you.' And Abraham rose early" (22:2-3). There are no recorded words until the third day, an exchange between son and father that echoes the initial dialogue between Abraham and God:

> And Isaac said to Abraham his father, "Father!" and he said, "Here I am, my son." And he said, "Here is the fire and the wood but where is the sheep for the offering?" And Abraham said, "God will see to the

---

[9]Nahum Sarna is an exception among commentators in observing this change in pattern, along with a hint of its significance: "The great difference between the two events is what constitutes the measure of Abraham's progress in his relationship to God. The first divine communication carried with it the promise of reward. The final one held out no such expectation" (*Understanding Genesis* [New York: McGraw-Hill, 1966], p. 63).

sheep for the offering, my son." And the two of them went together.
(22:7-8)

God had begun this visit with a spoken greeting, also something new
to this last visit: "Abraham!" God has said, and "Here I am," responded
the now-ready Abraham (22:1). "Father!" the son says, and "Here I
am," responds the now-ready father. "Here I am" in both cases suggests
utter availability and confidence.

Fourth Surprise: No Surprise

Abraham has begun this three-day journey of a lifetime with no reassurance from God, but he has been ready to offer reassurance to his
son: *God will see to* . . . God will provide. *Elohim* will see to it. Father
binds his son; the fire is ready; the knife raised. Only now, after Abraham has completed the test, does God respond, as *Yahweh*, with familiar promises, but with new language. *"By my own Self I swear,* declares
the LORD: *because* you have done this . . . I will *indeed* bless you"
(22:16-17, emphasis mine). Never before has God said, "By my own
self I swear." And never before, though always implied, any language
like *"because you have done this thing."* The language is precise. *Because*
you have done this, I will *greatly* bless you. *Because*, in fact, is repeated
as a frame to the promise:

> *Because* you have done this . . .
>   I will greatly bless you . . .
>   and all the nations of the earth will be blessed through your seed
> *because* you have listened to my voice. (22:16-18)

It's *because* Abraham obeyed that God can finalize the promise. The
delay of promise until after the perfected response now makes perfect
sense. If it's *because of* what Abraham does that God is enabled—by God's
own choosing—to follow through on the promise, then of course what
Abraham does has to come before God's guarantee of the promise. The
story has implied from the very start that Abraham's coming on board as
God's partner is critical to the implementation of the divine will. Now the
theme has become emphatic and explicit: *because* Abraham lived up to
his chosen role as partner, God will now swear for the first time by the
divine self that, *indeed*, the promise of blessing will happen.

Abraham's reoriented will is necessary for the fulfillment of God's will, but this human will cannot be forced—by God's sovereign choice. It all might have turned out differently. Perhaps it did, the first time, with an unknown nomad who listened once or twice to this God but finally grew hard of heart and tired of hearing. Nothing to write a story about there. What we *do* have is a worthy narrative, a tough-minded drama of a successful wrestling between God's will and Abraham's will. Religious sorts like myself may be uncomfortable with a God who waits, who comes to know, who says "because" you have done so-and-so, I will do such-and-such. Such language, from God's own mouth, clearly implicates Abraham as necessary to God's agenda. Though reported "in straightforward language," the meaning of the *because*-language is "often obscured by efforts to wiggle out of the implications," observes Terence Fretheim. *Because* is "twice spoken as if to ensure the point: *Because* Abraham has done this, previously spoken divine promises can be reiterated."[10]

There are two nearly continuous though separate communications from the messenger of Yahweh indicating that the test has been accomplished successfully. In the first, a messenger of the Lord calls out for Abraham to put down his knife, "for now I know that you fear God" (22:12). Then the messenger calls out a second time, with the *because-you-have-done-this* promise. Separate and repeated appearances of Yahweh, or Yahweh's messenger, raise a good question, asked by Mordecai Kaplan: "Why this repetition?" Always, when encountering repetition in biblical narratives, this is the right question: Why? To what effect? "The reason," Kaplan suggests, "is found in the concluding words, 'because you have done this.' These words place the Abrahamic promise in a totally different light. For, while hitherto the promise given to Abraham is mainly an expression of divine favor, it now comes for the first time as an acknowledgement of Abraham's faithfulness. This is the point where divine effort meets with full response in the human being."[11] Divine effort meeting full human response: this is the language of partnership perfected. The necessary role of the

---

[10]Terence Fretheim, *Genesis,* in *The New Interpreter's Bible,* Vol. 1, ed. Leander E. Keck et al. (Nashville: Abingdon, 1994), p. 498.
[11]Quoted in Plaut, *Torah,* p. 153.

human partner is emphasized by making the *because-you-have-done-this* speech stand alone.

Fifth Surprise: *Now* I Know, Says God

Sometimes my students and I get nervous when we realize how emphatic the biblical writer is about God's apparent dependence on human response. Doesn't this limit God? And doesn't it seem a bit like Abraham is earning a reward from God for doing well? We go back over the story, noting that in choosing Abraham as a partner, God chooses an ordinary human being who can choose poorly—can respond, in fact, by saying no to God. In that case, what would God do? Try another would-be partner? That seems to be what this story is suggesting, reinforced by what God says after seeing Abraham's raised knife: "*Now* I know that you fear God" (22:12, emphasis mine). In our human projections of God, our creations of a deity in our image, do we long for one who ultimately pushes magic buttons, regardless of human agency—who doesn't need to wait on truly right action from the human partner? And perhaps we don't like the thought of waiting on a God who waits for us, a God who says about us, if at all, "*Now* I know." Becoming sure about the direction and perfecting of Abraham's will "is not a game with God," argues Walter Brueggemann. "God genuinely does not know. And that is settled in verse 12, 'Now I know.' There is a real development in the plot. The flow of the narrative accomplishes something in the awareness of God. He did not know. Now he knows."[12] And now that God knows, God will act.

And what of my students' uneasiness regarding Abraham's "reward" for doing well? That's what it sounds like: "Because you have done this for Me . . . I will do so-and-so for you." Casting the question in terms of Abraham's reward, however, misses a premise of the story, that Abraham is being groomed as a blessing for the world. It's a reward neither he nor any of us normally choose. One's own seed, how grand! That's a natural response. Blessing for all peoples, how much more grand—but from God's point of view, not ours. Abraham would desire blessing

---

[12]Walter Brueggemann, *Genesis* (Atlanta: John Knox Press, 1982), p. 187. Fretheim, *Genesis,* p. 497, agrees with this perspective.

for himself and his family, surely. He would work for a great name and a great nation, of course. In this story, however, Abraham's ultimate "reward"—whether he initially wants it or not—will be to function as a blessing to others. There is no question of earning special favor or divine acceptance for merely personal gain. God requires the godly with whom to work in refashioning creation from its chaos to a new harmony. This is the long view, the theme of the story as a whole.

In the Fear of God Is No Fear
But for Abraham it comes down to the details of everyday, to the morning of saddling his donkey, to the moment of grasping the cleaver. In addition, the writer focuses on textual details of word play that an alert audience will hear, though Abraham might have missed it (and maybe not: he says one word, God speaks the other):

> And Abraham reached out his hand and took the cleaver to slaughter his son. And the LORD's messenger called out to him from the heavens and said, "Abraham, Abraham!" and he said, "Here I am." And he said, "Do not reach out your hand against the lad, and do nothing to him, for now I know that you fear [*yere*] God and you have not held back your son, your only one, from Me." And Abraham raised his eyes and saw and, look, a ram was caught in the thicket by its horns, and Abraham went and took the ram and offered him up as a burnt offering instead of his son. And Abraham called the name of that place YHWH-*yireh*, as is said to this day, "On the mount of the LORD there is sight." (22:10-14, emphasis mine)

What is it that God comes to know about Abraham? God says: "that you *yere* God." And what is it that Abraham has discovered about God? He names the place: "the LORD *yireh*." *Yere, yireh*: this distinct word play occurs at the most critical juncture of the plot. (*Yere* is pronounced with an emphasis on the second syllable, with a long *a* sound; *Yireh* is pronounced with the accent on the first syllable, and the *e* is a short *e*.)

Abraham's perfect response in this last visit, without promise, proves decisive for God: "Now I know that you fear [*yere*] God." And what does this mean, in the dramatic context of this story—to fear God? "Fear of God" is what God has just witnessed: such trust in provision as to do the right thing for only the doing's sake, with no promise.

The God who has promised blessing to all peoples through Abraham
has asked Abraham to let go of his son, to trust God for the whole
grand enterprise. Abraham does it. God has witnessed Abraham's bartering pleas on behalf of "all peoples" living in Sodom and Gomorrah.
To fear God is to pursue a righteousness and justice that always bursts
the boundaries of narrow allegiances. Loyalty to family and upholding
the honor of the tribe, in the normal scheme of things, take prece-
dence over any commitment to the well-being of other families or of
neighboring tribes. God asks Abraham for that which is not normal, to
relinquish that which is at the old man's heart of family. For what?
That "all the nations of the earth will be blessed through your seed."
And why? "because you have listened to my voice" (22:18).

Maybe, as some of my students conjecture, this is coerced action,
God reducing Abraham to "fear and trembling," as the philosopher
Søren Kierkegaard has put it in the title of his reflections on this
scene.[13] Perhaps God is actually pleased to discover that Abraham is
properly afraid or so deeply reverential as to do anything this God asks
regardless of whether that thing is righteous even by God's own standards. Then we look at the story as a whole, once again. All his life
Abraham has lived in fear. Everywhere the couple traveled, they lied
and risked Sarah's chastity because of Abraham's fear for his life
(20:13). Does God ask Abraham to overcome being afraid of others'
harm by being afraid of what harm God might bring—if Abraham
doesn't measure up? The drama as a whole supports no such thing,
and in fact suggests Abraham's growing confidence in God. Abraham
comes to a place of trust and dedication that overcomes all manner of
"being afraid."

There are many other words for "fear" in the Hebrew lexicon that
could have been used other than *yere*. Many of these indicate "terror"
or "dread" or "trembling" or "being afraid." None of them are used. It's
yere. The great psychological and spiritual break-through for Abraham
is focused in the conjunction of *yere* and *yireh*. What he names this
sacred place, *Yahweh-yireh*, is an expression of his *yere* of God. *Fear* of
God, then, is a deep reverential regard for God's character as a *provider*.

---

[13]See the introduction for a discussion of this.

"The LORD-sees-to-it" is Abraham's new confidence, his obedient trust—his fear, *yere*, of God. Fear of God, in this story, has nothing to do with what modern readers commonly associate with fear. It's the kind of trust that empowers action—in Abraham's case, action of the most "un-normal" sort: for the sake of global blessedness as envisioned by God, Abraham relinquishes an only and beloved son. Confidence that *Yahweh-yireh* is the essence of *"yere* of God"; it is in this scene that such a connection is spelled out in everyday terms. Ancient ears would not have missed the sound-play of *yere-yireh*.

We don't know if, at the beginning of the story, Abraham is afraid of God. But his growing friendship with God and the trust exhibited in this sacrifice scene rule out the possibility that by the end of the story, in this climactic scene, Abraham's fear of God has anything at all to do with being afraid. As E. A. Speiser understands, this fear of God doesn't even point to reverential awe—though certainly such awe is apparent in other biblical scenarios.[14] Speiser translates *fear* of God as *dedication* to God: "The manifest stress," he points out, "is not so much on fear, or even awe, as on absolute dedication."[15] All of Abraham's contemporaries and predecessors from any ancient culture that we know about certainly began and ended their response to the gods in being afraid, in a trembling sort of awe. They lived in dread of what the gods might do to them at this turn or that, and so they went through their frenetic rituals to placate the gods. What God wants from Abraham, however, is friendship, not fear; dedication, not dread; trust, not trembling. In fact, Abraham's fear of God is the opposite of ordinary fear. Trust is the antidote to fear. In confidence, Abraham answers his son's queries about the sacrifice, "*Yahweh-yireh.*" Abraham evi-

---

[14]Isaiah's experience with God comes to mind: "In the year that King Uzziah died, I saw the Lord sitting on a throne, high and lofty; and the hem of his robe filled the temple. Seraphs were in attendance above him; each had six wings: with two they covered their faces, and with two they covered their feet, and with two they flew. And one called to another and said: 'Holy, holy, holy is the LORD of hosts; the whole earth is full of his glory.' The pivots on the thresholds shook at the voices of those who called, and the house filled with smoke. And I said: 'Woe is me! I am lost, for I am a man of unclean lips, and I live among a people of unclean lips; yet my eyes have seen the King, the LORD of hosts!' " (Is 6:1-5).

[15]"Now I know how dedicated you are to God" (E. A. Speiser, *Genesis*, Anchor Bible [New York: Doubleday, 1964], p. 163).

dences nothing of ordinary fear of God, nor fear of any outcome. Rather, we witness confidence and dedication, commitment and action.

Fear of God is grounded in confidence and deed, not emotion. Generations after Abraham, after God has noticed Israel's good attitude and action, God says to Moses, "If only they had such a mind as this, to fear me and to keep all my commandments always, so that it might go well with them and with their children forever!" (Deut 5:29 NRSV). And Job, that mightily troubled man, wonders where in the world one can find wisdom. He concludes that

> God understands the way to it,
>   and he knows its place . . . .
> "Truly, the fear of the LORD, that is wisdom;
>   and to depart from evil is understanding."
> (Job 28:23, 28 NRSV)

"To depart from evil" is paralleled with "the fear of the LORD," just as "to keep all my commandments" is linked by God to "fear of me." God can be sure, finally, about Abraham's "fear of God" because of proper response: it was *because* he did what God asked that God is now sure that Abraham has a proper fear of God.

But, but . . . perhaps it's being afraid of God that prompts one "to depart from evil" and "to keep all [God's] commandments" and to let go of your son? No, the narrative leads us to an opposite conclusion, that what Abraham comes to internalize by the end of his story is a fear of God characterized by meeting the particular challenge, and a wisdom that knows to trust in God's provision.

Abraham comes to understand in the marrow of his bones that God will provide, and that obedience entails letting go of what one naturally fears to lose—in Abraham's case, not just his own life but that life magnified oh-so-much in the life of his son. His fear of God is a wisdom, a deep knowing that the God who calls for such relinquishment is Elohim, the God of all peoples, and that this God Elohim will provide, as he tells his questioning son about the sacrifice (22:8). Then it is an angel of Yahweh who stops Abraham from slaying his son in sacrifice, acknowledging to Abraham the divine surety about Abraham's fear of Elohim (22:12). Perhaps Abraham has put it fully together, here in his greatest trial, that the God who wears two different faces is one. Abraham's God is the God, as well, of all peoples. It is to be a blessing for all peoples that Abraham was chosen as a potential partner in the first place (12:3). Abraham has known something of these two aspects of God. Yahweh, the more familiar, has been appearing and speaking in each of the visits; it's after the second visit that Abraham "invoked the name of [Yahweh]" (12:8; 13:4) and in the fourth visit that Abraham utters his very first recorded words to God, "O my Master, [Yahweh]" (15:2). But Elohim, too, is known by Abraham. As we saw in the prior chapter, he has taken an oath before a foreign king "to [Yahweh], the Most High [El], possessor of heaven and earth" (14:22), and he has flung himself to the ground when Yahweh appeared, saying, "I am [El Shaddai]"—*El*, associated with, or the same as, the Elohim who goes on to change Abram to Abraham, "father to a multitude of nations" (17:1, 4). El, or Elohim, is the "possessor of heaven and earth," as Abraham put it earlier in front of Melchizedek. But it is Yahweh who has opened each of the six visits before this last one. For Abraham and for the reader, then, there are two faces of God. But there is no question of a dualism for the writer, no sense of incompatible wrestling within the God-head. Quite the opposite, as illustrated here in visit seven. The Elohim aspect of God is in keeping with the nature of the great challenge given Abraham, while Yahweh's comforting voice is appropriate to Abraham's trusting response. For the writer and for Abraham, these are two faces of one God.

For the sake of a multitude of nations, Abraham is being challenged to give up claim to his life, name and nation embodied in his son, a son whom he loves. The move beyond parochialism is crucial, and Yahweh/Elohim has been present in Abraham's journey, preparing him for this crucial choice on his part. After Sarah dies, Abraham has to choose a wife for his son, and he entrusts to a servant the responsibility of going to just the right place for just the right wife. He makes the servant swear an oath, "by [Yahweh, Elohim] of the heavens and [Elohim] of the earth" (24:3). God is One, indeed, for Abraham: Elohim, the cosmic and global God "of the heavens and . . . of the earth" is also Yahweh, his master, Lord. The capacity to embrace the God of all who is also his Lord appears to be at the heart of what Abraham comes to in his slow change of orientation from fear to trust. Surely Abraham has come to realize, as the writer of the Torah's last book puts it, that "YHWH our God, YHWH is One!" (Deut 6:4).[16]

Such an embrace of a God who is simultaneously and emphatically for you and for all others is not a luxury for those inclined toward spiritual matters. Rather, coming to trust in the God who is such a One enables life to be lived well by ordinary folk making otherwise normal and disastrous choices. For example, what has kept Abraham from such an embrace has been ordinary fear, a fear for his life and well-being that kept alive a subterfuge that risked Sarah's honor everywhere the couple traveled, and led to others' harm. Abraham has lost his wife to another man, Sarah has been dishonored, and "all the peoples" have been plagued. Crippled by this anxiety all his traveling days, Abraham hears in visit four the most stark and most central of all the challenges: *fear not.* How does one get rid of anxieties that hobble the self and harm others? Nothing short of transformation will do, says this story, a fundamental change of natural priorities based on a growing confidence that the Elohim who asks for relinquishment is the Yahweh who will provide.

For name, for status, for a sense of importance, for survival itself: Elohim will see to it—and so Abraham names the place of triumph, *Yahweh-yireh.* Overcoming ordinary fear for one's own—one's life, name, family—is made possible for Abraham when he comes to fear the God who calls on behalf of all families. And this is the same God who gives Isaac back, who works to restore Sarah's honor, and who tutors toward a final return of the wife to her husband. God waits, encouraging and challenging all the time, until Abraham can let go and trust in God's provision—of his life, his name. God doesn't act in a conclusive way until Abraham acts in a conclusive way. Such a way proves risky for both partners. As Eugene Roop sees, "God took the risk that Abraham would respond. Abraham took the risk that God would provide."[17]

---

[16]Translation by Everett Fox, *The Five Books of Moses* (New York: Schocken, 1995).

[17]Eugene Roop, *Genesis* (Scottsdale, Penn.: Herald, 1987), p. 151. In *The God Who Risks: A Theology of Providence* (Downers Grove, Ill.: InterVarsity Press, 1998)—which came to my notice as I was putting the finishing touches on this book—John Sanders explores this idea of God waiting, God risking, a God who "comes to know." Sanders is equally adept and painstakingly thorough with biblical exegesis, theological and philosophical discourse, and historical reflection—and practical applicability.

God and Abraham come to a perfected trust in each other, and they move toward a future being forged by mutual goodwill. Clyde Francisco suggests that "to be true to himself God cannot bless Abraham and his descendants unless they give themselves to righteousness and justice. He will even work with them to see that it happens!"[18] This is the great drama. It's hard to imagine higher drama than this story of divine will and human will doing business together. How can such a thing work out? At the climactic episode of the drama, God's challenge to Abraham to give back his son brings the dramatic tensions to an unthinkable breaking point. This dramatic tension "presents a test not only of Abraham's faith in God," as Terence Fretheim sees, "but of God's faith in Abraham as well, in the sense that Abraham's response will affect the moves God makes next." Fretheim goes on to underscore just what is at stake by emphasizing the risk factor. "Given his somewhat mixed responses to God up to this point, God took something of a risk to put so much on the line with this man."[19] *Because* Abraham has grown up as a partner, God can proceed with the good intended for all. Having witnessed Abraham's concern for this global good, when in the prior visit Abraham argued boldly for Sodom and Gomorrah's salvation, God has evidence that, in spite of the risk, Abraham is up to it, finally. By the same token, Abraham has sufficient evidence of God's worthiness as a partner, permitting the old man with a young son to work out in everyday terms a *yere* of Elohim which is a transforming trust that *Yahweh-yireh*.

All well and good, to get rid of fear's clutching by obedient trust in the One-Who-Sees-To-It. But toward what end? The answer is love, but a love so different from what the word conjures up as to warrant a different language. One way to view the Abraham and Sarah story is to understand it as a demonstration of a reorientation toward a proper love, toward a concern for the blessing of others—for the others' best interests. To be a blessing for all peoples requires relinquishment, and this letting go starts where it's most difficult, with the one we "love" best. Relinquishment is at the heart of the challenge that begins the story and the challenge that ends the story, as we see next. The end is in the beginning, and the end is love.

---

[18]Clyde T. Francisco, *Genesis,* in *The Broadman Bible Commentary,* Vol. 1, rev. ed., ed. Clifton J. Allen (Nashville: Broadman, 1973), p. 175

[19]Fretheim, *Genesis,* p. 497.

LOVE IS THE LAST THING WE MIGHT THINK ABOUT IN reflecting on Abraham's acceptance of God's challenge to relinquish an only and beloved son. The striking parallelism between the narrative's first and last visits forces thought about relinquishment—its point, its goal. Why let go? Why detach from what is dearest? Each successive visit has widened the scope of Abraham's vision and has deepened the intimacy of friendship between God and Abraham. God is challenging Abraham to change, to become "un-normal" in learning not to fear for his life and name, not to scheme for self-preservation and self-promotion at others' expense. Letting go of that which is dearest to you, beginning with your own life and name, is for the sake of a more expansive and inclusive way of life. As a son, Abraham begins by letting go of his father's house, but as a father he ends by letting go of his son. This is the biblical way of showing us God's vision for the human creation. Here is a vision of love that is rooted and finds its flowering in communal, political terms.

6

WHAT'S LOVE— AND FEAR—GOT TO DO WITH IT?

G O FORTH TO A LAND THAT I WILL SHOW YOU," GOD'S FIRST CHAL- lenge rings out. Must Abraham begin a journey, then, without know- ing his place of arrival? And why should he have to turn his back on family and all that is familiar? In the story's climactic scene, "Go forth" is heard once again, and again the destination is uncertain—"to a mountain I will say to you." The Hebrew word for *go-forth* occurs nowhere else in the Bible. Its paralleled use indicates something of the writer's care in connecting visits one and seven, the plot's beginning and ending.

In visit one (12:1-4), Abraham had to turn his back on homeland and father's house. Relinquishing his son Isaac in the last visit repre- sents the same letting-go, only much more forcefully. Abraham's jour- ney in between has not been very smooth. All the while Abraham has been clinging to his own life and name, however well he did in relin- quishing the securities of his life and name in Haran. In visit seven he is challenged to let go of that which is dearer even than his own life, to relinquish that which represents his only hope for a name. He must let go of his son, of his future.

Let's be skeptical for a moment. Perhaps the first moving-on "was

the ordinary motive of his day" to which God catered, God being reasonable. That is, God understands and accommodates Abraham's natural desires.[1] But such a reading ignores the story's details. Peter Miscall
turns on its head the apparent call to let go: Abraham is "an opportun-
ist who will take advantage of any situation and of anyone, including
God. Abraham is leaving Haran for his own personal reasons . . . with
the hope of gaining some benefit from the Lord."[2] On the other hand,
suggests another reader, such a move for Abraham would have been
most *un*-ordinary. "Leaving one's family, which is the source of law
and morality, as well as safety and security for the primitive would
seem to be an almost unthinkable act for a person in Abram's time. . . .
Abram was being asked to shift his identity from his land and family
for an identity with the Lord, who will bless those who bless Abram."[3]
Which of the two scenarios is more likely? Can we simply fit the
story's voice to the pitch of hearing at which our individual ears are
set? I don't think so. The biblical writer is too careful for that.

The delight and power of this story are in the story's details. The
challenge of relinquishment, the second view above, is emphasized in
the first visit and mirrored in the last visit by a triad of terms that in
each case zeroes in on the emotional heart of the matter. It is a
wrenching affair—more so in the second instance. Look closely at the
arrangement of the first challenge:

1. Go forth from your land
  2. and your birthplace
    3. and your father's house

"This is more poetry than geographic information," observes

---

[1]Perhaps, as we have conjectured in an earlier chapter, what hit Abraham was the
travel-bug, the itch to go forth and trade. Maybe, as one commentator asserts, "the
mere abandonment of his country in the hope of gaining a better one [was] the
ordinary motive of his day" and that "it was the *ground* of this hope, the belief in
God, which made Abraham's conduct original and fruitful. That sufficient induce-
ment was presented to him is only to say that God is reasonable" (Marcus Dods,
Genesis Commentary, in *The Expositor's Bible*, ed. W. Robertson Nicoll [New York:
A. C. Armstrong and Son, 1903], p. 89).

[2]Peter D. Miscal, *The Workings of Old Testament Narrative* (Philadelphia: Fortress,
1983), p. 20.

[3]Martha Rogers, "The Call of Abram: A Systems Theory Analysis," *Journal of Psychology and Theology* 9, no. 2 (1981): 119–20.

W. Gunther Plaut. "It emphasizes the difficulties of the challenge Abraham is about to accept," a progressive test. "It is difficult to leave one's land and to be an unprotected wanderer abroad"; but "it is even more difficult to abjure all that is most dear in one's accustomed house"; and certainly "it is most difficult of all to reject one's father's values and standards."[4]

The end is in the beginning.[5] The parallel between the end and the beginning is precise, not just in theme, but in detailed pattern. Listen to the echo:

1. Go forth from your land	1. Go forth . . . take, pray, your son,
2. and your birthplace	2. your only one,
3. and your father's house	3. whom you love, Isaac . . .

Just as in visit one, the emotional stakes are raised within the three successive phrases. *Take your son* is stunning in its request. But *your only one* twists the emotional dagger. Then, the ultimate hitting-home, the deepest psychic expression of longing and desire, *whom you love . . . Isaac.*

In both the first and last visits, the theme of relinquishment is made all the more powerful by an identical technique that focuses in on the emotional trauma. My college students often miss the significance and power of paired scenes like visits one and seven because they don't recognize the repetitive technique of this ancient narrative. Robert Alter often has had to go back hundreds of years to find a good eye for the exquisite poetic paralleling of scenes like this one.[6] Abraham's

---

[4]And all of this is just the beginning of challenges, as the author understands: "The passage makes it clear that God's demand represents a severe trial of faith for Abraham, the first of several fundamental choices he will have to make in his life" (W. Gunther Plaut, ed., *The Torah: A Modern Commentary* [New York: Jewish Publication Society, Union of American Hebrew Congregations, 1981], pp. 93–94).

[5]A central theme in T. S. Eliot's *Four Quartets*, about which more will be said shortly.

[6]"I have discovered," Alter says, "that some of the medieval Hebrew commentators were often more helpful than nearly all the modern ones" (Robert Alter, *Genesis: Translation and Commentary* [New York: W. W. Norton, 1996], p. xliii). Here is Alter's fine use of an eleventh-century rabbi, who rehearses the parallels between visits one and seven: "The divine imperative to head out for an unspecified place [12:1-3] resembles, as Rashi observes, God's terrible call to Abraham in chapter 22 to sacrifice his son on a mountain God will show him. Rashi also draws a shrewd connection between the triplet here—'your land and your birthplace and your father's house'—with the triplet in chapter 22—'your son, your only one, whom you love' " (p. 50).

moral maturation begins and ends with relinquishment. God's challenge in the first visit, as Walter Brueggemann notes, "is a call to abandonment, renunciation, and relinquishment. It is a call for a dangerous departure from the presumed world of norms and security."[7] The difficulty of the initial challenge to leave his father's house is affirmed throughout the story by the uncertainty of a "resting place." Relinquishment receives its exclamation point with the demand to let go of an only and loved son. As a son, Abraham begins the journey detaching from the world of his father; twenty-five years later, father Abraham must relinquish his son.

The blessing that flows from relinquishment is felt first at home with the relationship to one's spouse and with one's own self. True, relinquishment leads beyond the parochialism of me and my partner in a cozy nest, beyond and outward toward concern and blessing to all families. But this kind of detachment works the magic of blessing within a single family as well. In Abraham and Sarah's case, blessing had to start at home before it could move beyond. Abraham got stuck on self. He could not let go of concern for his name, his very existence. And at the end, he must prove that he has journeyed far beyond self-promotion, beyond self-preservation at another's expense. "Do not reach out your hand against the lad," says God to the knife-wielding father, "for now I know that you *have not held back* your son, your only one, from Me" (22:12). And again, just a bit later: "Because you have done this thing and *have not held back* your son, your only one, I will greatly bless you. . . . And all the nations of the earth will be blessed through your seed" (22:16, 18, emphasis mine). The Hebrew word for "holding back"—translated often as "withhold"—is *chasak*. It can mean "hoard," as a miser who withholds wealth from the public good. It can also mean "prevent," as in a person who prevents something from happening. God's dream is that Abraham will become unnormal in choosing not to hoard, prevent, clutch or hang on to. You have not held back your son, your only one, and therefore—ultimate reward—"all the nations of the earth will be blessed through your seed." Abraham must not *hoard* this seed, making it his private good at the expense of global

---

[7]Walter Brueggemann, *Genesis* (Atlanta: John Knox Press, 1982), p. 118.

good. He must not *prevent* the fulfillment of the promise. He must pass the test he has been flunking all his life, the clinging to his own personal safety and well-being. Failure to let go has led, as we have seen, to the constant hazarding of his wife's chastity and the very womb that would bear the seed of promise! As always, wrongdoing has ironically appropriate consequences. Preserve your own life and name, and you'll lose the chance for seed (Sarah remains barren) that will bring you that name!

    1. Go forth . . . take, pray, your son,

      2. your only one,

        3. whom you love, Isaac.

The last word of the last challenge that Abraham ever hears from God is *Isaac*. Is the father left rehearsing this name as he trudges off for those three days toward God-only-knows-where? God, not Abraham, knows the destination. He had begun his story by hearing a promise that his own name would be a matter of God's provision: "I will bless you and make your name great" (12:2). Shall an aged father be asked to overcome attachment to a name so much more dear than his own? The end is in the beginning, only much more demanding. Abraham comes full circle from his early failure. And it's all about blessing, a profound happiness that possesses a touch of ache for the beauty of the world. Only in these two visits, first and seventh, are the promises spoken to Abraham referred to as "blessing." In light of the first visit especially, the seventh is wonderfully climactic.[8]

Relinquishment is not an end in itself, a stoical withdrawal for the sake of the soul's cultivation and peace. Rather, it's about love. Letting go leads to a personal fulfillment that spreads out as blessing for others. Abraham is not only to "go forth"; he is to "be a blessing." J. Gerald Janzen offers a translation of the first visit (Gen 12:1-3) that underscores the connection between relinquishment and love, between letting-go and taking-hold for the sake of others—for the sake of the world.

---

[8]Nahum Sarna, whose analysis of these two visits is compatible with mine, points out that God's request for the binding of Isaac—the "Akedah"—serves as "the climactic event" of the entire story ("The Birth of Isaac and the Akedah," in *Understanding Genesis* [New York: McGraw-Hill, 1966], p. 160).

Go from your country and from your kindred and from your father's
    house . . .
  that I may make of you a great nation
  and that I may bless you,
  and that I may make your name great;
Be a blessing,
  that I may bless those who bless you
  —but the one who belittles you I will curse—
  and that by you all the families of the earth may bless themselves.[9]

Be a blessing. Whether it's "you shall be a blessing" (Alter) or "be a
blessing" (Janzen), the impact is nearly the same. You let go, says God,
and you will be—or you must be—a blessing, so that I can make good
on the divine dream, "that by you all the families of the earth may
bless themselves." Blessing spreads out, a happy infectiousness: the
outsiders who bless this blessing-bringing man will themselves be
blessed by God. And Abraham will himself end up bringing blessing in
three specific instances, which we will look at in a later chapter.

Why are Abraham and Sarah singled out for initial blessing? The
text suggests that God chose with the hope or expectation that the couple would say yes, rather than on the grounds of any preexisting greatness. But what did God have in mind with this choosing? Something
cozy between the divine and special people? Quite the contrary: God
chooses this ordinary couple to "be a blessing." Terence Fretheim puts
it nicely: "God's choice of Abram serves as an initially exclusive move
for the sake of a maximally inclusive end."[10]

To be a blessing requires a journey within, a reorientation. As Abraham begins, so he ends—by hearing God's radical challenge to let go of

---

[9]J. Gerald Janzen, *Abraham and All the Families of the Earth: A Commentary on the
Book of Genesis 12–50* (Grand Rapids, Mich.: Eerdmans, 1993), p. 15. The line
arrangement is my own. "Be a blessing" in verse 2 can be translated as result
rather than challenge, as in the NRSV, "I will bless you, and make your name great,
so that you will be a blessing." As in so many cases, the context has to determine
translation, and I think the double imperative, "Go forth" and "Be a blessing" fits
not only this immediate context but the story as a whole. In either case, result or
cause, relinquishment is linked with blessing to all families of the world.

[10]Also from Terence Fretheim: "This final phrase [blessing to all] presents the objective of all the previous clauses; God's choice of Abraham will lead to blessings for
all the families of the earth" (*Genesis,* in *The New Interpreter's Bible,* Vol. 1 [Nash-
ville: Abingdon, 1994], p. 424).

parochial interests in order to provide happiness for all families of earth. We can't understand the import of God's request for the son in the last visit without seeing it as an overlay of the first request, as a paralleled instance to let go of all that is normal, of what we hang onto as belonging to us. Primarily, of course, I feel that I belong to myself, to my possibility of importance in the world, to my very existence. Evidently that's what Abraham felt in failing to let go of his self, his name, with the consequence of forcing his wife into sexual jeopardy and shame. The story is all of a piece, probing the deepest fears and longings of the individual psyche but proclaiming the highest reaches of potential—and by the end of Genesis, actual—global blessing.

Let us remember that the letting go is for the sake of blessing, and that relinquishment represents a reversal of normal and destructive attitudes and actions. Blessing progressively replaces the curse humans have brought on themselves. Eve is cursed with subjection to a husband with whom she had enjoyed a reciprocal companionship (Gen 2:23-25; 3:16) while Adam is cursed by a miserable toil that once was gardening pleasure (2:15; 3:17). Cain is cursed for killing his brother, Lamech boasts to his wives of outlandish revenge (4:23-24), and God finally curses the created order with a flood. After the killing waters, God tries for world-wide blessing through Noah's family. This tack also ends disastrously, with Babel's tower-building, motivated by name-securing fear. Babel folk are cursed with that which they fear, dispersal and alienation. The peoples of the earth are scattered and their language confused. These nations, then, are among the very nations to whom Abraham is to bring blessing. A new way of blessing rather than curse is envisioned by God. Five times in these opening verses of this story we hear *bless* or *blessing*; five times in the Genesis prologue (1—11) we have had explicit reference to *curse*. "The biblical story of redemption, as it begins in Abraham, is a journey in blessing from a single person to all the families of the earth."[11]

---

[11]The five mentions of curse in the Genesis prologue are these: 3:14 (serpent); 4:11 (Cain); 9:25 (Canaan); 3:17 and 5:29 (ground). "When the so-called *salvation history* begins in 12:1-3," J. Gerald Janzen points out, "its agenda is announced in the fivefold repetition of the word *bless/blessing*. This fivefold repetition answers to the fivefold reference to "curse" in chapters 1—11, signaling that the agenda of the salvation history is to counteract the workings of evil in the world and to restore the world to its divinely intended blessedness" (*Abraham and All the Families of the Earth*, pp. 5, 15).

Relinquishment, then, is a reversal of the normal. God tells Abraham to go forth "that I may make your name great." Abraham is challenged to let God take care of his person and status, his name. The move beyond parochialism begins as close to home as possible, with one's very own self and concern for place in the world. Such reorientation of intuitive choices reaches the impossible moral heights of relinquishing that which is dearer even than one's own life, the life of an only child, a dearly loved child. Are we called to let go of one so close, whom we love? The purpose of Abraham's relinquishment is, after all, love. But God's kind of love, in this narrative and in Genesis generally, is an inclusive love. Relinquishment is letting go of an anxiety about what I might lose; it is letting go of the desire for what I might gain. Relinquishment is one side of a coin whose other and shining face is God's concern for blessing. Relinquishment is the necessary condition toward an embrace of blessing for all peoples everywhere and at all times.

This relinquishment is precisely the "detachment" of which the poet T. S. Eliot speaks. Relinquishment is

> not less of love but expanding
> Of love beyond desire. . . . Thus, love of a country
> Begins as an attachment to our own field of action
> And comes to find that action of little importance
> Though never indifferent.[12]

This is the terrain of Abraham and Sarah's journeying. Love has everything to do with this journey.

Eliot calls such love "the still point of the turning world." Timeless good, in Abraham and Sarah's story, is a "still point" taking a lifetime to learn. Timeless good, the still point, is a love that renews with blessing all that goes on in time, in the "turning world." We might demur: surely Abraham loved his son well. Yes—otherwise, he wouldn't have had any clue about what God wanted, which was to learn from that love and move beyond its exclusive object. Abraham couldn't have anguished over leaving his father's house back in Haran if he hadn't

---

[12]T. S. Eliot, "Little Gidding," in *Four Quartets* (1943; reprint, New York: Harcourt Brace & Company, 1971), p. 55.

known love in that house. Relinquishment-love "begins as attachment to our own field of action," Eliot observes, but it must move outward in concentric circles to stay alive as love. Attachment-love is love for a spouse, a son or daughter. But if attachment remains as love merely of one's own, such a love will shrivel up on itself. Given enough time, it atrophies into a suffocating loyalty, a vindicating honor. Relinquishment-love includes attachment but moves decisively beyond family and one's own. We are to "be a blessing to all peoples." True love is a centrifugal force whose initial and constant energy includes one's own and renews one's own only by continually expanding outward.

Abraham has to learn this love. It's not normal; the process, for Abraham, extends over the seven visits, as we have seen. "The revelations appear as stations in a progress from trial to trial and from blessing to blessing," Martin Buber points out. "[They] are seven stations on the way of a man from the beginning of the mutual relation between this man and God until its completion."[13] At the conclusion of his first "station," having left his father's house, Abraham arrives at a "teaching tree," the "Terebinth of the Oracle" at Moreh (12:6).[14] "Moreh" derives from the Hebrew *yarah*, to direct, point out, show, teach. "Torah" is related to this root term *yarah* as well. The Torah teaches. What it teaches above all is dramatized in this ultimate challenge to Abraham: Do right, and be a blessing. Bestow love. Learn love.

What prohibits love? Wrong responses to fear have kept Abraham from hazarding his own life by sacrificing his wife's chastity. Fear has prohibited love. If the tests of each visit are viewed chiastically—paralleled but in reverse order—the central visit, number four, would be the

---

[13]Martin Buber, "Abraham the Seer," in *On the Bible* (New York: Schocken, 1968), p. 36. "The seven revelations to Abram are precisely and significantly related both to one another and to the stories with which they are interspersed. Each one of the revelations and each one of the other stories has its particular place in the pattern, and could not stand in any other. . . . Not one of them can be transposed without disrupting the whole. . . . No theory of sources can explain this structure, which is so manifold in character and style and yet held together by a uniformly great vision" (pp. 36–37).

[14]J. Gerald Janzen points out nicely Abram's need of this teaching (*Abraham and All the Families of the Earth*, p. 22). "Moreh" is used by many translations, including Everett Fox.

"heart" of the chiasm. There we find the challenge "not to fear." This chiasm is suggested by what we have just seen as the repetition of elements in visit seven that were crucial in visit one. These parallels extend through the other visits, six repeating two, and five repeating three. The entire chiasm is framed by genealogies:

A *Frame: Genealogy*	(11:27-32)
B *Test 1* Go . . . from your country, kindred, father's house	(Visit 1, 12:1-6)
C *Test 2* Implied: Abram initiates response to promise	(Visit 2, 12:7-9)
D *Test 3* Walk . . . [the land]	(Visit 3, 13:14-18)
E *Test 4* Do not fear; cut animals	(Visit 4, 15)
D' *Test 5* Walk . . . [before Me; be blameless]	(Visit 5, 17)
C' *Test 6* Implied: Abraham initiates response to	
Presence	(Visit 6, 18;1-15)
B' *Test 7* Go . . . take your son . . . only son . . . whom you love	(Visit 7, 22:1-19)
A' *Frame: Genealogy*	(22:20-24)

As is true for other chiasms found in Genesis,[15] the second element not only repeats its counterpart, but provides a twist—an elaboration, or something more complex. In the case of the seven visits, each test gets successively more challenging, just as we have already discovered in the seventh test for Abraham, to relinquish his beloved son—and

---

[15]For Dixon Sutherland, the entire narrative is arranged chiastically ("The Organization of the Abraham Promise Narrative," *Zeitschrift für die alttestamentliche Wissenschaft* 95, no. 3 [1983]: 337–43).

Isaac Kikawada and Arthur Quinn have uncovered simple and fairly elaborate chiastic structures for the preface of Genesis. The following three-verse chiasm (7:21-23) illustrates the point that the repeated element elaborates or extends that which it echoes; this chiasm also has a "heart":

A And all flesh died that moved upon the earth
 B birds, cattle, beasts, all swarming creatures that swarm upon the earth
  C and every man
   D everything on the dry land in whose nostrils was the breath of life
    E died;
     F He
    E' blotted out
   D' every
  C' Man
 B' and animals and creeping things and birds of the air;
A' they were blotted out from the earth.
God is at the heart of the devastation (F). The destruction is pictured more graphically in the last element ("they were blotted out from the earth") than in the first element, which it echoes ("And all flesh died that moved upon the earth.") Isaac Kikawada and Arthur Quinn, *Before Abraham Was: The Unity of Genesis 1–11* (Nashville: Abingdon, 1985), p. 95.

not just his kinfolk, as in the first test. The implied test of visit six is more momentous than the implied test of visit two: to host God and to initiate conversation, in visit six, indicates an advanced stage of relationship from the initiating activity of altar-building in honor of this God, in visit two.

Similarly, the walk-challenge of visit five is of a much higher order than the walk-challenge of visit two: to walk before God, or with God, demands what is difficult even to imagine, whereas to walk a strange land as if claiming it for your own—while requiring faithful obedience—is at least doable during a given week or two. What this chiasm emphasizes goes beyond the escalating difficulty and greater reciprocity of relationship. It provides a focus, as well, on the middle test. This challenge "not to fear" appears as central to all the visits and all the tests. Indeed, Abraham's fundamental wrong has stemmed from a fear for his life, and a fear that led him not only to plead self-preservation to his wife, but self-promoting interests as well—"that it may go well with me." However normal such a response to one's life being risked, the consequences of Abraham's subterfuge prove him wrong, as we have observed. His has been a very narrow attachment-love, to himself.

To the exclusion or at the expense of others, we cling to our own— our own person, our mother, husband, sister, son, daughter; our neighborhood or country. We confuse such loyalty with virtue. Tribalism then and now, however normal, can lead to horror. Defining loyalty and honor exclusively in familial and national terms is commonplace, and inevitably destructive. Relinquishing such commitments to "what's ours" for the sake of others' interests is the scope of the journey that God offers Abraham and Sarah. For this couple, and all their children into our own day and beyond, it's a journey of a lifetime.

Though the major action of the story is concluded—all questions regarding Abraham and God and Sarah resolved, all threats to the promise overcome there is still an epilogue like ending to the narrative that helps the reader to reflect with pleasure on what has transpired, and what is to come. Without any more of God's visiting, Abraham must deal with a foreign people concerning a tricky land deal. Land? Yes, that part of the promise is still hanging, though the seed problem has loomed more in the plot's action. Must Abraham negotiate to get land, or will God simply hand it over to him? And in these negotiations, will Abraham bring curse or blessing? Added to Abraham's role in the world as a newly "completed" pilgrim, he must provide for his son's marriage. Sarah has died, and Isaac is passive, it appears: has he been traumatized by the near-sacrifice? In any case, he needs help and gets it, beautifully. God will be Isaac's God, too—the "God of Abraham, Isaac, and Jacob." And the God of Ishmael, too, with whose genealogy the story of Abraham, fittingly, closes. After all, Abraham was to be a blessing beyond his family, to all families.

SUCH LETTING GO AS ABRAHAM IS CHALLENGED TO undergo is unnatural and counterintuitive. Abraham's gestures of relinquishment indicate at least that the heart can be made willing. Well and good. But how in the world, in the real world, do you let go and at the same time take steps to accomplish anything? What does it look like to bring blessing? The epilogue of Abraham's story gives us three answers.

7

THE POINT
Abraham Brings Triple Blessing

WHAT DO YOU DO ABOUT YOUR HIRED HELP SQUABBLING WITH the neighbor's hired help—something that for moderns might threaten a nasty court battle?

☐ How do you bring blessing when faced with smooth-talking rascals who are trying to cheat you, in your hour of grief and need, over a little plot of ground in which to bury your wife?

☐ Most difficult of all, perhaps: What does an aging father do, without his wife, about a son who needs to get married but apparently lacks the capacity to act on his own?

Abraham faces all of this at a ripe old age, a widower in two of the three instances. How has a life-time of God's challenging and testing and grooming turned out? How does Abraham do in the real world at the tail end of God's visits and after, when God stops visiting him entirely?

Blessing One: God's Partner, Covenant-Maker

God has made a covenant with Abraham. Now, Abraham will walk with God by making a covenant with a foreigner regarding land. Partnership with God means walking before God, as God would walk. This is the way of bringing blessing.

Land squabbles: The first time (13:5-13). A long time earlier in his journeying, Abraham had been faced with squabbling shepherds in the land dispute with his nephew Lot. Land and seed have been twin staples of God's promises to Abraham, and each has been threatened throughout the story. With Lot, it was a matter of water rights. Abraham allowed his nephew first choice of land, and Lot chose the fertile land down in the valley. We can take two views of the matter. Abraham simply washed his hands of the issue and avoided conflict by enabling the nephew to exercise his greed in choosing first, thereby threatening God's promise of land—in effect "throwing it away." Or we can see Abraham's offer as a noble and generous act tinged with possible shrewdness: Abraham would be provided cover from enemies in the higher bush country with room for his flocks to graze and increase. In either case, the immediate conflict over land was resolved. The dynamics of such a territorial dispute would reappear years later.

Land squabbles repeated—and a treaty (21:22-34). The second dispute occurs after Sarah has given birth to Isaac, and before the seventh visit from God, the sacrifice scene. Abraham's handling of the repeated situation, late in his story, is quite different. It's more sophisticated in the political sense, and more clearly a blessing for both of the opposing parties.

Again we have squabbling shepherds and a land dispute, but to make matters a bit more ticklish, the offending servants belong to the same foreign king who had taken Sarah. Abraham had wronged Abimelech and his people, but interceded for them in his newly designated role as "prophet." Sensitive to Sarah's shame at the hands of her husband, Abimelech gave gifts specifically to honor Sarah so that she could "lift up her face" in public. Stay in the land, Abimelech had urged the couple, and now they make a pact that neither will deal falsely with the other. The two agree—but immediately there is trouble:

> Abraham upbraided Abimelech concerning the well of water that Abimelech's servants had seized. And Abimelech said, "I do not know who has done this thing, and you, too, have not told me, and I myself never heard of it till this day." (21:25-26)

Abraham challenges the king about the hostility over wells. It's diplomacy's first step, an important move toward any potential partnership between Abimelech and Abraham. But there needs to be more on Abraham's part.

> And Abraham took sheep and cattle and gave them to Abimelech, and the two of them sealed a pact. And Abraham set apart seven ewes of the flock, and Abimelech said to Abraham, "What are these seven ewes that you set apart?" And he said, "Now, the seven ewes you shall take from my hand, so that they may serve me as witness that I have dug this well." Therefore did he call the name of that place Beer-sheba, for there did the two of them swear. And they sealed a pact in Beer-sheba, and Abimelech arose, and Phicol captain of his troops with him, and they returned to the land of the Philistines. And Abraham planted a tamarisk at Beer-sheba, and he invoked there the name of the LORD, everlasting God. And Abraham sojourned in the land of the Philistines many days. (21:27-34)

In this vital second stage of diplomacy, Abraham makes a promise, sealing it with gifts from his flock. He has initiated a pact, a covenant of peace. Abraham stays in the land, in the same land along with Abimelech.

Neither party can simply walk away, as in the land dispute with Lot and his shepherds. This is the real world of politics, with pressing territorial concerns. Abraham's solution follows the pattern of God's covenant-making. The two parties have made a covenant of peace, with Abraham acting like God. The challenge of visit five was to "walk with Me" (or "walk before Me"), and here Abraham demonstrates getting in step with, or anticipating the step of, God. He has become a blessing.

Still an alien, Abraham has become a friendly alien. Through the stages of seven visits, God had been establishing with Abraham a covenant of peace that would extend to "all the peoples of the earth" (12:3). In this still-alien land, "Abraham planted a tamarisk"—a sacred tree— "and he invoked there the name of the LORD, everlasting God" (21:33). Perhaps the tree-planting—as opposed to a gathering and piling of stones for an altar only—is symbolic both of the treaty with Abimelech as stable, and of Abraham's confidence that the Lord is indeed an "everlasting" God.[1] For now, at least, Abraham is able to plant himself

---

[1] Terence Fretheim suggests, "Abraham plants a tree at Beersheba as a permanent sign of the treaty and worships God" *(Genesis,* in *The New Interpreter's Bible,* Vol. 1 [Nashville: Abingdon, 1994], p. 492).

in the land, because of the covenant he has established with a potential foe. He is growing as a partner of God by bringing blessing.

Blessing Two: God's Partner, Land Negotiator (23:1-20)

There have been promises of seed and of land. The seed promise has
been fulfilled. What of the land? Is it possible that Abraham, as God's
partner, will have to procure at least token land by purchase—in fact,
by paying too much for too little?

Much has happened since the seed promise was fulfilled. "And it
happened after these things" (22:1)—that is, after making the covenant
with Abimelech regarding land—that Abraham accepted God's challenge to let go of his son Isaac. It is here that God can say about Abraham, "Now I know"—that Abraham can be trusted as full partner, that
he acts in obedient trust. Here, too, Abraham demonstrates that he has
come to trust fully in God's provision. But with this plot resolve we
may well wonder about the land.

"And it happened after these things" is repeated (22:20). Now
Abraham hears that his brother Nahor has twelve sons by way of his
wife and his concubine, a possible anticipation of Jacob's twelve sons
(22:20-24). There will be other peoples—Abraham's brother's tribal
groups, for example—that are important; there are other clans to be
accounted for and blessed. The repeated "And it happened after
these things" has introduced and concluded the seventh visit, and
now we move out into a more ordinary world where God visits no
more, where Abraham must figure out what it means to be a blessing. The climactic action of Abraham's growth into partnership has
been achieved, and there now appears a second instance of bringing
blessing that helps put the entire Abraham and Sarah story into perspective.

Abraham has come back to the same alien land where he had initiated a covenant of peace with Abimelech—to Beer-sheba, "well's-oath"
in the Hebrew.

> And Sarah's life was a hundred and twenty-seven years, the years of
> Sarah's life. And Sarah died in Kiriath-arba, which is Hebron, in the land
> of Canaan, and Abraham came to mourn Sarah and to keen for her. And
> Abraham rose from before his dead and he spoke to the Hittites, saying:

"I am a sojourning settler with you. Grant me a burial holding with you,
and let me bury my dead now before me." (23:1-4)

What is an old landless man to do? Are we to wonder—does Abraham
wonder?—about the promise of land? The promise of seed, after all,
has come true.

Many years have passed since the sacrifice scene and the last of
God's visits. Nothing worth a story about the couple's lives has happened since. And now Sarah is dead. From a modern perspective,
Sarah has gotten short shrift in the narrative. But for an ancient audience, there must have been pleasure in the righting of wrong in regard
to Sarah, in the narrative vindication of her importance in the action.
Sarah has proven essential in God's vision of blessing for all peoples.
She has been fully honored as wife and seed-bearer. Her circumstances of shame have been wonderfully transformed. A foreign king
has honored her, God has honored her, and Abraham no longer
shames her. Now Sarah needs a proper burial. Abraham's time of
mourning is over.

For the writer, this little matter of burial plot must be of great
moment, a dramatic movement forward. After all, there has been no
story during the many years after the seventh visit.

And Abraham rose from before his dead and he spoke to the Hittites,
saying: "I am a sojourning settler with you. Grant me a burial holding
with you, and let me bury my dead now before me." And the Hittites
answered Abraham, saying: "Pray, hear us, my lord. You are a prince of
God among us! In the pick of our graves bury your dead. No man among
us will deny you his grave for burying your dead." And Abraham rose
and bowed to the folk of the land, to the Hittites. And he spoke with
them, saying, "If you have it in your hearts that I should bury my dead
now before me, hear me, entreat for me Ephron son of Zohar, and let
him grant me the cave of Machpelah that belongs to him, which is at the
far end of his field. At the full price let him grant it to me in your midst
as a burial holding." (23:3-9)

Abraham does not presume to ask for actual land, *erets,* which God
has promised. He doesn't even ask for the field, *sadeh.* All he wants is
the cave at the end of the field. On the other hand, the Hebrew for
"burial holding" indicates that, however minuscule the land, Abraham
wants legal possession. The little details are creating a very big story,

at least for the reader/hearer who knows that seed and land, *erets*, were the twin pillars of the promise in each of God's seven visits. Will a cave, not even a field—a little patch of ground—be the fulfillment to God's promise of land? Will it be given outright by potentially hostile Hittites? What does one do in the real world, once God leaves you on your own, with no more visits, no further directives?

The elaborate language of bargaining, so familiar to these people and times, gives the exchanges a dramatic edge. Abraham makes himself very clear: he wants to purchase, at the going rate—and he repeats that he wants legal possession, a "burial-holding."

> And Ephron was sitting in the midst of the Hittites, and Ephron the Hittite answered Abraham in the hearing of the Hittites, all the assembled in the gate of his town, saying: "Pray, my lord, hear me. The field I grant you and the cave that is in it. I grant it to you in full view of my kinfolk, I grant it to you. Bury your dead." (23:10-11)

Whatever the subtext of this bargaining is all about, Abraham will not take the land without paying for it:

> And Abraham bowed before the folk of the land, and he spoke to Ephron in the hearing of the folk of the land, saying: "If you would but hear me—I give the price of the field, take it from me, and let me bury my dead there." And Ephron answered Abraham, saying: "Pray, my lord, hear me. Land for four hundred silver shekels between me and you, what does it come to? Go bury your dead." (23:12-15)

Maybe Ephron was serious about the field as a gift, or maybe he was eliciting, in the method of his day, an offer from Abraham. Maybe Abraham could have taken him either way. But Abraham insists on purchase, just as he has insisted on legal possession. Everything is to be fair and square, in front of "the Hittites, all the assembled in the gate of his town," the legal court of those days.[2] But the four hundred silver shekels is highway robbery—a fortune not in any way reflecting the field's value! Much later in Israel's history, King David was to buy land for an altar site, at only fifty shekels of silver (2 Sam 24:24). Four hundred shekels for a cave is not so fair and square, after all. What is Abraham to do?

---

[2]Legal judgments and proceedings were always conducted before the town elders in the gate of the town.

> And Abraham listened to Ephron and Abraham weighed out to Ephron
> the silver that he spoke of in the hearing of the Hittites, four hundred sil-
> ver shekels at the merchants' tried weight. And Ephron's field at Mach-
> pelah by Mamre, the field and the cave that was in it and every tree in
> the field, within its boundaries all around, passed over to Abraham as a
> possession, in the full view of the Hittites, all the assembled in the gate
> of his town. And then Abraham buried Sarah his wife in the cave of the
> Machpelah field by Mamre, which is Hebron, in the land of Canaan. And
> the field and the cave that was in it passed over to Abraham as a burial-
> holding from the Hittites. (23:16-20)

Abraham's seed, he has been told by God, "shall be strangers in a land
not theirs and they shall be enslaved and afflicted for four hundred
years" (15:13), and yet it will be to the geographic area, including this
field, that they will come when finally entering their promised land.
At the very least, this purchase serves as a precursor to the greater fulfillment of the land promise.

Abraham has pursued diplomacy-plus in obtaining token claim to
the land. God promises, and Abraham does the negotiating. We can
view Abraham as a helpless pawn in the clutches of ruthless land-
holders. Or, more appropriate to the context of the preceding narrative, we see him as a blessing-bearer, a negotiator for land who does
what is more than generous. Why not? Abraham can afford it—he is
rich. But still, Abraham lets go of the normal human need for an
external sign of competitive edge. Such taking-hold requires a deep
trust in God's "seeing to it"—a letting-go. One can pay exorbitantly—
when the occasion requires—if one has a generous and trustworthy
sponsor. Abraham could have refused to dicker, waiting piously for
God to make good on the divine promise for land. In this scenario,
he could have played false with the Hittites, accepting Ephron's
offer of land for free, even though to do so would have been a
breach of the day's customary bargaining procedures. Ephron presumably never intended to give away the land. But Abraham could
have broken protocol, calling Ephron's bluff and counting on the
God-up-his-sleeve. But this would have been to play false, as well,
with his partner and Lord. God needs Abraham to walk, to go out
into the world of land-dealing and do it, having been educated about
what it means to walk with God. He strikes a covenant for land with

the foreigner by purchasing it at an exorbitant price, for the sake of peace and covenant (does Abraham sense that God has operated extravagantly with him?). Partnership with God is yielding the kind of blessing Abraham might never have dreamed of embracing, back in his self-protecting, self-aggrandizing days.

Blessing Three: God's Partner, Matchmaker (24:1-67)

God's ultimate promise to Abraham, a challenge also, lies in the bringing of blessing to others. At the end of his life, he does so by fashioning a covenant of peace with Abimelech, avoiding warfare. And he does so by paying foreigners exorbitantly for land rather than creating a fuss. Finally, he must bring blessing to his own son by providing for him what Isaac apparently cannot do for himself. Abraham will find Isaac a wife.

Abraham's son Isaac, as enterprising sons go, is a flop. He is so passive and inept that it would be impossible to have him featured in a story of his own. There is no major narrative about Isaac. There are only a few anecdotes that prove an important point: the God of Abraham is also the God of Isaac, and that God counts on Abraham to do for Isaac what he apparently can't do for himself. The God of Abraham, Isaac and Jacob is a God who countenances—or at least works with—a full range of human capacity and incapacity. What compensates for "incapacity" may be a good heart. The first we hear of any spouse's love for a spouse is Isaac's love for his wife, Rebekah, though he has nothing to do with obtaining her, and later will be outwitted by her in family struggles where individuals serve self-promoting interests at the expense of others.

For such an incompetent son, Abraham takes the reins, doing what a father has to do. He arranges a marriage. Abraham's excellence in letting go does not prevent him, and in fact enables him, to take hold, and to take hold in cunning, practical, God-fearing ways. An unwary reader might conclude that Abraham was over-protective, a meddler. Isaac's passive and fumbling character, which we will explore briefly, helps to explain why Abraham's matchmaking is an action that brings blessing.

Isaac, this one without a full story, nonetheless loves his wife. He

loves Rebekah, in fact, with complete abandon. It's the abandon part of
Isaac's love that highlights his foolishness. He, like father Abraham, is
afraid for his life in a foreign land because of men lusting after his
beautiful bride. So he revives the lie: Rebekah is a sister, not a wife.
But, having gone on record that, yes, Rebekah is his sister, he then fon-
dles her in public, in front of the foreign king's window! (26:6-11) The
king looks out his window (the reader sees this coming), and spies this
public display of affection between "brother" and "sister." The text
moves swiftly: "Abimelech . . . looked out the window and saw—and
there was Isaac playing with Rebekah his wife" (26:8). He calls Isaac in
to explain. The Hebrew syntax emphasizes the strangeness and wonder in all this, that the king sees Isaac first ("there was Isaac"), then the
fondling ("playing" with the connotation of sexual dalliance), and only
then, "Rebekah his wife"![3]

This would not film well, except in slapstick comedy. "After the dramatic high point in ch. 22," as J. Gerald Janzen sees it, "Isaac appears
to live out the rest of his days in a state of anticlimactic existential
exhaustion, capable only of imitating elements in his father's life."[4] No
wonder Abraham had to help jump-start the marriage. Perhaps the
father felt partially responsible for the son's ineptness. Whether Isaac
was born passive and a bit befuddled, or whether his being bound on
the altar under his father's raised knife had stunned and maimed him
for life, we can't know. What is clear is the man's inability to function
well in the real world.

Passive in his younger years, the blind old Isaac in the end lets himself get duped by his son Jacob, who, at his mother's prodding, dons
clothes of deceit and goes before father Isaac pretending to be Esau.
It's blessing time, before the father dies. Isaac is fooled into thinking
that he's blessing Esau, the eldest son, after checking Jacob's skin and
finding it hairy and rough like Esau's. Jacob has wrapped himself in
animal's skin. There's no father Abraham around to whisper in the
son's ear, alas. With such a son, the father will in the end be forced to

---

[3]See Robert Alter's comments on this passage in the introduction to his translation
(*Genesis: Translation and Commentary* [New York: W. W. Norton, 1996], p. xxxi).
[4]Gerald J. Janzen, *Abraham and All the Families of the Earth: A Commentary on the
Book of Genesis 12-50* (Grand Rapids: Eerdmans, 1993), p. 99.

make possible the blessing of a good wife.

In between these two short tales, we find a variation on the wells-dispute theme that we've seen between Abimelech's and Abraham's servants (26:13-22). Recall that when things got out of hand for Abraham, he confronted the king and initiated a pact of peace. But in Isaac's case there is no diplomacy. Rather, Isaac walks away from the problem, and walks away again, and again.

> And all the wells that his father's servants had dug in the days of Abraham his father, the Philistines blocked up, filling them with earth. And Abimelech said to Isaac, "Go away from us, for you have grown far too powerful for us." And Isaac went off from there and encamped in the wadi of Gerar, and he dwelled there. And Isaac dug anew the wells of water that had been dug in the days of Abraham his father, which the Philistines had blocked up after Abraham's death, and he gave them names, like the names his father had called them. And Isaac's servants dug in the wadi and they found there a well of fresh water. And the shepherds of Gerar quarreled with Isaac's shepherds, saying, "The water is ours." And he called the name of the well Esek, for they had contended with him. And they dug another well and they quarreled over it, too, and he called its name Sitnah. And he pulled up stakes from there and dug another well, and they did not quarrel over it, and he called its name Rehoboth, and he said, "For now the LORD has given us space that we may be fruitful in the land." (26:15-22)

Go away, says the king. Isaac goes away. He redigs wells that the neighbors have maliciously plugged up (if we can't use them, you can't either—so there!). Isaac does nothing to go on record about this abuse: he simply re-digs the wells. The first new well that Isaac digs on his own, however, leads to active *esek*, "contention," which is the name Isaac gives to the well. The second well, *Sitnah*, means "hostility." Isaac moves on. Not until the problem goes away—or, rather, not until Isaac walks far enough away from the problem—does he find satisfaction. Perhaps this is a way of making peace, by way of avoidance. However we interpret Isaac's motives, the story stands in conspicuous comparison to the "take-hold" action of his father Abraham, including the last of these actions. Abraham had to become matchmaker. On the other hand, Isaac is able to say at the conclusion of the wells-conflict, "For now the LORD has given us space that we may be fruitful in the land." Just before this revealing anecdote we read that "the LORD blessed him. And the man became ever greater until he was very great." Perhaps God takes by the hand those who can't quite cope, but whose heart is fine, though fragile. Perhaps Isaac, given his temperament, did the right thing in avoiding conflict by moving away until the conflict went away.

The whole business of why Isaac isn't up to having a story of his own is summarized by the biblical writer in a brief introduction to the non-story incidents of Isaac's life. Isaac lives off the laurels of his father's venturing faith—and that's OK. It will be the same God, the same blessing. Why? Because the father did what was right. God explains the matter to Isaac, giving explicit directions not to go down into Egypt to solve the famine problem (as his father Abraham had done):

> And the LORD appeared unto him and said, "Do not go down to Egypt. Stay in the land that I shall say to you. Sojourn in this land so that I may be with you and bless you, for to you and your seed I will give all these lands and I will fulfill the oath that I swore to Abraham your father, and I will multiply your seed like the stars in the heavens and I will give to your seed all these lands, and all the nations of the earth shall be blessed through your seed because Abraham has listened to my voice and has kept my charge, my commandments, my statutes, and my teachings." (26:2-5)

God tells Abraham to go forth, with very little in the way of stage directions after that. But to Isaac, "Do not go." Stay put. And don't worry about a thing, for "I will fulfill [through you, too!] the oath that I swore to Abraham your father." Isaac has his life stage-managed by God and by his matchmaking father.

Perhaps the essential truth of these non-story snippets from Isaac's passive life enable the writer to repeat the promises the Lord made to Abraham. God says to Isaac, "I will multiply your seed like the stars in the heavens, and I will give to your seed all these lands, and *all the nations of the earth shall be blessed through your seed because Abraham has listened to my voice and has kept my charge, my commandments, my statutes, and my teachings*" (26:5, emphasis mine). It's *because* again, and again: *because* Abraham has done this thing, I can do my grand

thing. I will bring blessing to "all the nations of the earth." Now the
son, who has done very little, hears the promise, and the reason for its
continuation: it's because his father listened to God's voice, and did the
right thing.

Abraham knows all about his son, his only son, the son whom he
loves, Isaac. He knows that Isaac is not aggressive, or even able, and
that he needs a marriage companion. Years earlier the father had
taken initiative to get the son married, with ingenious attention to
detail:

> And Abraham was old, and advanced in years, and the LORD had blessed
> Abraham in all things. And Abraham said to his servant, elder of his
> household, who ruled over all things that were his, "Put your hand, pray,
> under my thigh, that I may make you swear by the LORD, God of the
> heavens and God of the earth, that you shall not take a wife for my son
> from the daughters of Canaanite in whose midst I dwell. But to my land
> and to my birthplace you shall go, and you shall take a wife for my son,
> for Isaac." And the servant said to him, "Perhaps the woman will not
> want to come after me to this land. Shall I indeed bring your son back to
> the land you left?" And Abraham said to him, "Watch yourself, lest you
> bring my son back there. The LORD God of the heavens, Who took me
> from my father's house and from the land of my birthplace, and Who
> spoke to me and Who swore to me saying, 'To your seed will I give this
> land,' He shall send His messenger before you and you shall take a wife
> for my son from there. And if the woman should not want to go after
> you, you shall be clear of this vow of mine; only my son you must not
> bring back there." (24:1-8)

The servant, reasonably enough, wants to know if it's all right to bring
Isaac to the woman should she prove recalcitrant. Under no condition
will the father let the son go anywhere—just as God has forbidden
Isaac's going anywhere in the case of famine. "Watch yourself," says
Abraham to the servant, "lest you bring my son back there." Each
detail is crucial. "And the servant put his hand under Abraham's thigh
and he swore to him concerning this thing" (24:9). The servant's hand
on the master's genitals makes the agreement serious indeed. You
don't trust just any fellow to do so, and to carry out such a mission on
your behalf, on behalf of a son, an only son, a son whom you love. And
the promised nation will come from the seed of this marriage.

Abraham has chosen a very shrewd and God-tuned servant to be the surrogate groom.[5] That's clearly to Abraham's further credit, his "merit" (15:6)—that he can let go and trust in God, as he puts it to his servant, to "send His messenger before [me]." This is good, that Abraham can trust in a servant who trusts in God to "see to it." Once on his own, in an intriguing and lovely scene at the well, the servant demonstrates his own cleverness and trust in God's provision. The servant, having arrived in the land of Abraham's birthplace,

> made the camels kneel outside the city by the well of water at eventide, the hour when the water-drawing women come out. And he said, "LORD, God of my master Abraham, pray, grant me good speed this day and do kindness with my master, Abraham. Here, I am poised by the spring of water, and the daughters of the men of the town are coming out to draw water. Let it be that the young woman to whom I say, 'Pray, tip down your jug that I may drink,' if she says, 'Drink, and your camels, too, I shall water,' she it is whom You have marked for your servant, for Isaac, and by this I shall know that You have done kindness with my master." (24:11-14)

It's not just that the servant comes up with a plan that will test the mettle of Isaac's future bride, but that the particular challenge will reveal precisely those enterprising characteristics that the passive Isaac so desperately needs for a life's companion. Isaac needs a take-charge wife, which the take-charge servant of Abraham prays to God about. The servant leaves out of the equation the necessity that the wife be from Nahor's family, as Abraham had instructed him.[6] Perhaps God is taking charge as well, willing to work in concert with human planning.

> He had barely finished speaking when, look, Rebekah was coming out, who was born to Bethuel son of Milcah, the wife of Nahor, Abraham's

---

[5]Husbands meeting up with potential wives at wells is a repeated kind of scene in these biblical stories: Jacob, for example, will find his future wife at a well, as will Moses in Exodus. This little episode stands out conspicuously because of its difference from others in the convention: the bridegroom is missing! Robert Alter notes well that the scene, complete with an enterprising bride in lieu of a rather inept and missing bridegroom, underscores what is to come: "There is surely some intimation in all this," he says, "of the subsequent course of the marriage of Isaac and Rebekah—he in most respects the most passive of all the patriarchs, she forceful and enterprising" (Alter, *Genesis*, p. 115).
[6]I was reminded of this interesting detail by James Ackerman

> brother, with her jug on her shoulder. And the young woman was very
> comely to look at, a virgin, no man had known her. And she came down
> to the spring and filled her jug and came back up. And the servant ran
> toward her and said, "Pray, let me sip a bit of water from your jug." And
> she said, "Drink, my lord," and she hurried and lowered her jug onto her
> hand and let him drink. And she let him drink his fill and said, "For your
> camels, too, I shall draw water until they drink their fill." And she hur-
> ried and emptied her jug into the trough and she ran again to the well to
> draw water and drew water for all his camels. And the man was staring
> at her, keeping silent, to know whether the LORD had granted success to
> his journey. (24:15-21)

Rebekah is there first, before any of the other maidens. And she
doesn't simply do the tasks envisioned by the thoughtful servant, she
hurried to give him drink, and then she *hurried* again and *ran* to implement her offer of drink to the camels as well. She's not just capable—
she's energized! Lucky husband, especially if you're Isaac's sort.

> And it happened, when the camels had drunk their fill, that the man
> took a gold nose ring . . . and two bracelets for her arms, ten gold shekels
> in weight. And he said, "Whose daughter are you? Tell me, pray. Is there
> room in your father's house for us to spend the night?" And she said to
> him, "I am the daughter of Bethuel the son of Milcah whom she bore to
> Nahor." And she said to him, "We have abundance of bran and feed as
> well and room to spend the night." And the man did obeisance and
> bowed to the LORD, and he said, "Blessed be the LORD, God of my master
> Abraham, Who has not left off His steadfast kindness toward my mas-
> ter—me on this journey the LORD led to the house of my master's kins-
> men." (24:22-27)

"We have an abundance." Come. And that happens to be at the heart of
the rather large conception of God immediately following: a God of
abundance, of "steadfast kindness."

"Steadfast kindness"—*hesed*—is the key attribute of God in all these
Genesis stories.[7] Faithful love: this is the truly unchanging aspect of
God, that portion of God never subject to change or variation or
shadow of turning.

God's human partner, and this partner's partner, the servant, learn
to let go of anxieties that prohibit good action by relaxing into the con-

---

[7]And beyond, in King David's long and complex narrative, for example.

fidence that the *hesed* of God is the *hesed* of provision, a meeting of their rather significant needs. Such letting go is not sufficient, however. Without taking hold, without making it happen—shrewdly, as in the servant's case, shrewdly, as in Abraham's choice of the servant, and shrewdly, as in the very conception of this match-making business—without such taking-hold as a simultaneous motion along with the letting-go, God's will for global blessing would be stalled. God counts on the human partner for blessing number three: a good wife for Abraham's son.

For What, This Partnership?

And what does God want? The answer was there from the start, with the first promise to Abraham: happiness all around, states of blessedness for all peoples. It's no wonder that the Hebrews came to bless the name of the Lord, the God of Abraham, Isaac and Jacob. And it's no wonder they, along with two other major world religions, revere Abraham as father. All peoples. How appropriate, then, that the "falling off" action of Abraham's story, the *denouement,* is captured in these tidbits of God's partner acting as covenant-maker to solve a land dispute, as land-negotiator to purchase the land promised him by God and as matchmaker for a son who can't procure a wife on his own.

Blessing to all peoples: the Abraham narrative is brought to a final close with the genealogy of . . . Ishmael! Just before launching into the major narrative of Jacob, we read: "And this is the lineage of Ishmael, son of Abraham whom Hagar the Egyptian, Sarah's slavegirl, bore to Abraham." (25:12-18). We recall that God has visited Hagar twice, with just such promised blessing (16;10-11; 21:18). Through Abraham, all nations are to be blessed. That is the main point of the promises to him, and with just such a reminder his story concludes.

Family, and families of the earth: Abraham and the subsequent stories of Genesis are a unified and novel-like history of family origins, family disarray, and global possibilities. All of these very ordinary human beings, beginning with Abraham, go through a testing of one sort or another, appropriate to their own mischievous way of being in the world. Nothing less than transformation is needed, a change in normal ways of being in the world. For some, this change is more conspicuous than for others (Isaac, for example, seems stunned, wounded, utterly passive). But always with God's partners, up through the present tense of the implicitly ongoing story into our own third millennium of the common era (we are "all the peoples," after all), there is a coming-along of a recalcitrant human will to the beauty of divine goodness.

All peoples: all is gathered up into the promise . . . for now. Never is there a simple "falling off" of action in these grand narratives. Always there is the falling off but also a falling forward, an escalation of family members, of nation . . . and of trouble. The next major narrative dramatizes the striving for "name" and self-promotion between brothers Jacob and Esau, between spouses Isaac and Rebekah, between wives Leah and Rachel, and between uncle Laban and nephew Jacob. What happens to God's vision of recovery, of blessing to all families beginning with this very troubled family of Isaac and Rebekah?

CAIN KILLED YOUNGER BROTHER ABEL, WHOSE ONLY crime was having gained greater notice from God. The second major narrative after Abraham and Sarah begins with Esau wanting to kill younger brother Jacob, who, unlike Abel, wrongs his brother in a hateful way. Making matters apparently worse, Jacob, like Abel, is favored by God over his older brother, while father Isaac and mother Rebekah pander to their respective favorites. Meanwhile, it becomes clear that God wants Jacob as a partner toward the goal of blessing for all, but that Jacob isn't so sure about wanting God as a partner. What good can God and Jacob possibly work out together toward life and blessing, in the everyday world of self-aggrandizement, murderous intent and family breakdown?

8

JACOB WRESTLES FOR HIS BLESSINGS WITH ESAU, WITH GOD

THE STORY BEGINS, AS DO ALL GREAT STORIES, WITH BOTH PROMISE and problem. Brother is pitted against brother, and Jacob resists a God who makes him promises. These two plot complications appear unrelated until, late in the story, they intersect. Each difficulty bears on the other, just as the resolution of one requires the resolution of the other. With no narrator to explain things, the action manages its revelation of meaning with realistic and compelling power. There is reconciliation. What has Jacob learned? Has Jacob changed in his fundamental nature? Or has he kept his basic wile and strong will, changing instead the orientation . . . that will, its outlook and action?

> And this is the lineage of Isaac son of Abraham. Abraham begot Isaac. And Isaac was forty years old when he took as wife Rebekah. . . . And Isaac pleaded with the LORD on behalf of his wife, for she was barren, and the Lord granted his plea, and Rebekah his wife conceived. And the children clashed together within her, and she said, "Then why me?" and she went to inquire of the LORD. And the LORD said to her:
>
> "Two nations—in your womb,
>   two peoples from your loins shall issue.
> People over people shall prevail,
>   the elder, the younger's slave."

> And when her time was come to give birth, look, there were twins in her
> womb. And the first one came out ruddy, like a hairy mantle all over,
> and they called his name Esau. Then his brother came out, his hand
> grasping Esau's heel, and they called his name Jacob. And Isaac was
> sixty years old when they were born. (25:19-26)

Jacob is second, number two. Jacob, "heel-grabber" in this scene, will
go on to grab what he can in order to overcome his status as merely
number two. An entirely normal human being, he covets being number one. To become so, he swindles his older twin brother Esau out of
a birthright, and with the help of his doting mother deceives father
Isaac out of the first-born's blessing. And he resists a solicitous God
until such a time as suits him—when he is convinced God is worth
claiming as his own.

Jacob's struggle provides a more straightforward story of wayward-
ness and reorientation than Abraham's, but some of my students, and
sometimes I myself, find Jacob difficult to root for as a character. Abraham's offense against his wife, which jeopardizes her chastity, strikes
my students as quite bad, especially when the scheme gets repeated.
But there is enough in Abraham's story to suggest his likability: he cou-
rageously rescues Lot, for example, along with the five kings. Aren't
we drawn in as Abraham's growing partnership with God unfolds?
Abraham's consistent attentiveness regarding the God who visits rec-
ommends him to the reader. Jacob's character, on the other hand,
offers no redeeming feature until fairly late in the story—and even
then, we may not be sure how to take him. We may find it hard to
acknowledge Jacob's slow change of heart, indicated late in the story
by God's changing of Jacob's name from *Jacob*, "heel-grabber," to *Israel*,
"God-strives-with (or for)." Jacob ends up wrestling with God, a goodly
match that leads to blessing. But is this any way to treat God, by wrestling blessing away?

Other readers, however, identify with Jacob, and like him. Doug
Frank, for example, after reading the story and my introductory words
above, writes:

> I find Jacob the most interesting and likable character in Genesis. I like
> his feistiness. I like his doubt. I like it that he's going to test this God's
> voice that he hears. He sounds genuine, an actual human being. Why

should he trust? He's certainly heard the story of Isaac's experience—he's seen the wounds his father has sustained at the hands of a crazy grandfather [Abraham] and a crazy God. He's going to take care of himself. Sounds a lot like me.[1]

Perhaps at the heart of Jacob's scrambling efforts to take care of himself—at the other's expense—is a fear we can all identify with, a fear of insignificance, of not counting, of being number two.

Jacob Wrestles Esau: Bout One (25:27-34)

Jacob is "grasping Esau's heel" in the womb, and in the very next verses we proceed to the plot's point of horror.

"The lads grew up, and Esau was a man skilled in hunting, a man of the field, and Jacob was a simple man, a dweller in tents. And Isaac loved Esau for the game that he brought him, but Rebekah loved Jacob. And Jacob prepared a stew." (25:27-29). Father loves one son in particular; the writer sets this bare, ominous stage, proceeding immediately to a scene of how the family dynamics play out:

> And Jacob prepared a stew and Esau came from the field, and he was famished. And Esau said to Jacob, "Let me gulp down some of this red, red stuff, for I am famished." Therefore is his name called Edom. And Jacob said, "Sell now your birthright to me." And Esau said, "Look, I am at the point of death, so why do I need a birthright?" And Jacob said, "Swear to me now," and he swore to him, and he sold his birthright to Jacob. Then Jacob gave Esau bread and lentil stew, and he ate and he drank and he rose and he went off, and Esau spurned the birthright. (25:29-34)

Jacob's impulse to make a name for himself even at the expense of his own sibling is normal. Esau's impetuous nature is understood and maliciously played by Jacob to his own advantage. Famished Esau ate, he drank, he rose, he went off, he spurned: this is the action-oriented and appetitive brother Jacob had come to know, and knew how to outwit.

Jacob wrestles the birthright away from Esau, and later, wrestles both father and brother out of the first-born's blessing. To make a clean

---

[1]Doug Frank, in a letter, April 25, 2000. Frank is on the faculty of The Oregon Extension, an alternate semester program in Ashland, Oregon.

sweep of his elder brother's right of inheritance, Jacob needs both birthright and blessing—respectively *bekorah* and *berakhah*. With the help of his mother, Jacob has donned animal skins to replicate Esau's hairy skin in his successful bid to fool the blind Isaac out of Esau's blessing. Poor, passive Isaac, never too adept at anything, is now blind, and taken in by the disguise. He grants the blessing to Jacob, who he thinks is Esau. Jacob and his mother play on both the literal blindness and the impoverishment of wit that Isaac's physical blindness implies.[2]

Esau's cry of anguish, upon learning from his father of Jacob's swindle, is right on target:

> When Esau heard his father's words, he cried out with a great and very bitter outcry and he said to his father, "Bless me, too, Father!" And he said, "Your brother has come in deceit and has taken your blessing." And [Esau] said,
>
> > "Was his name called Jacob
> > That he should trip me now twice by the heels?
> > My *birthright* he took,
> > and look, now, he's taken my *blessing*." (27:34-36, emphasis mine)

Esau possesses some cleverness of his own. Even in the height of his despair he is able to allude to the meaning of Jacob's name, "heel-grabber," while providing a twist. As used by Esau, the name *Jacob* can also mean "crooked heart."[3]

Jacob Wrestles God: Bout One (28:12-22)

At this point Jacob must flee for his life. His mother helps him to jus-

---

[2]As we saw in the prior chapter, between the "stealing" of birthright and the theft of blessing, are two brief accounts that focus on Isaac. Why? In part, I think, the writer wants us to note Isaac's inability to operate well, with wit, in the real world. Isaac tries and fails to carry out the deception practiced by his father in pretending that his wife is his sister; Isaac fumbles the ruse, fondling Rebekah not only in public but in front of the window of the king he intends to dupe! And in a matter of wells-closing by hostile folks, Isaac's recourse is simply to move farther and farther away from the problem until it disappears—unlike his father's covenant-making solution.

[3]"Esau adds another layer . . . by making the name [Jacob] into a verb from *aquob*, "crooked," with the obvious sense of devious or deceitful dealing" (Robert Alter, *Genesis: Translation and Commentary* [New York: W. W. Norton, 1996], p. 142).

tify the flight by claiming the need to find a proper wife. For this, she claims, he must return to the original family home, back in Haran, Abraham's initial point of departure and the place where Abraham's servant found Rebekah, Isaac's wife-to-be. In his flight from Esau, Jacob is visited by God in a strange dream involving a ramp with "messengers of God" going in both directions. Jacob's response to the dream will be another form of flight, or distancing—from God!

> And, look, the LORD was poised over [Jacob] and He said, "I, the LORD, am the God of Abraham your father and the God of Isaac. The land on which you lie, to you I will give it and to your seed. And your seed shall be like the dust of the earth and you shall burst forth to the west and the east and the north and the south, and all the clans of the earth shall be blessed through you, and through your seed. And, look, I am with you and I will guard you wherever you go, and I will bring you back to this land, for I will not leave you until I have done that which I have spoken to you." And Jacob awoke from his sleep and he said, "Indeed, the LORD is in this place, and I did not know." And he was afraid and he said,
>
>   "How fearsome is this place!
>   This can be but the house of God,
>   and this is the gate of the heavens." (28:13-17)

Jacob is having a "boundary" experience; he's at that place where earthly and heavenly reality intersect. Later in the story, there is a second night vision. It is stranger than the first, with God responding to Jacob's wrestling nature by wrestling with him. Once again the boundary between divine and human realities will be blurred, and this time Jacob will proceed to act out in everyday life the significance of the interweaving between divine and earthly realms. But here, his response is strictly earth-bound. He is afraid, and wary.

Jacob's fear is a far cry from his grandfather Abraham's "fear of God," a trust in God's provision. The narrator stresses Jacob's fear, first, by stating it ("And he was afraid") and then by recording Jacob's own confession, "How fearsome is this place!" Far from trusting in God's provision with a proper "fear of God," Jacob is wary and fearful. God anticipates his charge's reluctance, and the fear: "Look, I am with you and I will guard you wherever you go, and I will bring you back to this land, for I will not leave you until I have done that which I have spoken to you." We may recall the strange challenge of the central fourth visit between God and Abraham. "Do not fear," God had said to Abraham, apropos of nothing immediately obvious to the reader. Here, the reader sees plenty of reason for fear. And yet the problem may lie deeper than God's dramatic appearance in the middle of the night. For Jacob, fear may be traced back to the root of all clutching—after a twin's heel, a twin's birthright, a twin's blessing. This fundamental anxiety, in any case, is dramatized in the narrative. It is a fear of not counting, of not having a name.

In those last words, *I will not leave you until I have done that which I have spoken to you,* God speaks of divine tenacity in the face of a would-be partner's grasping and possibly fearful tenacity. God "hangs on" as would a wrestler, waiting for and working toward partnership with this wily one.

But the withholding—Jacob's apparent stiff-arming of God—comes in the context of a promise made by Jacob to God. It's a conditional promise. Startled awake by this evening vision, Jacob recognizes his fearfulness. In the bright light of day, however, he moves from night-time terrors to skeptical calculation.

> Jacob rose early in the morning and . . . made a vow, saying, "If the LORD God be with me and guard me on this way that I am going and give me bread to eat and clothing to wear, and I return safely to my father's house, then the LORD will be my God. And this stone that I set as a pillar will be a house of God, and everything that You give me I will surely tithe to You." (28:18-22)

Jacob has abandoned home in fear of his brother, and the past night he has been in dread because of an encounter with God.[4] But he awakes with the presence of mind and temerity of spirit to counter

---

[4]J. Gerald Janzen captures the tension between Jacob's clutching fear and provision promise to God: "In the encounter between God and Jacob at Bethel, we see the beginning of the change in a person who out of existential anxiety has all his life attempted to dominate others in order to control his unknown future. Now he adopts a different approach to the future. He binds himself to a God he cannot control, trusting that God will be faithful to the promise God has freely made to him. The future is not thereby totally determined. It remains open to all manner of unforeseeable events. But whatever may happen, it will occur within the covenantal horizon of God's promise and Jacob's vow" (*Abraham and All the Families of the Earth: A Commentary on the Book of Genesis 12-50* [Grand Rapids, Mich.: Eerdmans, 1993], p. 112).

God by offering terms of agreement. In effect, Jacob stiff-arms God. He postpones any response to the Most High—but offers God a possible partnership, if . . . If God will indeed do all these things, *then the Lord will be my God.* I'll be a partner, maybe—but let's see how you do first, God. Is this any way to treat God? My students—and I!—are more comfortable with a God who doesn't choose such a person in the first place. We resist such a person who openly resists God. More outrageous still is the idea that Jacob, if blessed materially and given safe passage, will offer God a gratuity. *If* it all comes true as you say, God, then *everything that You give me I will surely tithe [give a ten-percent return] to You.* Gunther Plaut anticipates well our possible reaction to Jacob's bargaining with God:

> Jacob promises that if God will be his protector, he in turn will worship God, build a shrine for Him, and offer Him a tithe. This formal promise or vow is conditional, and, although other such vows are found in the Bible . . . it appears at first sight rather unusual. Jacob bargains with God: if God performs properly—and performs first—Jacob will accept Him as his God. Readers often find this a highly objectionable way of dealing with the Almighty, especially since Jacob is shown doubting God's word.[5]

What will it take for Jacob to "come around"? We have two great complications in the action: Jacob's flight from Esau, emphasizing the emotional distance and ill-will between the two, and Jacob's studied distance from God. Perhaps the messengers in perpetual motion up and down the ramp, in the night vision, hint at "real-life" messengers who will soon enter Jacob's life as mirrors of his own crooked and grasping heart.

With Abraham, God had employed the *if* factor: if you leave your land, I will bless you (12:1-3); if you let go of your son, I will surely bless you (22:1,12, 16-17). With Abraham, God's *if* is implied as a necessary ingredient in the relationship between divine challenge and divine promise, as we have seen. But here it is Jacob's *if,* put to God: *If you do this, God, then I will* . . .[6] God works with what God gets, which

---

[5]W. Gunther Plaut, *The Torah: A Modern Commentary* (New York: Jewish Publication Society, Union of American Hebrew Congregations, 1981), p. 196.
[6]I am indebted to student Jill Hohengasser for this insight (in her essay "Genesis: Learning to Walk Before God," February 14, 2000).

requires great divine flexibility. With Jacob, the divine *if* gets replaced by a human *if*, and God goes along. God's promise to Jacob is a reiteration of the promise made to grandfather Abraham, and carries the tone of utter reassurance, with no obvious strings attached. Does God anticipate Jacob's "wrestling" sort of response? If you do this for me, Jacob says to God, I'll do what you seem to want, an acknowledgment of you as my God.

How does one go from self-aggrandizement and God-resistance to being a blessing to all peoples? As it was with Abraham and Isaac before him, Jacob receives a promise from God, whose ultimate end is blessing for all peoples: "And your seed shall be like the dust of the earth and you shall burst forth to the west and the east and the north and the south, *and all the clans of the earth shall be blessed through you.*" This is God's desire, this global blessing. How can God help Jacob toward such a lofty goal, given Jacob's self-promoting deviousness? Will God act in spite of Jacob? The answer we are expecting, from Abraham and Sarah's narrative, is no. God will have to work with Jacob, not in spite of him. Indeed, there will be no divine magic of an override to Jacob's nasty disposition.

Will Jacob accept as *his* God the God he refers to as someone else's God—for example, "the God of my father, the God of Abraham and the Terror of Isaac"? He has bargained with God: if you do all these wonderful things for me, including safe passage back home, then you will be my God. "The most important point on which the Story of Jacob either revolves or gets stuck," observes J. P. Fokkelman, "is, will the God of Abraham and Isaac also be the God of Jacob?"[7] And so what? What has this "most important point" about connecting up with God got to do with anything "real"—like a possible reconciliation with Esau? The narrative provides an answer in a complicated but compelling manner.

Jacob Wrestles Esau: Bout Two, Round One (32:1-22)

Jacob's flight from Esau takes him to the land of his uncle Laban, where he will be cheated, consistently, for twenty long years. The

---

[7]J. P. Fokkelman, *Narrative Art in Genesis: Specimens of Stylistic and Structural Analysis* (Assen, The Netherlands: Van Gorcum, 1975), p. 191.

trickster is tricked. His marriage is troubled: two bickering wives vie for first place just as he has done with Esau. These matters will be taken up in the following chapter. For now, the assumption is that Jacob has learned a thing or two of major consequence for living as a whole person, as one who can bring blessing.

As soon as Jacob takes final leave of Laban, "messengers of God accosted him" (32:2). We're not told why. Perhaps, as a student notes, the accosting by God's messengers means that now "Jacob can no longer 'brush God aside.'"[8] That seems right: the accosting God is one who—at least in Jacob's perception—now wrestles as well.

Immediately, "Jacob sent messengers before him to Esau." There will end up being another sort of accosting:

> And he charged [the messengers], saying, "Thus shall you say—To my lord Esau, thus says your servant Jacob: With Laban I have sojourned and I tarried till now. And I have gotten oxen and donkeys and sheep and male and female slaves, and I send ahead to tell my lord, to find favor in your eyes." (32:5-6)

Does Esau feel *accosted*? "My *lord* Esau"? "Your *servant* Jacob"? Is this mimicry? If not, is it inflated and false? Mother Rebekah had been told that the elder would be the younger's slave (25:23). Will this be in any way true, that the "slave"—while remaining an outsider to God's focused attention on Jacob and his family—will be treated as a "lord" by the actual lord? Is that where this story is going? We keep in mind the ultimate promise: God's work with the family of Abraham is to bring blessing to all families of the earth. Esau and his family are to be blessed, in God's scheme of things.

The messengers return, telling Jacob that Esau is coming with four hundred men. In fear, Jacob prays to God. "God of my father Abraham and God of my father Isaac!" he cries out, "I am unworthy of all the kindness that you have steadfastly done for your servant." (32:10). Jacob may not have claimed this God as his own God, but he recognizes God's steadfast kindness. Jacob knows about God's *hesed*, this unchanging feature of God's character. Jacob reminds God of the divine promise to bring Jacob home safely.

---

[8]Hohengasser, "Genesis, Learning to Walk Before God."

And now Jacob mounts a campaign of gift-giving to beat all gift-giving.
Here, his messengers clearly *accost* Esau, but not toward ill. Jacob
devises an intricate plan to "placate" his brother Esau with wave after
wave of gifts and with the rhetoric of subservience. The extravaganza is
to take place in three consecutive waves, each contingent of greeter with
its own set of messengers bearing gifts, and speaking the same lines:

> And he charged the first one, saying, "When Esau my brother meets you
> and asks you, saying, 'Whose man are you, and where are you going, and
> whose are these herds before you?', you shall say, 'They are your servant
> Jacob's, a tribute sent to my lord Esau, and, look, he himself is behind us.' "
> And he charged the second one as well, and also the third, indeed, all those
> who went after the herds, saying, "In this fashion you shall speak to Esau
> when you find him. And you shall say, 'Look, your servant Jacob himself is
> behind us.' " *For he thought, 'Let me placate him with the tribute that goes before
> me, and after I shall look on his face, perhaps he will show me a kindly face.'*
> *And the tribute passed on before him.* (32:17-21, emphasis mine)

Jacob's emphasis on "face" indicates something more significant and
substantial than excessive formalities of reconciliation. He wants to
"look on [Esau's] face," hoping that "he will show me a kindly face."

The Hebrew here—and further on—makes a great deal of this "face"
detail that most translations obscure. Everett Fox renders the italicized
portion above in a way that emphasizes the word play:

> For he said to himself:
> I will wipe (the anger from) his *face [phanav]*
> with the gift that goes ahead of my *face [le-phanai]*;
> afterward, when I see his *face [phanav]*,
> perhaps he will lift up my *face [phanai]!*
> The gift crossed over ahead of his *face [al panav]*.[9]

---

[9]Fox illustrates the obscuring of such detail in most translations. He offers this, from
The New English Bible: "For he thought, 'I will appease him with the present that I
have sent on ahead, and afterwards, when I come into his presence, he will perhaps receive me kindly.' So Jacob's present went on ahead of him." Comments Fox,
"This is an accurate and highly idiomatic translation of the Hebrew, and the reader
will notice nothing unusual about the passage as it reads in English. The sound of
the Hebrew text, on the other hand, gives one pause. It is built on variations of the
word *panim*, whose basic meaning is 'face,' although the Hebrew uses it idiomati-
cally to encompass various ideas." All transliterations are Fox's *(The Five Books of
Moses* [New York: Schocken, 1995], p. xi).

Esau is being set up for something grand—if Esau is in a position to receive this sort of "grand." The gifts are an extension of Jacob's face— gifts going "ahead of my face." He wants to wipe the anger from his brother's face, to see Esau's face and have his own face lifted up.

Jacob Wrestles God: Bout Two (32:24-32)

The night before the fateful meeting with the brother whose murderous wrath had forced him to flee, Jacob sleeps. His sleep is fitful, to say the least. For a second time in the narrative there is a night visit between Jacob and a mysterious divine being. The two accost each other, and wrestle (32:24-32). "Let me go," says a man later identified by Jacob as God, "for dawn is breaking." Jacob, the master wrestler, refuses: "I will not let you go unless you bless me." So Jacob's name is changed, to Israel—"for you have striven with God and men," the mysterious wrestler explains, "and won out." But Israel can also mean "God strives," and not just "the one who strives with God." Perhaps, as Fretheim notes, "God's giving this name . . . has implications for God as well as for Jacob, [affirming] a divine commitment to stay with Jacob in struggle. God will be caught up in this relationship"[10]—just as we have seen God and Abraham in a partnership that is dynamic, and not static. For Jacob's part, there comes with victory a disability. He limps, because of a hip dislocation. Is this a reminder that walking will never again be the same, just as God had come to challenge Abraham, "Walk with Me"?

Jacob has "won out!" What goes on here? Winning, and winning rewarded? Rachel had exclaimed, "In awesome grapplings I have grappled with my sister and, yes, I *won out*" (30:8, emphasis mine). In Rachel's case, the winning was at the expense of a loser. This was not good, this rivalry, this spirit of one-upmanship. But here, winning out against men—and *God!*—is good because each wrestling partner seems to have won. Two winners, no losers. At the end of the struggle, Jacob said, "'Tell me your name, pray!' And he said, 'Why should you ask my name?' and there he blessed him. And Jacob called the name of the place Peniel, meaning, 'I have seen God face to face and I came out alive'" (32:29-30).

---

[10]Terence Fretheim, *Genesis,* in *The New Interpreter's Bible,* Vol. 1, ed. Leander E. Keck et al. (Nashville: Abingdon, 1994), p. 566.

Jacob has hoped that "when I see [Esau's] *face* . . . perhaps he will lift up my *face!*" and now he sees God *face to face*. Are we to expect good things, now, of the actual encounter between Jacob and Esau? Though limping, Jacob has won blessing and a new name.[11] God seems to have won, also, accomplishing the next step toward the divine will of establishing a nation, Israel: this partner-in-the-making God can now name *Israel*, "he strives with God."[12] The name can suggest, as well, "lordly."[13] Has Israel learned, in becoming lordly, not to lord it over Esau and others? The story moves on immediately to answer that question, as we will see, when the twins encounter one another. Has God achieved an ultimate "win" in regard to Israel, namely God's will that Jacob/Israel acknowledge God as *his* God? No, not yet. Jacob had said he wouldn't do so, not until God made good on all the promises, including safe passage home (28:20-22). Interestingly, in this story as for the larger story of Genesis, God won't "win" in this struggle of wills—won't realize the divine will— until the chosen human chooses God and God's way.

God leaves without disclosing the divine name to an inquisitive Jacob (32:30). This might appear strange, since God has already disclosed his name to Jacob, back in the prior night encounter ("I, the LORD [Yahweh], am the God [Elohim] of Abraham your father and the God [Elohim] of Isaac," 28:13). Does God's denial of a personal name in this second night encounter help to steer Jacob away from some kind of "pocket god," to be brought out like a magic genie, name mumbled, for emergency situations? Will God's denial help to nudge Jacob toward claiming allegiance to the God with whom he has already been making bargains and from whom he has been asking favors? Perhaps the writer wants us to con-

---

[11]Referring to this repetition of face in the two passages, Fox makes this observation: "The repetition suggests a thematic link with what has gone before. One could interpret that once the hero has met and actually bested this divine being, his coming human confrontation is assured of success" (Fox, *Five Books of Moses*, p. xii).

[12]Though more conventionally, "God strives with (or for)"—see Alter's note on 32:28-29.

[13]Alter, quoting the midrashist Rashi: "It will no longer be said that the blessings came to you through deviousness [*oqbah*], a word suggested by the radical of 'crookedness' in the name Jacob but instead through lordliness [*serarah*, a root that can be extracted from the name 'Israel'] and openness" (Alter, *Genesis*, note on 32:29).

sider the conspicuous lack of any acknowledgment by Jacob that this God is *his* God. Without such invoking of God's name, perhaps the danger of "using" God becomes greater. In any case, at this point the mysterious stranger of the night refuses to give Jacob the name he's looking for.

Jacob Wrestles Esau: Bout Two, Round Two (33:1-17)

Immediately following the second night visitation with God, "Jacob looked up and there was Esau, coming with his four hundred men" (33:1) Jacob has named the place of his night visit, *Peniel*, "I have seen God face to face and I came out alive." Now he will face Esau by bowing his face to the ground:

> [Jacob] bowed to the ground seven times until he drew near his brother. And Esau ran to meet him and embraced him and fell upon his neck, and they wept. And he raised his eyes and saw the women and the children and he said, "Who are these with you?" And he said, "The children with whom God has favored your servant." And the slavegirls drew near, they and their children, and they bowed down. And Leah, too, and her children drew near, and they bowed down, and then Joseph and Rachel drew near and bowed down. And he said, "What do you mean by all this camp I have met?" And he said, "To find favor in the eyes of my lord." And Esau said, "I have much, my brother. Keep what you have." And Jacob said, "O, no, pray, if I have found favor in your eyes, take this tribute from my hand, for have I not seen your face as one might see God's face, and you received me in kindness? Pray, take my blessing that has been brought you, for God has favored me and I have everything." And he pressed him, and he took it. (33:3-11)

Having seen God face to face, Jacob can face his brother. "If I have found favor in your eyes, take this tribute from my hand, for have I not seen your face as one might see God's face, and you received me in kindness?" We should recall the word-play on "face" that has preceded this climactic moment (32:20), when Jacob's intentions were revealed:

> I will wipe (the anger from) his *face [phanav]*
> with the gift that goes ahead of my *face [le-phanai]*;
> afterward, when I see his *face [phanav]*,
> perhaps he will lift up my *face [phanai]*!
> The gift crossed over ahead of his *face [al panav]*.[14]

---

[14]All transliterations are Fox's.

So, finally, the brothers can face each other, after long years of the most acute alienation. And they embrace, weeping.

Jacob has had to press Esau to take the gifts. Why? "What do you mean by all this camp?" Esau has asked. He's referring, apparently, to the three waves of gifts. *Take it all back*, Esau says; *I have plenty*. What could have seemed to be merely another of Jacob's tricks to get himself out of a jam, or into a good position, turns out to be crucial to the completion of a radical change in heart. Such a transformation does not mean, of course, that Jacob no longer looks out for himself—which clearly he does here. It's in his best interests not to get himself killed in his effort to appease Esau. The question here, as throughout Genesis, is this: How can one engage in proper care for oneself and one's interests without the self-promotion that harms others? How can one properly provide for oneself while simultaneously providing for others? How can the struggle, which life always seems to be in these stories, result in a win-win result, as in the immediately prior wrestling scene between Jacob and his partner-in-wrestling? Jacob understands the need to reverse wrong, and even to reverse roles as the world normally defines them. Lordly Jacob/Israel insists on being servant to his lord Esau. "If I have found favor in your eyes," insists Jacob, "take this tribute from my hand. . . . Pray, take my *blessing* that has been brought you, for God has favored me and I have everything." The blessing! Is Jacob returning the stolen blessing?

Yes, God has favored Jacob. The normal favor of the first-born will remain Jacob's, though second-born. God's purpose seems spelled out here: Jacob gets in order to give. The talented and tenacious Jacob is finally willing to redirect his energies, to bow down, to make possible face-to-face restitution—with tangible goods: "Take this tribute from my hand. . . . Pray, take my blessing that has been brought you."

But what are we to make of Esau, who acts so magnanimously? What credit does the narrative give him? The narrative focus is not on Esau, not on the dynamics of someone "naturally" gracious, as Esau appears to be. Rather, this is a story about a seemingly hopeless rascal who is greatly "gifted," but caught up in the normal syndrome of making a name for himself, of clutching, in his case, after the perks of the elder-born at the expense of that elder-born. In a story we don't have, Esau, too, has gotten past his rage at having his number-one position usurped. Perhaps, impetuous to the end, Esau has been susceptible to the "softening up" of Jacob's three-day barrage of gifts. In any case, it's a story that focuses on Jacob, who has wanted reconciliation and worked cleverly to achieve it with the three days' gifts. But facing intimately the other person with whom you have fought for standing is impossible without facing the ultimate Other—or so this story goes, in its intricately interwoven way. "Take this tribute from my hand," Jacob/Israel insists to the estranged other, "for have I not seen your face as one might see God's face?" Esau concludes their meeting with his own offer of blessing: "Pray, let me set aside for you some of the people who are with me." Jacob responds, gratefully. "Why should I find such favor in the eyes of my lord?" (33:15). "Esau's acceptance of Jacob's gift and Jacob's blessing of Esau," J. Gerald Janzen notes, "are a combined sign of Jacob's full restoration to a bilateral relation."[15] *Restoration*: the word reminds us, perhaps, of the ideal for marital companionship, an ideal of "bilateral relation" portrayed in the creation accounts and subsequently lost with such destructiveness from Eve and Adam on. Partnership with God is intended for blessing, and this is what blessing looks like.

At this most significant change for the good—Jacob's interior change, and the change in external circumstances—Jacob wrestles blessing from Esau, but not until he has wrestled blessing from God. Jacob's match with God produced two winners; here, with his twin brother, Jacob has successfully "wrestled" his way into Esau's favor. Once again, there are two winners. The brothers exchange hugs, tears, blessing, and a moment of face-to-face.

In the apparent warmth of this momentous reconciliation scene, Esau suggests that he accompany Jacob: "Let us journey onward and go, and let me go alongside you" (33:12). But journey where? Where does Esau think the two reunited brothers will end up, geographically? We recall that at Bethel Jacob had been promised safe passage by God "back to this land" (28:15). Is the goal of returning "back to this land"

---

[15]Janzen, *Abraham and All the Families of the Earth*, p. 134.

promised by God in Jacob's mind when he gently refuses his brother's offer? Gently, but with either deceit or with a subsequent change of mind. To the solicitous Esau, Jacob says that he'll travel separately, behind Esau and more slowly—but that he'll meet Esau back at Esau's home in Seir. Either Jacob never intended to keep his word, or he decides later not to keep his word. Jacob never goes to Seir. He goes "back to this land" promised by God—or at least to the general area. There, a more momentous resolve to a strained relationship will occur than even the reconciliation with his brother Esau.

God has promised not only land to Jacob, but seed that will "burst forth to the west and the east and the north and the south, and all the clans of the earth shall be blessed through you, and through your seed" (28:14). In refusing a common geographical destination, Jacob may be insisting as well that each brother have his own seed of significance, with appropriate land for that seed. There may have been a better way to handle saying no to his brother. In fact, as we will see later in Joseph's story, Jacob's transformation is far from complete, though at this point the narrative insists on the remarkable turning-around of Jacob's youthful self-promotion at his brother's expense—which change of heart includes, apparently, a detour of many miles in order to meet up with his brother. Jacob has left the far-north country of his uncle Laban, in Haran, and traveled far south of where he wants to end up—back up north, in Shechem, the area to which God had promised him safe passage. For peace with his brother, and to make restitution, Jacob has gone out of his way, apparently—and gone a dangerous way, since he still fears Esau's murderous intent.

When Will Jacob Agree on God as His Partner?

What could be more important than this, reconciliation between brothers after long years of sibling wreckage? Well, we haven't heard about the final resolve to a complication that, given Abraham's story, might intrigue us. Will Jacob come around to accepting this God as *his* God? Jacob consistently refers to God as his fathers' God, never as his God. And he told God that this would be the case, that only *if* God came through on all the promises at Bethel would Jacob acknowledge God as his God. I ask my students where this second plot line finds its resolve, and they seldom find it because they aren't looking for it. If we are to appreciate the power of this story and its deep truth about reconciliations human and divine, we need to take seriously Jacob's stiff-arming God back at Bethel. *If you do this for me, God, I'll let you be my God.* Immediately after the resolve with Esau, "Jacob came in peace to the town of Shechem," where he buys a parcel of land from the sons of Hamor, the father of Shechem. "And he set up an altar there and called it El-Elohei-Israel," which means "God-the-God-of-Israel" (33:18-20). Jacob has finally acknowledged this God as his own God.

Jacob has been growing into his transformed self, indicated by the name change. Now at last Israel claims as Israel's God this Elohei. And so Jacob/Israel confirms the partnership that God has been seeking and cultivating. Israel will continue to be Jacob, the two names alternating through the rest of Genesis. But here, Jacob has come home as Israel, and come home to his God, the God of Israel. He has come home, as the text suggests, "in peace"—or, "whole."[16] Jacob is a boundary-man. In the two night-visits with God, he has been stretched to the edge of heavenly and earthly realms. And now the boundary-man has achieved at least the foundation for peace. He has integrated God-truth and human-truth, God's face and the other's face, in his one person. If "whole" is a good translation here, then it's a wholeness that proves to be a basis for dealing with further transformation needs. Still ahead of him, for example, will be a major test, to relinquish a son—a challenge he is initially quite reluctant to meet.

The paralleled problems, between Jacob and Esau and between Jacob and God, have been resolved in the intersection of those parallel lines: Jacob sees Esau's face as he has just seen God's. But we have left out a crucial chunk of the story that indicates just how arduous and lengthy any such healing is, within an individual and within a family, toward blessing for all families. After fleeing Esau and before his return and reconciliation, Jacob undergoes dark and difficult years characterized by mirrors. Everywhere he turns, for years, a mirror on the wall asks. Who is troubled most of all? What does Jacob see, in being wrestled out of goods, and even a wife? In being confronted with wives who seek to wrestle position and status away from each other, what does Jacob see?

---

[16]Alter translates *shalem* as "peace" though acknowledging that "elsewhere *shalem* means 'whole.'" I think "whole" works better in the context (*Genesis*, p. 187).

JACOB HAS WRESTLED HIS WAY BACK INTO ESAU'S
*favor, as he has done with God, to obtain divine bless-
ing. What goodness is suggested in these plot resolu-
tions has been hard to come by, and come by honestly.
Between the initial problems and their resolve are
many years of mirrors and hard labor for Jacob. The
greatest mirror of all is that of his contentious wives. In
the Genesis view, women are not exempt from the
insidious impulse to make a name for themselves, and
at another's expense. "In awesome grapplings I have
grappled with my sister and, yes, I won out," exclaims
wife number one in affection but number two in fact.
This gloating of Rachel over older sister Leah encapsu-
lates all of the wrong choices in this story, and in Genesis. Is there any hope that the spirit and reality of
winning out over another person, jockeying for the
number one position, can be changed? Is it possible to
have a winner with no losers?*

9

THREE MIRRORS
FOR JACOB

J ACOB WRESTLES WITH GOD, WITH MAN AND—UNWILLINGLY—WITH
woman. His tenacity and shrewdness can be very bad, as in the self-aggrandizing deceiving of his father and the cheating of his brother.
But such a nature can be turned to good ends as well. Perhaps his bargaining with God that first strange night—If you do well by me, God,
I'll let you be my God—is neither all bad nor all good. His struggle with
God during the second night visitation, however, and the clever
"worming" of his way back into favor with Esau are unambiguously
good. Between these pairs of wrestling scenes lie many years of
extreme difficulty for Jacob. He has fled from Esau, from home. As
soon as he comes to Uncle Laban's land in Haran, he engages in a sort
of wrestling with the local shepherds and, in fact, with a huge inert
object that thwarts his designs.

After Cheating, a Promising New Start (29:1-14)
Jacob is seeking out the home of his mother's brother, Laban, for a
daughter of Laban's to marry. His struggle at a well reveals something
positive, for the first time, in Jacob's character. We may think, finally,

that God's choice of one fetus over the other was a good one.[1]

> And [Jacob] saw and, look, there was a well in the field, and, look, three
> flocks of sheep were lying beside it, for from that well they would water
> the flocks, and the stone was big on the mouth of the well. And when all
> the flocks were gathered there, they would roll the stone from the
> mouth of the well and would water the sheep and put back the stone in
> its place on the mouth of the well. (29:2-3)

Jacob makes inquiry of the shepherds regarding his uncle, and the
men tell him that the uncle's daughter Rachel is now approaching.

Something bothers Jacob about this scene: "And he said, 'Look, the day
is still long. It is not time to gather in the herd. Water the sheep and take
them to graze' " (29:7). Though a stranger to these men, Jacob suggests that
they're wasting precious grazing time. He's bold, but on behalf of the truth.

> And they said, "We cannot until all the flocks have gathered and the
> stone is rolled from the mouth of the well and we water the sheep." He
> was still speaking with them when Rachel came with her father's sheep,
> for she was a shepherdess. And it happened when Jacob saw Rachel
> daughter of Laban his mother's brother and the sheep of Laban his
> mother's brother that he stepped forward and rolled the stone from the
> mouth of the well and watered the sheep of Laban his mother's brother.
> And Jacob kissed Rachel and lifted his voice and wept. (29:8-11)

Esau is the huntsman, but Jacob himself—this mother's boy dwelling
in tents—turns out to be quite robust, as well as bold of spirit. Whether
to impress Rachel or simply to help the shepherdess water her father's
sheep—or both—Jacob wrestles from the well's mouth a boulder usually handled by several men.

We may recall Abraham's servant finding a bride for Isaac at a well.
Jacob outdoes his father Isaac by making an appearance at his own well
of betrothal. Isaac had a surrogate groom seeking him a bride, while
Jacob finds his own bride. Like his energized mother Rebekah, who hus-

---

[1]Though back in 25:27, Jacob is described as a man who is "simple" [from *tam*,
"integrity" or "innocence"—"or blamelessness"!], "a dweller in tents," while Esau
"was a man skilled in hunting." Robert Alter notes the possible irony here (see his
note on this verse), given the scene which these descriptions introduce: Jacob cons
Esau out of the birthright, playing to his older twin's impetuous appetitiveness. I
think the irony is clear.

tled about giving water to Isaac's surrogate groom and his camels, Jacob does the watering for his prospective bride, and with minor heroics. Is it possible to convert such energy from evil intentions to positive ends? We don't know quite what to make of Jacob at this point. But undoubtedly he possesses physical strength, boldness of spirit—and an extensive emotional range, a kiss of greeting along with weeping.

First Mirror: Deceiver Deceived (29:14-25)

It will be an uphill struggle for Jacob from this point on, even as his fortunes slide downhill. Jacob is smitten by Rachel but gets struck down—out-maneuvered, out-wrestled—by Uncle Laban:

> And [Jacob] stayed with him a month's time, and Laban said to Jacob, "Because you are my kin, should you serve me for nothing? Tell me what your wages should be." And Laban had two daughters. The name of the elder was Leah and the name of the younger Rachel. And Leah's eyes were tender, but Rachel was comely in features and comely to look at, and Jacob loved Rachel. And he said, "I will serve seven years for Rachel your younger daughter." And Laban said, "Better I should give her to you than give her to another man. Stay with me." And Jacob served seven years for Rachel, and they seemed in his eyes but a few days in his love for her. (29:14-20)

Fair is fair, from Laban's point of view: Jacob left home, presumably with no money, so he can't afford the bride-price. He pays the seven years' worth of wages. "And Jacob said to Laban, 'Give me my wife, for my time is done, and let me come to bed with her.' " (29:21)

Seven years is a long time to wait, and Jacob is frank about his desire. "Let me come to bed with her." Uncle Laban preys, perhaps, on Jacob's sexual longing. Jacob, who counted on the appetites of his ravenously hungry brother, swapping mere stew for the precious birthright, now falls victim himself to a crafty uncle who understands Jacob's sexual appetite, however honorable.

> And Laban gathered all the men of the place and made a feast. And when evening came, he took Leah his daughter and brought her to Jacob, and he came to bed with her. . . . And when morning came, look, she was Leah. (29:22-23, 25)

Jacob the trickster is tricked; the deceiver is deceived. "What is this you have done to me?" asks Jacob of his uncle. "Was it not for Rachel that I served you, and why have you deceived me?" (29:25).

Did Jacob call out Rachel's name that evening of consummation, or murmur the name Rachel during a tender moment of touch with Leah? Whatever the mumble, whatever the response, Leah successfully carries out her father's ruse. Does Jacob recall, the morning after, the scene with his blind father, befuddled, asking for touch, for the true identity? "Come close, pray," Isaac had asked Jacob, "that I may feel you, my son, whether you are my son Esau or not." Jacob has touched Leah, and has been duped. Perhaps Leah had whispered something, and perhaps Jacob hears an echo of his father's confusion, "The voice is the voice of Jacob and the hands are Esau's hands" (27:21, 22). Jacob would have been taken in by both voice and hands.

How do any of us get to see ourselves, to peel back the layers of what we unconsciously provide for ourselves as defense against unseemly truth? Shakespeare's Hamlet used the mirror of a mini-drama so that his murderous and incestuous uncle and his too-ready mother could view their own treacherous wiles and be exposed in their reaction. Jacob will have mirror after mirror held up for him. He had duped Esau at the high point of the elder brother's appetite. Does Jacob, the morning after, catch the irony of being done in at the point of his own appetite—the feasting, the drinking, the desire?

Second Mirror: Younger Versus Older (29:26-28)

Laban proves to be an unsavory character, but he has the kind of reason on his side that may have struck a nerve with Jacob. Obviously upset, Jacob has asked, "What is this you have done to me? Was it not for Rachel that I served you, and why have you deceived me?"

> And Laban said, "It is not done thus in our place, to give the younger girl before the firstborn. Finish out the bridal week of this one and we shall give you the other as well for the service you render me for still another seven years." And so Jacob did. And when he finished out the bridal week of the one, he gave him Rachel his daughter as wife. (29:26-28)

"It is not done thus in our place, to give the younger . . . before the firstborn." Jacob remains silent, and agrees to terms. Jacob had usurped the birthright of the eldest, and now an eldest daughter is forced upon him.

Third Mirror: Contentious Siblings, Desperate Wives (29:29–30:24)

The work is physical labor, but it's emotional labor as well. Jacob has to contend with the unhappy dynamics between his two wives—a very large mirror to be held up for many strife-filled years.

> And he came to bed with Rachel, too, and, indeed, loved Rachel more than Leah, and he served him still another seven years. And the LORD saw that Leah was despised and he opened her womb, but Rachel was barren. And Leah conceived and bore a son and called his name Reuben, for she said, "Yes, the Lord has seen my suffering, for now my husband will love me." (29:30-32)

So God doesn't like it, this plight of the despised and "cheated" elder daughter. "And the Lord saw that Leah was despised." Will unfavored Leah find satisfaction in this child? She hopes that "now my husband will love me." These are very sad words.

Lacking her husband's notice, Leah suffers. She wants to count. She understands that God has seen her pain, but the child is not enough. Jacob loves Rachel. And so Leah comes to understand in the painful depths of her heart that it didn't work, that Reuben, the child she had given her husband, has not provided her a name murmured lovingly from her husband's lips.

> And she conceived again and bore a son, and she said, "Yes, the LORD has heard I was despised and He has given me this one, too," and she called his name Simeon. And she conceived again and bore a son, and she said, "This time at last my husband will join me, for I have born him three sons." (29:33-34)

Restless heart, Leah can't stop the longing, fill the void. Not with one child, not with two, not with three. She wants to be told in language of body and voice that she is solid and valuable. And so she names this child Levi in the hope that "This time at last my husband will join me, for I have born him three sons." As if this were not enough, Leah conceives again and bears a fourth son, Judah, meaning "This time I sing praise to the LORD" (29:35). Sing praise for what reason? Is the struggle over? The readers waits.

Meanwhile, what of Rachel, she who is loved? Is being loved enough? Does it automatically stop the craving for significance? Rachel may be loved, but she is barren. She envies. Eve and Adam envied the god-like state. It's not enough to be loved, to be the person you were created to be and have that suffice:

> And Rachel saw that she had born no children to Jacob, and Rachel was jealous of her sister, and she said to Jacob, "Give me sons, for if you don't, I'm a dead woman!" And Jacob was incensed with Rachel and he said, "Am I instead of God, Who has denied you fruit of the womb?" And she said, "Here is my slavegirl, Bilhah. Come to bed with her, that she may give birth on my knees, so that I, too, shall be built up through her." (30:1-3)

Where does this jealousy come from? Where does any jealousy come from, if not from a sense that I'm somehow number two relative to some other, a number one? Jacob appears sick and tired of the whole mess. Does this normal but disastrous dynamic sink home for him?

Perhaps a surrogate womb will do, thinks Rachel, just as grandmother Sarah had thought:

> And she gave [Jacob] Bilhah her slavegirl as a wife, and Jacob came to bed with her. And Bilhah conceived and bore Jacob a son. And Rachel said, "God granted my cause, yes, He heard my voice and He gave me a son." Therefore she called his name Dan. And Bilhah Rachel's slavegirl, conceived again and bore a second son to Jacob. And Rachel said, "In awesome grapplings I have grappled with my sister and, yes, I won out." And she called his name Naphtali. (30:4-8)

"Yes, I won out." Does the wrestling-minded Jacob take note? Naphtali, his new son's name: "in awesome grapplings I have grappled with my sister and, yes, I won out." These may be the saddest words so far in the story, this expression of Rachel's heart, words that might very well have penetrated Jacob's heart upon hearing "Naphtali": *"Yes, I won out"*—but to what ultimate satisfaction? Jacob, who loves Rachel, has snapped at her most furiously. Leah is jealous of Rachel's being loved, while Rachel is jealous of Leah's being fertile. Each scrambles for whatever sense of name they can muster. Jacob may be the victim here, but he is guilty as well. He has victimized Esau, in response to the same sort of struggle now being played out in front of him by his wives.

Again, where does jealousy come from? What causes it to lodge and fester in the human heart? And what is the normal way of dealing with jealousy? All the answers are here in the story. Jealousy lies in the fear of not winning, of not being important as compared to at least one other person. Winning takes care of jealousy, as our world turns in its ordinary way. We long to be at least one other person's better. Even through a surrogate womb, Rachel can taste victory: "In awesome grapplings I have grappled with my sister and, yes, I won out." Sad cry of victory, somber grappling for position. And it doesn't stop. Leah, apparently, no longer shares her husband's bed. And Rachel does not have a true share in her husband's children. Neither of them, in Leah's words, feels "joined." "This time my husband will join me," Leah hopes in naming her child Levi, "for I have bore him three sons" (29:34). But there is no satisfaction for either of them, no resting in a sense of their own significance.

Enter new drama: a love potion, a fertility drug—and jockeying for further position. The weary Jacob trudges onto the scene, weary from the fields of labor in which Laban has been cheating him of wages. Does this scenario of scheming and name-securing hit home for Jacob?

> And Reuben went out during the wheat harvest and found mandrakes in the field and brought them to Leah his mother. And Rachel said to Leah, "Give me, pray, some of the mandrakes of your son." And she said, "Is it not enough that you have taken my husband, and now you would take the mandrakes of my son?" And Rachel said, "Then let him lie with you tonight in return for the mandrakes of your son." And Jacob came from the field in the evening and Leah went out to meet him and said, "With me you will come to bed, for I have clearly hired you with the mandrakes of my son." (30:14-16)

Laban has hired Jacob for services Jacob had not envisioned, and now Leah will hire him for that which, presumably, he'd rather not perform.

> And he lay with her that night. And God heard Leah and she conceived and bore Jacob a fifth son. And Leah, said, "God has given my wages

because I gave my slavegirl to my husband," and she called his name
Issachar. And Leah conceived again and bore a sixth son to Jacob. And
Leah said, "God has granted me a goodly gift. This time my husband will
exalt me, for I have born him six sons." (30:17-20)

Tilting the balance in my direction, making things right, giving me a
place to stand . . . Leah thinks that now, now with her fifth son, "God
has given my wages." And yet again, a sixth son, whose name once
again hits the target of what is normal, and devastating, "This time my
husband will exalt me, for I have born him six sons." It's the same beat
of every normal heart, *This time I will be exalted in the eyes of at least
one other person.*

God finally gets around to Rachel, and she has a son by Jacob.
Finally the loved wife is also the fertile wife. Rachel would appear to
have it all:

> And God remembered Rachel and God heard her and He opened her
> womb, and she conceived and bore a son, and she said, "God has taken
> away my shame." And she called his name Joseph, which is to say, "May
> the LORD add me another son." (30:22-24)

The name *Joseph* can mean two contradictory things that might
describe the complicated state of Rachel's heart. First, "God has taken
away my shame," but then this: "May the LORD add me another son."[2]
Shame and disgrace indicate the distinct lack of being favored by
another, or others. Loved by her husband, Rachel yet needs deliver-
ance from the shame of her childlessness, a sure mark in her culture
of not counting for much, if for anything. Son born, shame gone. But
no, the shame is not gone, not entirely.

As Rachel herself notes, *Joseph* can also mean "May the LORD add
me another son." Rachel wants more? How much will be enough? Both
women frequently bring God into the name of the child, but each
appears to be using God as a champion against the other, as if to say,
"Look what God has done for me, rather than for you!" Rachel's naming can seem to escape this charge. But in the context of struggle, it
would appear that she names her son first for the elevation of standing

---

[2]"Taken away," from *asaf*. "Add" is a meaning of *yosef*, "a perfect homonym in
Hebrew for Joseph" (Robert Alter, *Genesis: Translation and Commentary* [New York:
W. W. Norton, 1996], note on 30:23-24).

she feels in her own person ("God has taken away my shame") and second for the prospect of even greater standing ("May the LORD add me another son"). Perhaps Rachel is properly reverential; more likely, and fitting the context of strife much better, is the view that Rachel is self-consumed, naming Joseph not by a name intrinsic to who he is—or is before God—but rather, what this child has done or can do for *her*. Attributing such elevation to God would be the farthest thing from being pious or reverential.

With the birth of a second son, Benjamin, Rachel dies. "Son of my vigor" or perhaps "son of my sorrow," the name appears ambiguous in establishing any progress for Rachel beyond self-absorption.

What does it take for the human heart to rest, to let go and to take hold of something better? Genesis consistently provides the answer: radical transformation from what's normal. And for that change to take place, God must stay on the scene, prodding, coaching, being available. God needs Jacob, and, if blessing is to come, Jacob needs to change. It will have to be a blessing that spreads out from his own person to include his wives. And it must keep spreading, to include all peoples of the earth—which is, for Jacob as for Abraham and Isaac, the ultimate promise.

The story suggests that Jacob has been faced with himself by way of several "mirrors." The deciever is deceived. Usurping brother Jacob sees younger sister Rachel supplanted by elder Leah. And he witnesses—and suffers from—conflict between the sisters, his wives. Jacob has been taught. It remains to be seen if any good will come from these experiences, ordeals that resemble the self-promotion and resulting havoc of Jacob's youth. We have seen the carefully nurtured partnership between God and Abraham, but nothing so promising here thus far. What is to come may look like a strange partnership in the making, but a partnership between God and Jacob nonetheless. The one capable of cunning deceit must now discover ways of using shrewdness for good ends, including the wooing of his wives as if they were one.

JACOB IS READY TO LEAVE THE LAND OF MIRRORS AND
hard labor, to put behind him the long years of being
deceived and cheated. Is he ready for the difficult
encounters lying ahead with his brother and with God?
And what of Jacob's contentious wives: will God's blessing for this family proceed in spite of their self-promoting and haggling ways? Abraham stopped lying about
his wife and subjecting her to sexually compromising
circumstances—and then, and only then, did God bless
the couple with a child. What evidence do we find of
Jacob's reorientation of heart, toward blessing others
rather than acquiring for himself?

Jacob tricks Uncle Laban and ends up with just
wages, and it appears that God helps him in this trick-
ery! Jacob maneuvers his wives into speaking and acting in one voice, with his own clever speech and game-
plan for the family's future. Lastly, Jacob successfully
flees once again; unlike his flight from Esau, however,
his stealthy leave-taking from Laban appears to be
sanctioned by God. After all this come face-to-face
encounters with God and his brother, and reconciliation. But then, the story doesn't end happily ever after:
disaster strikes, as Jacob is confronted with the horror
of his own sons' deceitful destructiveness in response
to a daughter's rape. The end, like the beginning and
everything in between, suggests real life, the depths
and range of its difficulties. And still there is hope,
which comes across as realistic and compelling.

10

THREE BREAKTHROUGHS— AND DISASTER

J ACOB HAS SWINDLED HIS BROTHER, ESAU, OUT OF BOTH BIRTHRIGHT and blessing. In Haran, Jacob gets swindled on a grand scale over a long period of time by his uncle Laban. By this time Jacob has had fourteen-plus years to consider what it means to cheat and be cheated.[1] He has had enough.

Turning Turned Tables: Out-Wrestling Laban (30:25–31:3)

> And it happened, when Rachel bore Joseph, that Jacob said to Laban, "Send me off, that I may go to my place and to my land. Give me my wives and my children, for whom I have served you, that I may go, for you know the service that I have done you." (30:25-26)

Laban knows, indeed, the good labor of Jacob, as we can tell from his response: "If, pray, I have found favor in your eyes, I have prospered and the LORD has blessed me because of you. . . . Name me your wages

---

[1]Seven years for Leah, then seven more for Rachel, plus several years if we count the seven childbirths of Leah and the "few years hiatus between the fourth and fifth sons" (Robert Alter, *Genesis: Translation and Commentary* [New York: W. W. Norton, 1996], note on 30:26).

that I may give them" (30:27-28). Is Laban asking Jacob to stay?

Jacob stalls, elaborating on just what his labor has meant for Laban. The reader may sense that Jacob is up to something here. Is Laban wary? "You know how I have served you," Jacob repeats, "and how your livestock has fared with me. For the little you had before my time has swollen to a multitude and the LORD has blessed you on my count. And now, when shall I, too, provide for my household?" Again Laban asks, "What shall I give you?" (30:29-31) Cleverly, Jacob has gotten Laban to listen twice to the truth of Jacob's good labor, which forces the uncle to ask each time what it is that Jacob wants. Going home may still be Jacob's ultimate agenda, but what is he really asking?

> And Jacob said, "You need give me nothing if you will do this thing for me: Let me go back and herd your flocks and watch them. I shall pass through all your flocks today to remove from them every spotted and speckled animal and every dark-colored sheep and the speckled and spotted among the goats, and that will be my wages. Then my honesty will bear witness for me in the days to come when you go over my wages—whatever is not spotted and speckled among the goats and dark-colored among the sheep shall be accounted stolen by me." And Laban said, "Let it be just as you say." (30:31-34)

Jacob seems to be setting himself up for loss. He offers to take from the flock as wages the few odd-colored sheep and goats (most sheep are white, most goats are black). Is this what it means to undergo transformation of heart? Does transformation include a letting-go that benefits someone who has wronged you? Must Jacob become a doormat? Does God want Jacob to take next to nothing for his family's provision, assuming that God is still with Jacob as God promised back at Bethel?

We expect change for Jacob after all the mirrors that have been held up to him; he himself has suffered the same fate as he inflicted on his brother, Esau. And we expect change because the preceding narrative recounted Abraham's change and growth into partnership with God. Does Jacob need to change his conniving nature, his cleverness? The biblical writer, characteristically, is laconic, clipped—moving along with hardly time for the reader to ask these little questions until it's too late and we realize we've missed something we need to go back over. There seem to be two obvious options: one, that Jacob display a broken spirit in taking only the leftovers; or two, that Jacob rise up with his wily spirit from younger days and get the better of Laban. But is there a third option, that Jacob take charge, cleverly and properly, in order to provide for his household? Shouldn't he try to get what he rightfully can from the wealthy Laban, who has cheated him of wages all these years?

Laban need come up with no liquid assets. Has Jacob anticipated that his uncle would not have been very generous in giving him "wages" sufficient for his immediate departure? Laban agrees to the proposal, which seems foolproof in his favor. Why not let Jacob have the few odd-colored flock? Laban agrees, and does the separating himself, then gives the strangely colored stock to his sons for safekeeping—at three days distance. Does Laban want to insure that Jacob won't trick him by crossbreeding the pure-colored and the off-colored? Jacob is left tending the purely colored stock. Jacob proceeds with a strange breeding scheme. He peels tree branches, making them appear streaked and spotted, and places them at a watering trough so that when the females are in heat, and come to drink, they and the mounting males will be looking at the now-flawed branches. Jacob takes the heartiest stock to breed, leaving the feeble for Laban. Does the scheme rest on some strange notion of embryo influence, following perception at moment of conception? There would also have to be something like recessive genes in the otherwise pure-colored sheep and goats. The writer doesn't explain, but does give us the results. The pure-colored flock diminish in number and in strength, while Jacob comes away "with many flocks and female and male slaves and camels and donkeys" (30:43). Laban and his household are upset at the results—so much so that Jacob becomes aware of the unrest:

> And [Jacob] heard the words of Laban's sons, saying, "Jacob has taken everything of our father's, and from what belonged to our father he has made all this wealth." And Jacob saw Laban's face and, look, it was not disposed toward him as it used to be. And the LORD said to Jacob, "Return to the land of your fathers and to your birthplace and I will be with you." (31:1-3)

Now it's time for Jacob to make his move. Does God approve of this deceiving of the deceiver?

New Partners (31:4-18)

In order to leave, there's something else Jacob must take care of, a serious matter indeed. His wrestling ways must be applied not only to the good of getting his proper pay from Laban but to getting his bickering wives to become one. Will the two of them leave their father and cling to him? Will the two of them become one in purpose, one in voice, one in action? Jacob calls Rachel and Leah together to plead with them. How will he put this matter? How strongly can he make his case to the contentious wives? Can he simply presume on their good will? Apparently not, if his carefully rehearsed and very clever speech is any indication. Jacob anticipates all the main features of what might sway his wives, finally, to come together. He saves God as his trump card:

> And Jacob sent and called Rachel and Leah out to the field, to his flocks, and he said to them, "I see your father's face, that it is not disposed toward me as it used to be, but the God of my father has been with me. And you know that with all my strength I have served your father. But your father has tricked me and has switched my wages ten times over, yet God has not let him do me harm. If thus he said, 'The spotted ones will be your wages,' all the flocks bore spotted ones. And if he said, 'The brindled ones will be your wages,' all the flocks bore brindled ones. And so God has reclaimed your father's livestock and given it to me. And so, at the time when the flocks were in heat, I raised my eyes and saw in a dream and, look, the rams mounting the flocks were brindled, spotted, and speckled. And God's messenger said to me in the dream, 'Jacob!' and I said, 'Here I am.' And he said, 'Raise your eyes, pray, and see: all the rams mounting the flocks are spotted, brindled, and speckled, for I have seen all that Laban has been doing to you. I am the God who appeared to you at Bethel, where you anointed a pillar and made me a vow. Now, rise, leave this land, and return to the land of your birthplace.' " (31:4-13)

Jacob tells them, in effect, that the breeding scheme whereby he has increased his flocks, tricking their father Laban, has been God's idea! Rachel and Leah can see that Jacob's holdings at this point are impressive. That their husband has no less than God on his side is, presumably, doubly impressive. It appears that Jacob's delay in going home, after the idea first occurred to him, is not only to give the breeding scheme time to "provide for [his] household." In addition, the impressive results might help to persuade the wives that their husband, an obviously superior fellow, is worth leaving home for. It works. The two wives, previously at odds with each other, band together for the first time in the story. They speak literally and emphatically with one voice, in support of their husband's leaving.

> And Rachel and Leah answered and they said to him, "Do we still have any share in the inheritance of our father's house? Why, we have been counted by him as strangers, for he has sold us, and he has wholly consumed our money. For whatever wealth God has reclaimed from our father is ours and our children's, and so, whatever God has said to you, do." (31:14-16)

Jacob's desire to "provide for his household" is shared by the wives, and they accept as proper the divine role in turning the tables on their father. Their unified allegiance to Jacob and to the good of the family replaces their contentious ways, at least for now. In fact, we have no evidence that the wives ever again struggle against one another to "win out."

Jacob has wanted to leave; God wants Jacob to leave. Jacob has wanted to provide for his household with increased flocks. Has God, indeed, allowed him a scheme to acquire those flocks? And to turn the tables on Laban? "I have seen all that Laban has been doing to you," says God (31:12). We can't be sure about God's role. We only hear it from Jacob. Maybe Jacob, who has lied to deceive his father out of Esau's 'blessing, is lying still to lure his wives away. After all, the reader hasn't heard of God's dream-instruction until after the breeding success had been reported. So how is the reader to know, to evaluate actions and character? It's a serious question, because even our idea of God is at stake.

The dynamic of the narrative suggests that Jacob is telling the truth. God had promised, in the night visit back at Bethel, to protect Jacob and increase his wealth and bring him back home. Perhaps the strange breeding trick is an actual law of nature, unknown by ordinary shepherds, to which God allows Jacob access. Perhaps, as W. Gunther Plaut surmises, "[Jacob] comes to know God not only in His immediate manifestations but also in the long-range processes of nature." Such privileged information would show that "God is concerned with Jacob and the latter knows this concern, which here is expressed in a non-miraculous way: Jacob is favored in that he learns the secrets of nature and utilizes them in accordance with God's will."[2] Jacob has already been granted some sort of "insider's" track with God and divine realities. There was the night visit with God when fleeing Esau, complete with messengers going up and down a ramp between earth and heaven, crossing the boundary between earthly and heavenly realities (28:10-22). There will come another liminal experience for Jacob, as we have seen. He will wrestle at night with a strange man whom he takes for God—a fact the writer seems to affirm since it will prove pivotal in what happens next between Jacob and Esau. There are key junctures, then, where Jacob experiences reality at the threshold between "natural" and supranatural. So it should not come as a surprise to the reader that God has come to Jacob in a dream with "secrets" at the boundary between natural law and bizarre breeding—bizarre, at least, from the perspective of Laban and his sons.

We have seen that, for the first time in the story, the wives speak as one, with one voice and purpose. This is a very good sign in and of itself, and an indication perhaps that Jacob is speaking the whole truth about God's help in out-scheming Laban. We have heard God's own words telling Jacob that it's time to leave and go back home (31:3), and Jacob repeats these words to his wives along with details about God's breeding savvy. His story about God's help hangs together for the reader, as it obviously has for his wives.

Once Again, Flight—and Deception (31:19–32:1)

It appears, then, that Jacob has used God as a trump card—with integrity. The wives accept their husband's version of events, understanding as well the pattern of their father's cheating ways. Jacob and his wives sneak off as one united family. They leave for home, as God had wished. Does God approve, however, of deceit? "And Jacob deceived Laban the Aramean, in not telling him he was fleeing. And he fled, he and all that was his, and he rose and he crossed the Euphrates, and set his face

---

[2]W. Gunther Plaut, *The Torah: A Modern Commentary* (New York: Jewish Publication Society, Union of American Hebrew Congregations, 1981), p. 206.

toward the high country of Gilead" (31:20-21). These human dimensions of doing God's will—including the breeding scheme and deceit in leaving—may amuse us or disturb us. Even a daughter gets in on the deceit: "And Rachel stole the household gods that were her father's" (31:19). The questions may persist: Where is God in all of this? What of the characters, their normal ways of being in the world—of self-promotion even at the expense of others? And does God care about reorientation of will—or just about forging ahead according to a divine blueprint for the world?

Another way to ask the question is, Is anything different? Have Jacob and his wives changed, from self-promotion and harm to others toward a more generous way of being in the world? If so, to what extent is God involved? The answers will come in the quotidian of life as represented in the narrative; in the everyday matters of breeding that leave an uncle the inferior stock; or, earlier, the making of a porridge that will prove irresistible to an appetitive brother who is conned out of his birthright. Where is God in all of this? Disapproving of the birthright scam? Approving or even initiating the breeding scheme? Or indifferent to such questions? We've begun to see God's possible role in the breeding scheme. Could it be that the great Master of the Universe has whispered nature's secrets in Jacob's ear, providing a bit of "righting the scales" for his years of being cheated by Laban? What about Jacob's deceitful flight, and Rachel's theft of her father's idols?

Some possible answers emerge in Laban's deportment, and the ensuing exchanges, after his daughters and Jacob leave:

> And Laban caught up with Jacob, and Jacob had pitched his tent on the height, and Laban had pitched with his kinsmen in the high country of Gilead. And Laban said to Jacob, "What have you done, *deceiving me*, and driving my daughters like captives of the sword? Why did you *flee in stealth* and *deceive me* and not tell me? . . . And so, you had to go because you longed so much for your father's house, but why did you *steal* my gods?" (31:25-30, emphasis mine)

Laban feels that he's been played the fool, as his staccato references to being deceived indicate. Yet he turns this anger around at the end of his little tirade, exclaiming to Jacob, "O, you have played the fool!" (31:28) How's that, the reader wonders? Who looks foolish here? Does the reader note with pleasure the deceitful uncle getting his comeuppance? "I have seen all that Laban has been doing to you," God has said. The reader has seen the same.

But what are we to make of the household gods being stolen? Rachel has been cheated by her father: She has been deprived of concord by having sister Leah thrown surreptitiously into the matrimonial mix. Now Rachel cheats her cheating father, and with the greatest guile. As Laban searches the compound for his gods, Rachel is sitting on them. They're hidden under her camel cushion. "Let not my lord be incensed that I am unable to rise before you," Rachel pleads to her father, "for the way of women is upon me" (31:34-35). She claims that her time of menstruation disallows her rising. Why does the writer include this little snippet of unseemly deception? Perhaps for the sheer delight of it, the pleasures of poetic justice. In addition, idolatry is implicitly condemned in Genesis by the presence of a living God. Except for their gold, these stolen god-idols are worthless, especially in terms of this story's vision of worthy and unworthy.

Rachel's deception of her father, which Jacob knows nothing about, seems to underscore Jacob's out-maneuvering Laban with the breeding scheme and stealing off in flight. Rachel belongs, now, to Jacob. "Rachel makes off with, or steals, the household gods," notes Robert Alter; "Jacob deceives—literally, 'steals the heart of Laban.'"[3] Indeed, it is likely that Rachel and Leah have been their father's "heart," stolen away by Jacob. What is clear from the text is Laban's mistaken notion about the relationship between Jacob and his wives. Far from "driving [his] daughters like captives of the sword"—wounded heart speaking?— Jacob has won them over completely, as wives who together have agreed with their husband's plans for departure. Among other things, Rachel's theft of the idols may be an exclamation point to her recent resolve with Leah to leave father and homeland at the request of a departing husband.

After Laban's fruitless search for the golden figurines, Jacob explodes in a poetic fit of rage. "And Jacob was incensed and voiced his grievance to Laban." Does he give vent to the twenty years of being cheated?

---

[3]Alter, *Genesis*, note on 31:20.

> What is my crime, what is my guilt,
>   that you should race after me?
> Though you rummaged through all my things,
>   What have you found of all your household things?
> Set it here before my kin and yours
>   and they shall determine between us two.
> These twenty years I have been with you,
>   your ewes and your she-goats did not lose their young,
>   the rams of your flock I have not eaten.
> What was torn up by beasts I've not brought you,
>   I bore the loss, from my hand you could seek it—
>   what was stolen by day and stolen by night.
> Often—by day the parching heat ate me up
>   and frost in the night,
>   and sleep was a stranger to my eyes. (31:36-40)

Is this merely rhetorical overkill, or are we being drawn into the truth of Jacob's faithfulness to Laban? Jacob claims that he's done his job with complete honesty and abandon, and that, in fact, he has gone beyond the normal shepherd's call of duty in bearing the loss of flock, even though the loss was not due to his negligence.[4] This is change of the highest and most transformational order, an example of what is expressed in the Genesis story with consistency and persuasiveness.

Jacob's outrage is impressive in its poetic expression, more expressive than the prose overview that follows, with its mathematics of Jacob's good case against Laban:

> These twenty years in your household I served you, fourteen years for your two daughters and six years for your flocks, and you switched my wages ten times over. Were it not that the God of my father, the God of Abraham and the Terror of Isaac, was with me, you would have sent me off empty-handed. *My suffering and the toil of my hands God has seen and last night He determined in my favor.* (31:41-42, emphasis mine)

Laban has repeated God's warning that the reader has already heard from the narrator, that Laban should watch himself lest he "speak to Jacob either good or evil" (31:24). "Last night [God] determined in my

---

[4]"Both biblical and other ancient Near Eastern codes indicate that a shepherd was not obliged to make good losses caused by beasts of prey and thieves, where no negligence was involved" (Alter, *Genesis,* note on 31:39).

favor," Jacob asserts. The reader—and Laban—know the truth of Jacob's judgment regarding the divine determination. That Jacob has been cheated on one hand, and hard-working and honest on the other, cannot be contested by Laban. The uncle can say nothing in his own defense, or to impugn Jacob's honor. So he suggests a peace pact between them, to which his son-in-law agrees. "And Jacob took a stone and set it up as a pillar" and has his men gather stones for a "mound [of] witness" (31:45-46).

We have seen the huge boulder removed by Jacob at the well of betrothal, when he meets Rachel, and we have seen the stone placed as a pillar to God after the night visit at Bethel, where God made promises and Jacob responded with a qualified vow. Now there are more stones. The one stone is for a pillar, possibly to invoke God's witness to the pact; the gathered mound of stones serves as a communal witness to peace between potentially warring clansmen. In love, then, and in politics, and in matters divine, Jacob's wrestling ways involve, symbolically and literally, a working with the unwieldy and weighty—with stone.[5] His journeying has been marked with stones to be lifted and with stones to be placed. He concludes his outburst with true words: "My suffering and the toil of my hands God has seen and last night He determined in my favor." That Laban does not refute a single word helps to confirm for the reader a growing partnership between God and Jacob. The two have worked together in successfully duping the duplicitous uncle.

Jacob's leaving Haran may remind us that his is a journey that is external as well as internal, as was the journey of his grandfather Abraham, who also journeyed to Haran and from Haran (11:31; 12:4). So far we have at least faint signs of Jacob's reorientation, including—and aided by—his recognition of God's kindness. There are the integrity and grit of his labor for Laban. And perhaps, in the case of his

---

[5] J. P. Fokkelman notes well the motif of stones in Jacob's story in his extremely detailed analysis of the literary connectedness of this narrative ("Jacob in the Service of Laban," in *Narrative Art in Genesis: Specimens of Stylistic and Structural Analysis* [Assen, The Netherlands: Van Gorcum, 1975], pp. 123-98). See also Robert Alter's brief note on Genesis 31:45, where Jacob takes the stone for a pillar in Laban's presence.

wives, we can count as salutary the redirection of Jacob's native wit toward the good end of unity between Rachel and Leah. He calls them together and speaks, and they then speak as one. As one, they will leave their homeland and father's house, casting their fortunes with Jacob. We await, however, the inevitable meeting-up with Esau. How possibly can there be reconciliation, blessing? Have the Laban years, in fact, been "mirror years" for Jacob? Has he taken stock of himself by witnessing and participating in the sad drama of his wives' efforts to be number one, and in Laban's lording it over him? The answer lies in what we have seen: the reconciliation with Esau effected by Jacob's tenacity and good will, and in Jacob's tenacious wrestling for blessing with God.

Disaster (34:1-31)

This story is over, and a goodly end we might think. But immediately ahead is heartache for Jacob and many others. This is the way it goes, this rare but compelling and realistic history—realistic, certainly, on the human level of interaction. The drama pushes relentlessly and ruthlessly onward in chapter 34. Jacob has bought land from Hamor, father of Shechem. Shechem rapes one of Jacob's daughters. Jacob's sons retaliate, dealing treacherously with Shechem and his people, turning their goodly intentions against them most horribly. Shechem has raped Dinah, yes, but he falls madly in love with her. He wants to marry her, and goes about making the proposal honorably. Fine, say Jacob's sons, but first all the foreign males in this clan must have the foreskin of their penises cut off, as all of Abraham's male offspring have had to do. Shechem's people agree, and all their males are cir-cumcised. But Jacob's children had schemed "deceitfully" (34:13)—Jacob's normal impulses surfacing now in his children. While the foreign males are hobbled by the cutting, they are slain brutally by two of the sons. Jacob is distraught at the treachery. He doesn't seem to know what to do, and does nothing. It's all so normal, this revenge of the brothers, this getting back, this coming out on top. With this ominous epilogue the larger Genesis story now moves on toward its concluding narrative, the story of Joseph.

A few matters remain: Jacob reaffirms God as his God by putting away all other gods, at God's command (35:1-7); Jacob again is renamed and again receives the promise of becoming nations—while being challenged to be fruitful and to multiply (35:9-15), this latter quite important for the story to come, since Jacob's clutching will stand in the way of multiplying and being fruitful; beloved Rachel dies in giving birth to a second son, named Benjamin by his father—again, an important detail for the story to come; a genealogy for Jacob along with notice of Isaac's death, and a much longer genealogy for Esau—both twins are to be blessed, given the promise beginning with Abraham that all families on earth are to be blessed (35:23—36:43). The worked-for harmony between Jacob and Esau was no fluke. It has continued. Together, they bury the father who had helped, in his blindness and in his befuddlement, to split them apart. "And Isaac breathed his last, and died, and was gathered to his kin, old and sated with years, and Esau and Jacob his sons buried him" (35:29).

Any Conclusions?

More. Rachel wants more, and still more. Is the everyday and normal heart so insatiable? Does it long and scratch and claw for significance, as we have seen it do with Rachel, with Leah, with Jacob, with Laban, and even with Esau? What makes a person like Jacob so deceitfully self-promoting at another's expense? Is it nature, or is it nurture? Is it in the genes, or in the home—or in the lack of a home? From the perspective of the Genesis stories, these are the wrong questions. It makes no significant difference how you answer questions of how this awful person came to be so awful. The question implied by Genesis is this: What am I or you going to *do* about our normal and sad state of self-aggrandizement? For Jacob, the wrong seems to begin with something like genetic disposition, back in the days of womb-wrestling. The twins seem doomed to strife. But then, all twins, all siblings, all spouses, all in-laws—all are doomed in the same manner, with myriad variation. It's all so normal.

But still . . . does God play favorites? What looks like luck of the draw turns out to be God's sleight of hand! The outcome between Jacob and Esau is a struggle that looks mighty unfair from the start, with their mother Rebekah moaning, Why me? Her belly proved to be a battleground for "fighting fetuses." With psychological realism and spiritual suggestiveness, Genesis explores these questions. If the impulse to make a name for ourselves is normal, and is compounded by the "givens" in life, including God's own choosing, how then shall we make our way? Joseph's story deals with that question head on.

Joseph's story offers a most convincing "conclusion" to the story of Genesis, and to the most fundamental questions that we can ask of life. The "chosen ones" are characters cursed with difficult lives for the sake of blessing. They must move beyond their normal attitudes and actions. There is no wishful thinking, no divine magic. It's all hard work. It's a struggle to the end, between what God wants and what humans want. God's will—God's choice-making—is finally done here on earth, in everyday circumstances. That's how Genesis ends. The complicated resolution to the dilemma of being human, toward global blessing, may strike us as improbable, but also as the only paradigm for the truly good life.

SITUATIONS THAT WERE PROBLEMATICAL FOR
*Abraham and Sarah worsened in the family of their
son Isaac and his wife, Rebekah, where there was
strife between the two; between their twin sons, Esau
and Jacob; between wives Rachel and Leah; between
Uncle Laban and nephew Jacob; and between God
and the would-be partner, Jacob. Now, in the last story
of Genesis, family confusions and hurts are brought to
their most excruciating pitch. It's the familiar problem
of making a name for oneself at the expense of others,
among a family of twelve brothers and between the
brothers and their father Jacob. Joseph's brothers hate
him, with good cause. Their younger brother is a tattletale and a braggart. Their father Jacob favors
Joseph above all of them, a position flaunted by Joseph
himself. God, too, seems to favor Joseph. It's normal to
hate someone like Joseph. Joseph's brothers, however,
are also hateful toward those outside the family. "You
have stirred up trouble for me," Jacob laments to his
sons, "making me stink among the land's inhabitants"
(34:30). And Joseph himself comes in for reproach by
the doting father. The story opens with Joseph's setting
himself up, only to be brought down. Something similar happens for Judah in the first part of this story.
Judah descends into his own darkness, surfacing as
the family's voice for understanding and upholding the
interests of the other person. All of the brothers,
including Joseph, jockey for position. If Joseph is to
help, he'll have to be cast down. He is, three times.
That's how the story begins.*

11

THREE DESCENTS
FOR JOSEPH, ONE
FOR JUDAH

W E BEGIN WITH A SENSE OF *DÉJÀ VU*, BACK TO THE VERY BEGIN-
ning, with Eve and Adam, Cain, Lamech, and Babel—and continuing
through Abraham and Sarah and Hagar, Jacob and Esau, Rachel and
Leah, Jacob's sons and the men of Shechem. Self-promotion, jealousy
and revenge are normal, according to Genesis. Nowhere is this sad-
ness so conspicuous as in the last narrative, that of Joseph and his
brothers.

The Need for Being Cast Down (37:1-11)
Favoritism of a parent and maybe even of God seems to compound the
problem of one-upmanship that crescendos here in the last story of
Genesis. This seemingly hopeless family scene of favoritism, mutual
disregard and dysfunction is captured deftly, with graphic detail, in a
few opening sentences:

> Joseph, seventeen years old, was tending the flock with his brothers,
> assisting the sons of Bilhah and the sons of Zilpah, the wives of his
> father. And Joseph brought ill report of them to their father. And Israel
> loved Joseph more than all his sons, for he was the child of his old age,

and he made him an ornamented tunic. And his brothers saw it was he
their father loved more than all his brothers, and they hated him and
could not speak a kind word to him. And Joseph dreamed a dream and
told it to his brothers and they hated him all the more. And he said to
them, "Listen, pray, to this dream that I dreamed. And, look, we were
binding sheaves in the field, and, look, my sheaf arose and actually
stood up, and, look, your sheaves drew round and bowed to my sheaf."
And his brothers said to him, "Do you mean to reign over us, do you
mean to rule us?" And they hated him all the more, for his dreams and
for his words. And he dreamed yet another dream and recounted it to
his brothers, and he said, "Look, I dreamed a dream again, and, look, the
sun and the moon and eleven stars were bowing to me." And he
recounted it to his father and to his brothers, and his father rebuked him
and said to him, "What is this dream that you have dreamed? Shall we
really come, I and your mother and your brothers, to bow before you to
the ground?" And his brothers were jealous of him, while his father kept
the thing in mind. (37:2-11)

What can be done about hatred and its cause? It's like a drumbeat:
they hated him and could not speak a kind word to him; again, they
hated him all the more; then again, they hated him all the more; even
his father rebuked him; and finally, if it isn't already dreadfully clear,
his brothers were jealous of him.

And worse still: Joseph, just a lad, an apprentice to his shepherd
brothers,[1] brings a bad report of the brothers back to a father who
"loved Joseph more than all his sons," who, in fact, rubs his fatherly
doting in the other brothers' faces by bestowing on Joseph "an ornamented tunic." And the kid brother demands that the brothers pay
attention to him: "Listen, pray," he says to them about these dreams of
his. To what point is Joseph's rehearsal of the dreams? Is Joseph just
an innocent, excited kid—a spontaneous burst of can-you-believe-this?
Is he merely "naive and guileless," as one might think?[2] In sibling relationships, even with children half Joseph's seventeen years, there's no

---

[1]"The Hebrew for 'lad,' *naar*, has a secondary meaning of assistant or subaltern. The
adolescent Joseph is working as a kind of apprentice shepherd with his older
brothers" (Robert Alter, *Genesis: Translation and Commentary* [New York: W. W.
Norton, 1996], p. 208).

[2]See Walter Brueggemann, for example, *Genesis* (Atlanta: John Knox Press, 1982), p.
336.

such thing as "innocent" when it comes to sibling rivalry. Normal behavior, certainly. Innocent, no. And so the brothers hated Joseph. Even the fawning but exasperated father has no recourse but to rebuke Joseph.

Earthly parents favor this one or that one, compounding the already normal drive of each sibling to be number one. Mother Sarah favors Isaac over Ishmael; Rebekah coddles the home-body Jacob while father Isaac, who likes to eat fresh game, has a special place in his heart for Esau the hunter; now it's Jacob making a special fuss over Joseph, son of his beloved Rachel. But God seemingly compounds the problem by showing divine favoritism: Abraham chosen from among many; Jacob picked over Esau. And it's possible that these dreams of Joseph reflect a divine favoring; if this is true, then once again the favoritism business is both divine and human. If the impulse to jockey for a favorable position in life lies at the heart of human wrong, how is it that we find major characters whose harmful striving after favor is complicated not only by a human parent's doting ways, but by a heavenly parent who purposefully favors one over another?

Joseph gets special notice from his earthly father and apparently from God as well, but any presumptuousness on his part about such "standing" will be seriously challenged. The brother who blabs to his brothers about their bowing down to him will be made to plead for his life by these same brothers (42:21). Has he had to bow down to them in this pleading? Joseph will be brought very low indeed. Before Joseph's gifted father Jacob was able to offer anything worthwhile, he had to be "put away" for twenty years in a living death, an imprisonment of sorts with Uncle Laban. Before Joseph can give anything worthwhile to his brothers and family, he must also be "put away," for twenty-plus years—put down into a pit, put down into a foreign country, and put down into a prison in a foreign land.

God wants something better than the normal family chaos with which the story opens. But God won't force things, we see insistently in Genesis. God won't make choices that the human has to make. What if Joseph's dreams have been given him by God—or at least reflect a reality that will unfold in the brothers' lives? The narrative insists that we entertain the very real possibility that these dreams are serious, both in their immediate and in their future significance. So we might wonder, as good listeners: In the event and to the extent that these dreams come true, will Joseph crush his brothers on the spot? Will the brothers cringe? We suspect that for anything good to come out of this dream business, it will mean that the dreams' dreamer must be transformed, along with the brothers who have been unnecessarily subjected to hearing the obnoxious dreams. What chance of such change from normal, in the real world? These are questions that the prior narratives have prepared us for, and the present narrative raises right at the beginning. To rise up, Joseph must be cast down. There is a triplet of such descents into darkness.

Cast Down: Pit Number One (37:12-35)

Joseph proves hateful to his brothers, but when Joseph is sent by his father on a mission to check on these brothers, we are reminded of how hateful they are even before Joseph or we find them. His brothers had gone "to graze their father's flock at Shechem" (37:12-14). Shechem! They're in the land of the man Shechem, who had raped and loved and wanted to marry the brothers' sister, Dinah! Shechem, who with all his male companions was brutally deceived and murdered by the vindictive and treacherously deceitful sons of Jacob! We remember the father's consternation (Genesis 34). The references to Shechem are conspicuous. The narrator has told us the brothers have gone to *Shechem*; Jacob now speaks it: "You know," says the father to Joseph, "your brothers are pasturing at *Shechem*" (37:13). Then, once again we hear it from the narrator: "[Joseph] came to *Shechem*" (37:14). After all this mention of *Shechem,* a mysterious stranger appears to Joseph out of nowhere with the information that the brothers are not here in Shechem! They have gone to Dothan. Physical details are always sparse in these stories. Why hammer away at Shechem, when the brothers aren't in Shechem, after all? Is it to prepare the reader— and Joseph?—for the treachery just ahead at the hands of the sons of Jacob? Could it be a reminder about just how grim things can get in normal everyday life? It was at Shechem that these brothers perpetrated in the name of family loyalty and honor a most heinous deception and murderous rampage. They're not at Shechem, but perhaps they have taken their hating, and hateful selves to Dothan. From afar the brothers see Joseph, whom they refer to derogatorily here as "that dream master" (37:19). The brothers come up with a plan, even as Joseph draws near: let's diminish his standing. Let's kill him, in fact. We'll throw him in a deserted pit—"and we can say, a vicious beast has devoured him, and we shall see what will come of his dreams" (37:20).

Two brothers come up with competing plans to avert this calamity. But each plan includes possibly self-promoting interests. Reuben seeks to fool his brothers by simply having them fling Joseph into a pit, alive—"that he [Reuben] might rescue him from their hands to bring him back to his father" (37:22). That sounds like an entirely positive thing, on the surface. Meanwhile, Judah proposes monetary gain: "Come, let us sell him to the Ishmaelites. . . . And his brothers agreed." The brothers like Judah's two-for-one suggestion, his idea that they might receive monetary gain as well as fulfill their initial desire for "satisfaction" in an ascendancy over a diminished brother. "And they took him and flung him into the pit, and the pit was empty, there was no water in it. And they sat down to eat bread." (37:24-25). Death, and life; an empty darkness with no water, and a smug circle with bread: "Be fruitful and multiply and fill the earth," God had challenged Adam and Eve, and then Noah (1:28; 9:1). The brothers, however normal in their responses to the tale-bearing braggart, fling the detestable brother into a kind of death, waterless and bare, while feeding themselves.

"And they raised their eyes," the text moves on, "and [they] saw and, look, a caravan of Ishmaelites was coming from Gilead . . . on their way to take down [goods] to Egypt" (37:25). But then "Midianite merchantmen passed by and pulled Joseph up out of the pit and sold Joseph to the Ishmaelites for twenty pieces of silver" (37:27-28). If we accept the discordant mix of Midianite and Ishmaelite here,[3] the out-

---

[3]*Midianites* and *Ishmaelites* are terms used, apparently, for the same peoples, though—as Robert Alter points out (in his note on 27:28)—from differing time periods (see Judg 8:22, 24). Whatever sometimes seems awkward in the composite artistry of these Genesis texts is usually highly effective in making a point. Although not all interpreters agree on who pulled Joseph from the pit (see Gen 37:28 NIV), Alter's rendering of the Hebrew suggests the irony of anticipated gain foiled. The reader is presumably to understand this chain of events in the later reference (37:36) to the Midianites selling Joseph to the Egyptian Potiphar.

come is a pointed irony: Judah's plans for monetary gain are foiled by the Midianites, who manage to beat the avaricious brothers to the pit. And Reuben? He's distraught at this turn of events. Why? For whom is he truly concerned? His cry at having his plan ignored is for himself, not Joseph nor father Jacob: "And Reuben came back to the pit and, look, Joseph was not in the pit, and he rent his garments, and he came back to his brothers, and he said, 'The boy is gone, and *I, where can I turn?*'" (37:30, emphasis mine). Reuben, as firstborn, sounds as if he's had something personal at stake, as if his bid to impress Dad has been undermined, to say nothing of the bad humor Dad will be in, with Joseph gone. First-born Reuben had slept with his father's concubine (35:22), incurring Jacob's displeasure (49:3, 4). Is Reuben protecting his birthright, trying to ingratiate himself by presenting Joseph to his father, promoting himself as Joseph's savior? Knowing what we do about the Genesis version of normal human attitude and action, we can assume the self-interested motive of Reuben, along with the obvious calculation for gain on the part of Judah and all the agreeing brothers.[4]

What does Joseph experience down in this first pit, in this time of darkness, emptiness, and no water? Is the reader expected to parallel this pit experience with the dark and difficult years of Joseph's father, Jacob, in the land of Laban and forced labor and sorrow? Jacob emerged with a tenacity for reconciliation with his estranged brother, Esau. Can we hope for the same, or even better, from Joseph—if and when the brothers all find themselves together again?

Cast Down: Pit Number Two (37:36; 39:1-6)

The end result of the sibling maneuvering is that Joseph, having been flung down into the pit, must now go down into Egypt. This is the second descent. Echoing this descent are the words of Jacob. Presented with the bloodied coat, Jacob "refused to be consoled and he said,

---

[4]James S. Ackerman discusses these possibilities very nicely in an extended focus on the Reuben-Judah comparison and the function of this "doubling" (two brothers with differing plans, in accounts that admittedly do not flow seamlessly in the story) in the larger story ("Joseph, Judah, and Jacob," in *Literary Interpretations of Biblical Narratives*, Vol. 2, ed. Kenneth R. R. Gros Louis, with James S. Ackerman and Thayer Warshaw [Nashville: Abingdon, 1982], pp. 98-102).

'Rather I will go down to my son in Sheol mourning' " (37:35). Joseph hasn't made it all the way down to Sheol, but Egypt is definitely "down."

The account of Joseph's arrival down in Egypt is delayed by a sordid tale involving brother Judah. It is a story about the precarious balance between death and life, between being fruitful and multiplying, and being the cause of no progeny. What this interruption means beyond its own intrinsic interest will be taken up in a moment.

Bracketing this Judah episode are references to Joseph going down to Egypt (37:36; 39:1). The latter of these "brackets" emphasizes by way of repetition that Egypt is "down," for Joseph:

> And Joseph was brought *down* to Egypt, and Potiphar, courtier of Pharaoh, the high chamberlain, an Egyptian man, bought him from the hands of the Ishmaelites who had brought him *down* there. (emphasis mine)

What does it mean to be cast down this second time? Sorrow, we might expect: wouldn't Joseph feel cut off from family and father's house—cast out, and down? In fact, we find out that this is precisely the case, revealed years later in Joseph's naming of his sons by his Egyptian wife:

> And Joseph called the name of the firstborn Manasseh, meaning, God has released me from all the debt of my hardship, and of all my father's house. And the name of the second he called Ephraim, meaning, God has made me fruitful in the land of my affliction. (41:51-52)

Apparent death—the darkness and emptiness and lack of water in that first pit—is overcome with fruitfulness right here "in the land of my affliction." God and Joseph—the two working in concert—will make a very good thing out of a very sorry situation.

Joseph rises to prominence in Egypt. Whatever happened to Joseph in the pleading before his brothers in that first pit experience (42:21), whatever happened on his journey down to Egypt, the result of both descents is announced in no uncertain terms by the narrator:

> *And the* LORD *was with Joseph* and he was a successful man, and he was in the house of his Egyptian master. And his master saw that *the Lord was with him, and all that he did the* LORD *made succeed* in his hand, and Joseph found favor in his eyes and he ministered to him, and he put him in charge of his house, and all that he had he placed in his hands. And it

happened from the time he put him in charge of his house that *the LORD blessed the Egyptian's house for Joseph's sake* and *the LORD 's blessing was on all that he had in house and field*. And he left all that he had in Joseph's hands, and he gave no thought to anything with him there save the bread he ate. And Joseph was comely in features and comely to look at. (39:2-6, emphasis mine)

God is with Joseph. Theirs is a partnership in operation. But folks in Egypt are normal, too, of course. Joseph faces a temptress and her easily duped husband.

"Joseph was comely in features and comely to look at"—gifted, even in appearance. We didn't know about this aspect of his being favored. Singled out by a parent, selected by God for special dreams—plus, good looking? How do ordinary people handle being considered exceptionally beautiful, or handsome? Joseph has "found favor in [Potiphar's] eyes," but now Joseph finds favor in the wife's eyes, too.

Cast Down: Pit Number Three (39:7—41:13)

Potiphar's wife comes after Joseph, and after him, and after him. Day after day, Joseph refuses her sexual advances. Finally, her aggressiveness leads to action: she seizes him by his garment, which he leaves in her hands as he flees (39:7-18). He has let go of a garment of favor, whereas earlier he had paraded his garment of favor in front of his brothers (37:23). To Potiphar, the wife concocts a tale that incriminates Joseph. In the face of these sexually problematic circumstances, Potiphar—possibly a eunuch[5]—chooses, of course, to believe his wife. Just as Jacob was deceived by a garment falsely presented, the lord of this house is taken in by the garment presented by his wife. Potiphar sends the handsome young manager down into a prison-house (39:19-20). That this is yet another instance of being cast down into a "pit" is reflected by Joseph himself, who refers to the prison-house as a pit: "I was stolen from the land of the Hebrews," he points out to fellow prison residents, "and here, too, I

---

[5]The Hebrew term designating Potiphar's status ("courtier," or "officer" in NRSV) is in other places translated "eunuch," or one who is castrated. See Esther 2:3, 14-15; Isaiah 56:3; see also Laurence A. Turner, *Genesis* (Sheffield, England: Sheffield Academic Press, 2000), p. 169.

have done nothing that I should have been put in the pit" (40:15).

The narrator emphasizes the riches to rags nature of the descent with a linkage between Potiphar's house and prison-house.[6] In each "house"—away from his father's house and feeling that loss (41:51)— Joseph comports himself in such a way as to rise up into a position of responsibility:

> And he was there in the prison-house, and *God was with Joseph* and extended kindness to him, and granted him favor in the eyes of the prison-house warden. And the prison-house warden placed in Joseph's hands all the prisoners who were in the prison-house, and all that they were to do there, it was he who did it. The prison-house warden had to see to nothing that was in his hands, as *the LORD was with him*, and *whatever he did, the LORD made succeed*. (39:21-23, emphasis mine)

Whatever he did: Joseph does good things that need doing, and doesn't do things that should not be done. God isn't pushing him or pulling strings like a puppeteer. At an extremely vulnerable sexual stage in his life, Joseph resists Potiphar's presumably attractive wife.

Abraham played loose with the sexual chastity of his own wife and prospered unjustly, it seems, at the hands of the man who took her for a wife. Joseph suffers unjustly for respecting his master and the sexual chastity of a wife who is playing loose with him. The good work begun with Abraham—focused, as we saw, on his terrible treatment of Sarah—is coming to full flower in Abraham's great-grandson Joseph. The final resolution to the destructiveness of what "normal" looks like throughout Genesis is all the more impressive in this last story because of its focus, in the beginning, on what the worst of ordinary life can be.

"Whatever he did" in the prison-house, Joseph did it with wisdom and grace. There is no God visiting Joseph in this third pit experience, but there is a God with him, nonetheless. God-with-him and whatever-he-did are two sides of the Joseph reality, of this final portrait in Genesis, a portrayal of the perfect partner to God. Joseph acts in such a way as to please God, and to please the head jailer.

It took seven visits with Abraham before God could retire from the

---

[6]As Alter notes in *Genesis*, p. 20.

earthly engagements with Abraham, finally knowing for sure that Abraham would trust in God's provision rather than fearfully attempt to provide for himself at Sarah's and others' expense. In Joseph's case, descents into the darkness—down into the wilderness pit, down into Egypt, and now down into the prison-house—reveal no interaction between Joseph and God. Joseph's ascendancy is clear, however, and seems linked by the writer with the descents. In the first major story of Genesis, it took a while before we, and God, could be sure that Abraham would be the blessing to others that God wanted him to be. Here, relatively early in the last story of Genesis, blessing is brought to Potiphar's house and into the prison-house because of Joseph.

Do we still have questions about what exactly it means, that "the LORD was with Joseph"? Does one go trance-like into each day, waiting for divine directives before acting? "Whatever he did, the LORD made succeed." It helps that Joseph says no when that is needed and yes when appropriate. He has accepted the responsibility of managing the houses of Potiphar and prison. "Walk with Me," God challenged Abraham; Joseph does just that.

Also cast down into the prison-house are a cupbearer and baker of the Pharaoh's. Joseph now has an additional responsibility: "And the high chamberlain assigned Joseph to them and *he ministered to them*, and they stayed a good while under guard" (40:4, emphasis mine). Whatever he did: what Joseph does is to manage well and, now, to minister well.[7] Do we hear the echo? In the other house, Potiphar's, the narrator tells us that "Joseph found favor in [Potiphar's] eyes, and he ministered to him"—with the result that Potiphar "put [Joseph] in charge of his house, and all that he had he placed in his hands" (39:3-4). Managing with his hands, and ministering. When the cupbearer and baker have dreams they cannot interpret, Joseph notices their depression. "Why are your faces downcast today?" he asks. (God vis-

---

[7]Robert Alter tackles those historians of the text who claim a discrepancy (differing sources) between Joseph's managing role at the end of chapter 39 and the ministering role here in 40:3. "Joseph's 'ministering' to the two courtiers need not imply a menial role. . . . [I]t makes perfect sense that they should be singled out for special treatment in prison, to be attended personally by the warden's right-hand man" (Alter, *Genesis,* p. 229).

ited Cain in a ministering sort of way, when Cain was "downcast," 4:5-7). "And they said to him, 'We dreamed a dream and there is no one to solve it.' And Joseph said to them, 'Are not solutions from God? Pray, recount them to me' " (40:7-8). Solutions are from God—so tell *me!* Joseph is like God, God's stand-in. God is with Joseph. Since Joseph is like God, perhaps God is like a good manager and minister—or perhaps God is mightily interested in managers and ministers who choose to spread God's blessing around.

With Abraham, God manages at first, but without any particular ministering. There are challenges and promises in the first three visits, but with no sense of intimacy. Not until visit four do we read of Abraham's talking with God. He questions a God who is willing to listen, a God who answers, entertaining questions from Abraham that express doubt and anxiety (15:1-15). By visit six, God's ministering to Abraham is reciprocated as Abraham at first provides nourishment to God and the other two divine beings. Then, after a feast, Abraham's word comes to God, who stands in Abraham's presence (18:22-23). These are two friends, Abraham and God, ministering to each other. Joseph is like God, able to move from the managerial role in the prison-house to the ministering role with Pharaoh's worried servants. Joseph manages in superior fashion by providing food for his family, but in his testing of the brothers, as we will soon see, he is ministering as well.

God is with Joseph, who has enough presence of mind to watch out for himself. He uses the good news of the cupbearer's dream to his own good advantage:

> But if you remember I was with you once it goes well for you, do me the kindness, pray, to mention me to Pharaoh and bring me out of this house. For indeed I was stolen from the land of the Hebrews, and here, too, I have done nothing that I should have been put in the pit. (40:14-15)

Two years later, having forgotten Joseph, the cupbearer suddenly remembers him when Pharaoh has two dreams no one can interpret. "And Pharaoh sent and called for Joseph, and they hurried him from the pit" (41:14). The narrator links prison-house with "pit," just as Joseph has done: the connection with being cast down, and pits, is clear.

Third Rising, Most Blessing (41:14-57)

Joseph has had his wits about him in trying to get out of this last pit by asking the cupbearer to remember him to Pharaoh. God's being with him does not mean, apparently, that Joseph can turn off his brain or refuse to take action on his own behalf. Pharaoh tells Joseph that he has heard "that you can understand a dream to solve it." Joseph protests, "Not I! God will answer for Pharaoh's well-being" (41:15-16). Pharaoh's two dreams are parallel: seven lean cows eat up seven fat cows, and seven lean ears of grain eat up seven fat ears of grain. After solving the dreams—there will be seven years of plenty, then seven years of famine—Joseph tells Pharaoh something that sheds light on how he has come to understand his own paralleled dreams, back home as a youth: "And the repeating of the dream to Pharaoh two times, this means that the thing has been fixed by God and God is hastening to do it" (41:32). If it has been fixed by God, what can be done about it by Joseph? The point is: Something will have to be done by Joseph.

Does Joseph entertain the possibilities of his own dreams, "repeated" and therefore "fixed by God"? Does he wonder how he and his brothers will respond to the dreams being fleshed out in reality? What he wants now may be different from then; what his brothers desire may be changing; what God wants could still be unclear to Joseph and the brothers. The relationship between God's will and human will is of great concern to the biblical writer of Genesis. Here, God has determined it; so what can Pharaoh do? Joseph not only interprets the dreams. The law of lean years following abundant years may be fixed, but "God will answer for Pharaoh's well-being" through the agency of Joseph, who discusses with Pharaoh the challenges and solutions, and offers advice. Pharaoh can take it or leave it—he can choose. And the person he chooses can go on to do a good job of it or bad. Joseph offers advice:

> And so, let Pharaoh look out for a discerning, wise man and set him over the land of Egypt. Let Pharaoh do this: appoint overseers for the land and muster the land of Egypt in the seven years of plenty. And let them collect all the food of these good years that are coming and let them pile up grain under Pharaoh's hand, food in the cities, to keep under guard. And the food will be a reserve for the land for the seven years of famine

which will be in the land of Egypt, that the land my not perish in the famine." (41:33-36)

Pharaoh is impressed. No one, including the reader, has any evidence of God whispering instructions into Joseph's ear. "And the thing seemed good in Pharaoh's eyes and in the eyes of his servants. And Pharaoh said to his servants, 'Could we find a man like him, in whom is the spirit of God?' " (41:37-38). Egypt's ruler recognizes what we've been told frequently: this is a man in whom the spirit of God resides and acts. "And Pharaoh said to Joseph, 'After God has made known to you all this, there is none as discerning and wise as you. You shall be over my house, and by your lips all my folk shall be guided' " (41:39-40). Find a "discerning, wise man and set him over the land of Egypt," the discerning and wise Joseph has advised. Pharaoh takes the hint, borrowing, in fact, the very superlatives he has just heard, praising Joseph and appointing this prison-house foreigner second in command, for handling national affairs.

But the reader is aware that this story of Genesis is more than any one national affair, that God has promised blessing to all nations of the earth. One nation is still struggling to be born, back in Canaan. It is time for the reappearance of the brothers, who with their father face death from starvation. Joseph has what his first family needs. Meanwhile, brother Judah has gotten himself in trouble. This powerful little story seems to interrupt the drama but in fact proves essential to the forward action we will see next, with the brothers coming to Egypt on behalf of life.

Judah's Descent, Tamar's Rising (38:1-30)
Out of the darkness of his three pit experiences, Joseph will come to understand well and rule rightly. Meanwhile, "interrupting" the story of Joseph being cast down—between the first and second descents—is a story of brother Judah's own personal darkness, and his coming out of that darkness to see rightly, and to do well, through a woman he has wronged. Is this a microcosm of Joseph's change?

Judah has married, and has three sons, Er, Onan and Shelah. He finds a wife, Tamar, for his oldest son. "And Er his firstborn was evil in the eyes of the LORD, and the LORD put him to death" (38:7). Following proper obligations of his day, Judah arranges for his second son to marry Tamar: "Come to bed with your brother's wife," he says to Onan. But the second son spills his semen on the ground "so to give no seed to his brother." God is displeased, and Onan dies also (38:9). Afraid that his third son Shelah will meet the same fate as the prior two sons, Judah deceives Tamar. He holds onto his son, his only remaining son, telling Tamar, with false intent, to wait until the boy is all grown up— "for he thought, Lest he, too, die like his brothers" (38:11).

Time passes. Judah's wife dies, and Tamar hears that Judah is coming to town. She disguises herself with clever wrapping and a veil, deceiving the deceiver; an echo of what father Jacob experienced with Laban. Judah and the brothers had deceived their father with Joseph's coat, dipped in blood. Jacob had been taken in by the ruse, assuming his beloved Joseph dead. Judah here is taken in by Tamar's similar ruse, the use of a deceptive garment. As always in the Genesis narrative, such detail is not just for the literary "fun of it." Rather, the paralleled garments of deception suggest the serious matter of reaping what you sow, and possibly learning from it. The deceived Judah sleeps with Tamar, his daughter-in-law, but not until after she has extracted payment from him.

> "What will you give me for coming to bed with me?" And he said, "I personally will send a kid from the flock." And she said, "Only if you give a pledge till you send it." And he said, "What pledge shall I give you?" And she said, "Your seal-and-cord, and the staff in your hand." And he gave them to her and he came to bed with her and she conceived by him. And she rose and went her way and took off the veil she was wearing and put on her widow's garb. And Judah sent the kid by the hand of his friend the Adulamite to take back the pledge from the woman's hand, and he did not find her. And he asked the men of the place saying, "Where is the cult-harlot, the one at Enaim by the road?" And they said, "There has been no cult-harlot here." (38:16-21)

Three months later Judah hears tales that Tamar has been whoring about, and is pregnant. "Take her out to be burned," says Judah (38:24).

Tamar's deceit comes full circle, as she had hoped. She presents her father-in-law with the evidence of his having slept with her—the pledge of Judah's seal-and-cord, and his staff. "And Judah recognized them and he said, 'She is more in the right than I, for have I not failed to give her to Shelah, my son?' " (38:26). For anything good to happen in this story, there must be change in the brothers who hate, and a change in Joseph, who gives reasons to be hated. The change has begun for Judah, a key brother, one whose reorientation of outlook and action will be realized in his brothers' lives and in his father's as well. Judah's extraordinary goodness will bring Joseph to tears.

The Judah-Tamar episode prepares the reader for what is to come. Small details emphasize the continuity and development of the action: (1) Joseph's garment, used for deception and death-dealing; (2) Tamar's garment and veil, used for deception and life-extending; and (3), Judah's personal accoutrements, taken by Tamar and presented back to Judah for life-extension, toward his own reorientation of will. Down in Egypt, Joseph's garments again come into play—and again, in a context of deception and death-dealing at the hands of Potiphar's wife. But then he will once again, and for good, don a royal garment of a lord who provides blessing to all. Such parallels and resemblances underscore the continuity of individual transformation that leads to family reconciliation.

Does Tamar, the wronged woman who does rightly, demonstrate an abbreviated version of the fruitfulness a changed Joseph can bring? The scenario of twisted relationships and crooked hearts at the beginning of Joseph's story couldn't be more filled with the human heart of darkness. Among other functions of the Judah-Tamar episode is the hope it offers for a widow who suffers unjustly and a father-in-law who is instructed in doing the right thing by a harlot. Like God, Tamar promotes life.

Joseph can't effect change in his family merely because he has changed, although his role will be primary. Judah must take the lead for all his brothers in turning away from normal name-seeking and toward the blessing of others. Joseph, however, is the godlike brother whose actions promote the final stage of Judah's astonishing turn-around. But what Judah has learned in this first stage of reorientation is to confess wrong in the light of a woman who does rightly. What Tamar does is in behalf of life, over against death, a multiplying and being fruitful as opposed to acquiescing to an enforced barrenness. In this she would have the creator God's blessing. Judah moves in this first phase of reori-

entation from protecting himself at the expense of progeny to embracing another, and fruitfulness. Will Joseph conclude his reorientation
along the same lines? Here is the most telling resonance between the
Judah-Tamar "interruption" and the larger plot: Joseph will have to
yield, as Judah has, a self-promotion at the expense of his family in
favor of a providing for others' well-being, and life.

*The brothers, on behalf of their family, will come bowing before Joseph for
food, for the continuation of life itself. At thirty years of age, Joseph is managing all the land and people of Egypt. Joseph will finally reveal himself to his
brothers, reassuring them after a series of outrageous and successful tests
that "it is not you who sent me here but God, and he has made me father to
Pharaoh and lord to all his house and ruler over all the land of Egypt" (45:8).
Joseph brings blessing to his own family. But, fulfilling the challenge-promise
to Abraham about being a blessing to all peoples, he has brought blessing to a
foreign nation. Joseph not only manages Pharaoh's affairs; he acts, in addition, in a fatherly role. He ministers to the potentate whose affairs he manages. Joseph is like God in managing good things out of bad, while helping
the weak become strong. That's how Joseph's brothers will come to a recognition of and repentance for the grievous wrong done their brother Joseph—
through the managing and ministering agency of Joseph himself! Transformation of the heart is, with Joseph and his brothers, still something that takes
human effort and divine help, but unlike the stories of Abraham and Jacob,
God works through Joseph and then through Judah without visiting, and
without speaking—except in dreams and dream interpretation. God has
become a spirit residing in the human, as Pharaoh has observed.*

*Fine. But here is Joseph, and far away, back home, are his brothers and
father. The realism of Genesis demands much more than resolution of family strife through separation—a course of least resistance taken early in his
life by Abraham with nephew Lot. How ready is Joseph for his brothers?
They are forced by famine down into Egypt where they will bow down
before Joseph. This is no fairytale of the disdained stepdaughter Cinderella
triumphing over morally flawed siblings and parent. There is no resolution
in Genesis without long and painful years and descents. Will his brothers,
too, have to be cast down? These are stories with moral rigor and realism,
which the story of Joseph makes more clear than any. Here there will be no
happy ending marked merely by happiness. But there will be blessing.*

THOUGH GOD NEVER APPEARS TO JOSEPH, AS HE did to Abraham and Sarah, Isaac, and Jacob, we are told repeatedly that the Lord was with him. A foreign potentate sees Joseph as one in whom the spirit of God resides. And yet, when Joseph finally gets the chance to embrace his brothers after many years, he not only refuses, but puts them through experiences the brothers themselves find extremely difficult. He is very clever at making life miserable for these brothers who have wronged him. Joseph's aged father Jacob falls victim as well to the scheming. Is this what it looks like to have God with you? In the end, there are hugs all around. But at what price? Have we gotten past the normal choices to improve our own standing at the expense of others? As Genesis winds down, where are we with the possibility of partnership with God, and blessing to all peoples on earth?

12

OLDER BROTHERS BOW
Does Joseph Tease or Test?

A ND ALL THE EARTH CAME TO EGYPT, TO JOSEPH, TO GET PROVI-
sions, for the famine had grown harsh in all the earth" is followed
immediately by "Jacob saw that there were provisions in Egypt." He
asks his sons to go down to procure food (41:57—42:1). The dramatic
stage couldn't be better set. Joseph is lord of the land; his brothers will
be beggars. The dreams from Joseph's youth . . .

Blessing to All Nations—but This Torn Family? (41:53—42:14)
From out of the grazing-field pit of his youth, from out of the prison-
house pit of his young adult experience in Egypt, from the very
descent itself down into Egypt, Joseph has risen to splendid heights,
clothed in garments of glory. Having interpreted well the two dreams
of Pharaoh, and having demonstrated to Pharaoh his shrewdness of
recommendations, Joseph has been chosen by Pharaoh to assume
leadership with grave responsibilities.

> And Pharaoh said to Joseph, "See, I have set you over all the land of
> Egypt." And Pharaoh took off his ring from his hand and put it on
> Joseph's hand and had him clothed in fine linen clothes and placed the
> golden collar round his neck. And he had him ride in the chariot of his

> viceroy, . . . setting him over all the land of Egypt. (41:41-43)

Joseph is favored by Pharaoh, and wearing garments and jewelry to prove it. It's been a long road from the garment of favor given him by Potiphar, which was stripped from him as he fled the lustful hands of Potiphar's wife. And a still longer road from father Jacob's garment of favor back when the youthful Joseph, however naively, set himself up in the land of his brothers only to be stripped of his prized garment and placed in a pit. But now he wears the rich linens and golden collar around his neck as one who has been set over all the land of Egypt.

The gaudy show is warranted. "And Joseph laid open whatever had grain within and sold provisions to Egypt. And the famine grew harsh in the land of Egypt. And all the earth came to Egypt, to Joseph, to get provisions, for the famine had grown harsh in all the earth" (41:56-57). Joseph provides, masterfully.

God promised provision of different sorts to Abraham and Jacob. God provided when Abraham relinquished his son Ishmael to the desert under Hagar's care. More encompassing than survival alone, God said to Hagar about the boy, "A great nation will I make him" (21:14-21). In the end, in relinquishing his second son, Isaac, Abraham came to know God as *Yahweh-yireh*, "the LORD-sees-to-it." God had provided a ram; and because of Abraham's trust in God's provision, God could swear by the divine self to move ahead with provision on a larger scale: "All the nations of the earth," God concluded, "will be blessed through your seed because you have listened to my voice" (22:16-18). Now, toward the end of Genesis, God provides for the survival needs of Jacob and his seed through a mature partner, Joseph. "All the earth came to Egypt, to Joseph, to get provisions." The initial and most fundamental promise in the beginning of Abraham's story is fulfilled toward the end of Joseph's story: "All the nations of the earth will be blessed through your seed." Why? "Because you have listened to my voice." Joseph has been listening also.

This happens because Joseph has been doing God's work. For the past seven years Joseph had been busy doing good. "He collected all the food of the seven years that were in the land of Egypt and he placed food in the cities, the food from the fields round each city he placed within it. And Joseph piled up grain like the sand of the sea, very much" (41:48-49). Providing takes foresight, planning, hard work—and by now in the Genesis narrative, we know that it's what God wants and that God is with Joseph. "Could we find a man like this [Joseph], in whom is the spirit of God?" Pharaoh had asked (41:38).

Testing, Phase One: A Descent, a Pit (42:15-17)

As we have seen, the text moves immediately from "all the earth came to Egypt, to Joseph" to Joseph's own family back in Canaan. "And Jacob saw that there were provisions in Egypt, and Jacob said to his sons, 'Why are you fearful?' And he said, 'Look, I have heard that there are provisions in Egypt. Go down there, and get us provisions from there that we may live and not die' " (42:1-2). Joseph's first dream had the brothers' harvested sheaves of grain bowing down to his, and now they come for the provision of grain. There's one conspicuous piece missing that was in that first dream:

> And the ten brothers of Joseph went down to buy grain from Egypt. But Benjamin, Joseph's brother, Jacob did not send with his brothers, for he thought, Lest harm befall him. . . . As for Joseph, he was the regent of the land, he was the provider to all the people of the land. And Joseph's brothers came and bowed down to him, their faces to the ground. (42:3-6)

The dream was right, then—or almost, since one of the "sheaves" is missing. While that first dream didn't specify "eleven" sheaves bowing, the reader nonetheless notes that not *all* the sheaves, not *all* the brothers, are here bowing down. Joseph picks up on the missing eleventh soon. How will Joseph respond to these brothers, bowing before him? And how will the brothers respond to Joseph's response?

Joseph is shrewd and capable. He can resist the wiles of an available woman who happens to be the wife of a boss who isn't home, while keeping sufficiently good humor to run a prison-house where he is interned unfairly. There he can interpret prison-house dreams on behalf of downcast prisoners; he is resilient enough in the end, when finally brought up on the whim of the needy monarch, to offer Pharaoh interpretation of his dreams. Joseph has been on his way to becoming a provider. Joseph will become like God. But what's this? Joseph "saw his brothers and recognized them, and he played the stranger to them and spoke harshly to them" (42:7). All the cards are in Joseph's hands. He recognizes his brothers, but they don't recognize him—a fact the narrator repeats. He can "play the stranger"—but to what point? He speaks harshly to them—but why? We're told that he remembers the dreams. "You are spies!" Joseph exclaims. "To see the land's nakedness you have come" (42:9).

At first glance it can seem that Joseph, who has spoken harshly and offered a stinging accusation, is going to relish a bit of one-upmanship. This normal way of being in the world will be all the sweeter to Joseph for its postponement since those brutish days of long ago. Referred to later by the brothers as "lord of the land" (42:30) and addressed repeatedly as "our lord" and "my lord," Joseph is now in a position to lord it over his brothers. On the other hand, as far back as the Potiphar and prison-house days, we have been informed by the narrator that "the LORD was with [Joseph]" (39:2), and that "his master saw that the LORD was with him" (39:3), that the LORD's blessing was on all the house because of Joseph (39:5)—and that, even down in the prison-house after being accused falsely, "the LORD was with him, and whatever he did, the LORD made succeed" (39:23). In this moment of revenge possibility, has Joseph abandoned the Lord who has been with him? Is the growing partnership suddenly challenged, so that we're back to square one, back in bad old days of family discord? What of Pharaoh's observation, just prior to this episode: "Could we find a man like [Joseph], in whom is the spirit of God?" (41:38)?

Joseph remembers the dreams and knows his place in those dreams and knows that ten of the eleven other players of the first dream are here. How do dreams work in this narrative? Is it simply a matter of "here's the prediction, now here's the fulfillment"? Is God's will like a blueprint in heaven which, in God's inscrutable way and with God's mysterious timing, gets played out on earth? Or are these dreams a divine occasion—a testing device—that intrudes in such a way as to force all the brothers, including Joseph, to deal with themselves? Joseph's two dreams indicate God's interaction with Joseph and his family, yes, but these dreams function more importantly in exploring and exposing how Joseph and his family will react to the dreams: they all have significant choices.

To appreciate what is going on within Joseph and his brothers here, so late in their life, we need to be reminded of their beginnings—perfectly normal beginnings, as families go. Once upon a time, long ago, Joseph had blurted out—needlessly and thoughtlessly—his dreams of superiority: "My sheaf arose and actually stood up, and look, your sheaves drew round and bowed to my sheaf" (37:7). Whether or not Joseph thought these dreams came from God, he must have known that his brothers already hated him and that to report the dreams would not only be pointless—they're all about future business, after all—but that this dream-report would cause an increase in present sibling strife. "And his brothers said to him, 'Do you mean to reign over us, do you mean to rule us?' And they hated him all the more, for his dreams and for his words" (37:8). Not for just the dreams did his brothers hate him, but "for his words." Another night, another dream, another telling of the dream, and presumably more words, to the same effect—only now it's "the sun and moon and eleven stars," parents and siblings bowing to Joseph. Even his doting father rebukes Joseph. How does one wear well a garment of favor? How does one respond well to the person so favored? The drama turns on the meeting-up of these two questions, when the gifted and the not-so-gifted come face to face, when the one with discerning recognition meets up with those who lack such discernment. The story's climactic sequence of events begins at this moment, when Joseph knows them who know not him, when Joseph remembers the dreams that made his brothers loathe him and cast him down. Joseph is lord of the land. "Do you mean to reign over us, do you mean to rule us?" the brothers had asked the young braggart. Rather than providing any simple solution to prior complications at this point in the narrative, the dream's partial realization initiates an unfolding of the narrative's most tense drama, a mini-drama with its own extremely complex complications. The immediate question has to do with how Joseph is going to handle the first dream's coming nearly true (again: there is one missing brother).

"You are spies!" Joseph exclaims. We presume that he's still speaking harshly. "To see the land's nakedness you have come" (42:9). Perhaps Joseph is filled with sudden anger and the need for revenge. The Lord may have been with him for many years, but maybe this is a

moment of truth that gives the lie to it all—or maybe this is just one
last challenge to cement the partnership between God and Joseph.
Yes, it's been difficult for Joseph, this family feuding and dysfunction.
Look again at what he's named his two sons by his Egyptian bride:

> And Joseph called the name of the firstborn Manasseh, meaning, *God
> has released me from all the debt of my hardship, and of all my father's
> house.* And the name of the second he called Ephraim, meaning, *God has
> made me fruitful in the land of my affliction.* (41:51-52, emphasis mine)

He has been carrying a psychological weight around, about which we
knew nothing, but could have suspected. The memory has been a
"debt of hardship," the pain "of all my father's house." But in Manasseh
he claims release. Just like that? We have not read of any attempt by
Joseph to contact his father or brothers during the many years in
Egypt. The "release" from his father's house is reinforced by the name
given son number two. *Ephraim* means "fruitfulness in the land of my
affliction." The "debt" of home has been compounded by his years
away-from-home in this "land of affliction." Have these two sons
proven enough to dispel from Joseph any lingering regret, any deep
longing? Had Joseph felt oppressed by the father's doting ways?
Maybe the harsh challenge "You are spies!" is expressed with vindictive anger toward everything associated with "the debt of my hardship,
and of all my father's house," of being subjected to this land of his
affliction.

Whether or not there is repressed or recognized rage, perhaps the
psychological fact is more complex: that Joseph is also stalling for time
with his brothers, accusing them of being spies so that he can come up
with a plan to challenge them toward recognition of their normal and
destructive ways, and toward a more life-giving response. Again, God
is with Joseph, as attested to by the narrator, Potiphar and Pharaoh.
Perhaps this is still the case. We can't see into Joseph's heart nor read
his mind. And of course the narrator, as is so often the case in much
biblical narrative, is silent. What else besides simple rage and revenge
could be going on here? The brothers have responded to Joseph's accusation that they are spies by protesting, with an integrity Joseph would
recognize, their innocence and honesty. "And they said, 'Your twelve
servants are brothers, we are the sons of one man in the land of

Canaan, and, look, the youngest is now with our father, and one is no more' " (42:13). Even at this point they include Joseph in their family! They have not forgotten that they are twelve.

Joseph seizes on the mention of a missing brother as evidence that they are spies—an irrational charge. How does acknowledgment of a missing brother implicate the brothers in some surreptitious act? Maybe Joseph has been intentionally irrational—for lack of a better point to buttress his contention, discerning all the while that his undiscerning brothers will not recognize the irrationality. If not intentionally, Joseph looks uncharacteristically silly in his blustering attempts to prove their treachery. He comes to the point, an announcement of a test of the greatest magnitude, a test that goes beyond even *his* powers to test.

> "In this shall you be tested—by Pharaoh! You shall not leave this place unless your youngest brother comes here. Send one of you to bring your brother, and as for the rest of you, you will be detained, and your words will be tested as to whether the truth is with you, and if not, by Pharaoh, you must be spies!" (42:15-16)

By Pharaoh, by Pharaoh: is the repetition meant to imply God, by way of the higher power, Pharaoh? Are we to think of God's testing of Abraham, of God's striving with Jacob?

All ten brothers are put in the guardhouse for three days (42:17). Why? Wasn't the test to be the incarceration of all but one, who would go and return with Benjamin and so provide release of the nine from prison? Does Joseph want the brothers to experience merely the pain of what he went through in the prison-house, in the pit, down here in Egypt? Or might Joseph be hoping they would experience what happened to him through these descents, a reorientation of his self-promoting ways as a youth? Is the bare "truth" of the brothers' account all that he's after? But he already knows that truth, and that the brothers have spoken truly. "Your twelve servants are brothers, we are the sons of one man in the land of Canaan, and, look, the youngest is now with our father, and one is no more."

In any case, for Joseph there won't be any immediate disclosure and satisfaction of proving his dreams as true, that he is, indeed, number one. He will not indulge himself impetuously, as he certainly did back in his youth, bursting to a youthful brim with news of his own sibling and family superiority. In all this, might Joseph want merely the satisfaction of delayed gratification at having, in fact, all eleven brothers—not just ten—bowing down to satisfy his egomania? The three days give the brothers time to ruminate, and time perhaps for Joseph to think further.

Testing, Phase Two: You Wanted the Silver? (42:18-38)

After the three days of prison for the brothers, Joseph changes the plan that would have sent one brother back to Canaan to get Benjamin, while the other nine stayed under guard. Now he will allow all the brothers, except one, to leave. Has this been a change in plan, or the plan all along? Whatever Joseph has had in mind for his brothers these three days of their being cast down, the immediate effect is better than any mere affirmation of factual truth, which in any case Joseph already possesses from the truth-saying brothers. With the announced change in plans, "they said each to his brother, 'Alas, we are guilty for our brother, whose mortal distress we saw when he pleaded with us and we did not listen. That is why this distress has overtaken us'" (42:21). The remorse is not shared by all, however. Reuben blurts out, in his own defense, "Didn't I say to you, 'Do not sin against the boy,' and you would not listen? And now, look, his blood is requited" (42:22).

Joseph, who has been speaking through an interpreter, understands what the brothers are saying. "And he turned away from them and wept." (42:24). This is the first of seven weeping sessions for the lord of Egypt.[1] This one who is bowed down to, and who could have pounced in pride, waits and weeps. Away from public view, he gives way to his deepest feelings. Is this one who merely longs for revenge of the highest order, to have the dream come true to his own satisfaction?

The one who waits and weeps also ups the ante of his testing, making his brothers' life even more miserable. He plants silver in their sacks, which, discovered on their way back home, frightens the brothers. Devious, clever Joseph? Whether for good or for ill, the

---

[1]The others are 43:30; 45:2, 14-15; 46:29; 50:1, 17.

answer is yes, Joseph is devious and clever.

The brothers had purchased Joseph's grain in silver. Joseph must anticipate his brothers' predictable dismay on discovering the intended payment tucked away in their sacks. With this unsettledness of his brothers, is Joseph hoping for further clarity and change of heart for his brothers? If so, one can be devious and clever toward good ends. It may not be a bad thing in the right spot to be devious and clever.[2]

The brothers had intended monetary gain by selling Joseph into Egypt. But the Midianites got the money, pulling Joseph out of that first pit and selling him to the Ishmaelites (37:28).[3] Now, years later, they receive silver from the brother whose sale they had hoped would bring them silver. Whatever Joseph's motives, he never asks for a return of the silver. Joseph may be setting a stage of difficulty wherein the players can learn better roles, better ways of being in the world than those of the past. Back home, in any case, father Jacob laments the incriminating presence of the silver; he also agonizes over the absence of the one brother in Egypt, Simeon. Jacob's anguish leads to fresh grief over the past loss of Joseph, and over the present threat of Benjamin's loss (42:36). The father refuses relinquishment of his most beloved son, Benjamin. "My son shall not go down with you," the father insists, "for his brother is dead, and he alone remains, and should harm befall him on the way you are going, you would bring down my gray head in sorrow to Sheol"—which echoes the lament over Joseph, assumed by Jacob to be dead (42:38). To the ten sons Jacob says that only one son—the only one who really counts—remains: how do sons, however grown, respond to that sort of parental favoritism? What can be done? How much work do Joseph and God have cut out for them in working what they can for family reconciliation, for family members including the father to move beyond self-aggrandizing ends? The family languishes; the famine is severe.

---

[2]Isn't God devious and clever in the test of Abraham, in the seventh visit? Jacob is surely devious and clever—apparently with God's help!—in maneuvering Laban out of wages by way of increased flocks.

[3]See n. 3 (p. 181) on the matter of who pulls Joseph out of the pit.

Testing, Phase Three: Relinquishment and Glory (43:1-14)

Whatever the goal of his testing, Joseph can't fully anticipate the consequences of his testing—or his teasing, if we continue to hold to that possibility. If testing, and the testing is for the good, a question: Is he like God in this matter of testing insofar as the tester can't know the results ahead of time, nor guarantee specific results? We recall that not until the last test of seven could God say about Abraham, "Now I know." Joseph can't control human choices and their likely outcomes; he can only arrange certain circumstances. Maybe something good can come out of testing. If Joseph is living up to his demonstrated capacity as a clever manager and sensitive minister, then perhaps we are meant to discern here the mind of God in testing God's potential partners. In both cases the testing has effected a family's rehearsal of past wrongs and sad consequences. The famine has gotten worse, the need for provision back in Canaan more acute. Jacob resists letting go of Benjamin—which surely Joseph would have anticipated, having been favored himself by the same father. Jacob is passionately attached to this second and last son of the beloved and deceased Rachel. Even for the sake of life over death, even for the sake of future generations, Jacob will not let go of his beloved son. He clings, though all the rest of his family suffer from the famine. Are we to remember the great and final test of Abraham, who let go of his "beloved" Isaac for the sake of a God promising provision, promising blessing for all the clans of earth? Famine and the threat of death notwithstanding, Jacob stands firm: "My son shall not go down with you, for his brother is dead, and he alone remains, and should harm befall him on the way you are going, you would bring down my gray head in sorrow to Sheol" (42:38). The details and nuances of how the test will play out are out of Joseph's control.

Before the first trip down to Egypt during the famine, Jacob had urged the brothers to "go down there, and get us provisions from there that we may live and not die." Live, and not die. But now Jacob settles for death over life. He clutches his own life, embodied in son Benjamin, at the expense of others. This is the normal way, according to Genesis. But one who is learning something better than "normal" rises up. Judah, who for his own interests had been willing to part with the life of Joseph and had thwarted the life of his own and Tamar's line, now places himself on the side of life and future generations, as he had in the end with Tamar. To do so, as Genesis suggests repeatedly, one's own life and name must be relinquished—which Judah urges upon his father and accepts for himself.

> And Judah said to him, saying, "The man firmly warned us, saying, 'You shall not see my face unless your brother is with you.' If you are going to send our brother with us, we may go down and buy you food, but if you are not going to send him, we will not go down, for the man said to us, 'You shall not see my face unless your brother is with you.'" (43:3-5)

Let go, Judah urges his father, let go. Judah speaks as he must, with integrity and urgency. Jacob claims personal harm and passes judgment on the brothers.

> And Israel said, "Why have you done me this harm to tell the man you have another brother?" And they said, "The man firmly asked us about ourselves and our kindred, saying, 'Is your father still living? Do you have a brother?' And we told him, in response to these words. Could we know he would say, 'Bring down your brother'?" (43:6-7)

Now Judah rises up even further. Relinquish your claim to what you conceive of as your future, Father; do this for "our little ones" and the greater future of many peoples:

> And Judah said to Israel his father, "Send the lad with me, and let us rise and go, that we may live and not die, neither we, nor you, nor our little ones. I will be his pledge, from my hand you may seek him: if I do not bring him to you and set him before you, I will bear the blame to you for all time. For had we not tarried, by now we could have come back twice." (43:8-10)

Reuben had already tried to budge his father by offering his own two sons to be put to death if the brothers didn't come back from Egypt with Benjamin (42:37). But Judah offers himself, willing to bear for all time the blame—and consequences?—in the event that Benjamin is lost. If acting self-consciously like God, could Joseph have hoped in the testing of his brothers for something this grand?

The narrator has switched in the above passages from *Jacob* to *Israel*. Does this call attention to the *Israel* who needs to choose for future Israel, for family and for life? For "the little ones"? Just prior to this switch by the narrator to *Israel*, a deep moan of self-absorption and self-pity has come from Jacob: "And *Jacob* their father said to them, 'Me you have bereaved. Joseph is no more and Simeon is no more, and Benjamin you would take! It is I who bear it all' " (42:36, emphasis mine). Does the narrator suggest, by contrast in this later plea from Judah, that *Israel* live up to his new name as father of a family on its way to becoming a nation, toward blessing and life for all peoples of the earth? "And Judah said to *Israel* his father, 'Send the lad.'"

For the blessing of peoples and the future, represented in these "little ones," Judah is willing to offer himself as pledge. And Jacob agrees, mournfully, to let go of his life, embodied in beloved Benjamin. Perhaps Joseph had hoped for something like this in his testing, but the results will become greater still, as Joseph relentlessly ups the ante of his challenges to the brothers. For the readers of Abraham and Sarah's story, and Jacob and Esau's, too, this will be a familiar story of escalating challenges for the sake of the other—of understanding and upholding the other's best interests. Such reorientation depends upon, and calls the would-be partner to, the living God, a God who desires blessing for all peoples. Jacob sacrifices Benjamin; all the brothers leave for Egypt.

Does It Get Worse, or Better, Than This? (43:15—45:15)
Phase one of the testing has been: stay in the guardhouse three days, a modest wake-up call, perhaps. Phase two: receive silver that isn't properly your own, who sought to gain silver so improperly from no less than the sale of a brother. Phase three: father, relinquish your beloved son; and brother (who will it be?), relinquish yourself in the interest of another—a father who favors another over you.

Now, back in Egypt with Benjamin, the brothers face one more test, perhaps the most difficult. This will be the fourth and final phase of Joseph's testing. What more can Joseph want from his brothers? What can he come up with now, for challenges? There's another silver-in-the-sack trick, but the silver is more precious and the test is more serious in consequence. After festivities that include drinking freely together (Joseph is still incognito, 43:31-34), the brothers, all eleven of them, are sent back home, with provisions. But this time Joseph has had his silver divining cup—not just silver coins—put in one brother's sack. He then sends his steward after the brothers to search their sacks. No, no, the brothers protest, we would never do such a thing: "He of your servants with whom it be found shall die, and, what's more, we shall become slaves to our lord" (44:9). The lord's cup is found in Benjamin's sack. "And they rent their garments," a death-lament (44:13). What more can Joseph want to extract from his brothers? Or is he possibly thinking of their provision, but at a more significant level than just grain?[4] Is Joseph going for a trump card as God did with Abraham in asking for that which was dearer than his own life, nudging his brothers toward the willingness to relinquish their own lives on behalf of the greater good?

The brothers turn around, and return to Joseph. Benjamin must become his slave, Joseph says, while the rest of the brothers may return home. Judah speaks for the brothers.

> Please, my lord, let your servant speak a word in my lord's hearing and let your wrath not kindle against your servant, for you are like Pharaoh. My lord had asked his servants, saying, "Do you have a father or brother?" And we said to my lord, "We have an aged father and a young child of his old age, and his brother being dead, he alone is left of his mother, and his father loves him." And you said to your servants, "Bring him down to me, that I may set my eyes on him." And we said to my lord, "The lad cannot leave his father. Should he leave his father, he would die." And you said to your servants, "If your youngest brother does not come down with you, you shall not see my face again." And it happened when we went up to your servant, my father, that we told him the words of my lord. And our father said, "Go back, buy us some food." And we said, "We cannot go down. If our youngest brother is with us, we shall go down. For we cannot see the face of the man if our youngest brother is not with us." And your servant, our father, said to us, "You know that two did my wife bear me. And one went out from me and I thought, O, he's been torn to shreds, and I have not seen him since. And

---

[4]One might argue, as J. Gerald Janzen suggests, that Joseph is a split personality throughout these dealings with the brothers, showing compassion by returning their money for the second time, but then later giving way to spite in sending someone to accuse them falsely of taking the money. I don't think this is the case, as will become evident by the end of the chapter (*Abraham and All the Families of the Earth: A Commentary on the Book of Genesis 12-50* [Grand Rapids, Mich.: Eerdmans, 1993], p. 173).

> should you take this one, too, from my presence and harm befall him,
> you would bring my gray head in evil to Sheol." (44:18-29)

We have already heard what Joseph hasn't heard, and we delight in
hearing again Judah's turned-around concern toward both the father
who favors and the son whom the father favors. Judah has come all
the way "home" and can only speak for himself at this point:

> And so, should I come to your servant, my father, and the lad be not
> with us, for his life is bound to the lad's, when he saw the lad was not
> with us, he would die, and your servants would bring down the gray
> head of your servant, our father, in sorrow to Sheol. For your servant
> became the pledge for the lad to my father, saying, 'If I do not bring him
> to you, I will bear the blame to my father for all time.' And so, let your
> servant, pray, stay instead of the lad as a slave to my lord, and let the lad
> go up with his brothers. For how shall I go up to my father, if the lad be
> not with us? Let me see not the evil that would find out my father!"
> (44:30-34)

That Judah will let go of his own life for another's life is one thing. But
that such relinquishment embraces and even promotes the fortunes of
a son favored above himself by an aging parent? This is too good to be
true, and yet the psychological realism of this narrative makes us
believe it as true, while reveling also in its quality of being too-good-to-
be-true.

And Joseph, the tester: how is it with him when Judah has pleaded
on others' behalf? How would God respond? Joseph may have been
lost to the brothers, but they have also been lost to him. Now, at this
point of their journeying, they are found; they are found out, sounded,
and found finally to be true of heart, whole. Away from Canaan, they
have come home to the truest of all homes. How would the waiting
God respond? I think we are being given a picture of the heart and
mind of God:

> Joseph could no longer hold himself in check before all who stood [in]
> attendance upon him, and he cried, "Clear out everyone around me!"
> And no man stood with him when Joseph made himself known to his
> brothers. And he wept aloud and the Egyptians heard and the house of
> Pharaoh heard. And Joseph said to his brothers, "I am Joseph." (45:1-3)

This third weeping of Joseph in regard to his brothers is the loudest. Is this a cathartic cry of someone who longed for such a thing to happen but who feared it might not?[5] He couldn't be sure. Neither could God, with Abraham, until that final test when Abraham came home to where God had hoped he would: Now, says God, I know that you fear Me . . . and now indeed, by my own Self I swear, I will move ahead with the promises (22:12, 16).

The testing is over. Hurry, bring Father down, says Joseph (45:9). Does Joseph simply want the second dream fulfilled, vaingloriously to have his one parent bow down, too, along with the brothers? His mother is dead, he knows, so technical fulfillment is impossible. In one breath will he insist on the letter of the dream for self-satisfaction—to have his father bow, too—while, in the same breath, weeping? Joseph breaks down and exposes his heart: "And he fell upon the neck of his brother Benjamin and he wept, and Benjamin wept on his neck. And he kissed all his brothers and wept over them. And after that, his brothers spoke with him" (45:14-15). This is, in part, what blessedness looks like. Apparently such fulfillment, for Joseph, has nothing to do with dreams coming true. Basking in the glow of being bowed down to, and seeing youthful dreams of superiority come true, seem quite beside the point in this series of challenges Joseph has put to his brothers.

The actual happy arrival of father Jacob will be more a delightful denouement shared by all than any delivery-of-the-goods craved by lord Joseph. When Jacob is summoned by the brothers to come down to Egypt, Joseph travels out some distance to meet his father, rather than waiting on some throne of royalty for genuflecting obeisance. "And Joseph harnessed his chariot and went up to meet Israel his father in Goshen, and appeared before him and fell on his neck, and

---

[5]Some, like Walter Brueggemann, take an exclusively negative view of Joseph's motives in the testing that leads up to this moment. With the brothers, Joseph is "a ruthless and calculating governor [who] understands the potential of his enormous office and exploits his capacity fully. He not only manipulates the scene but seems to relish his power to intimidate and threaten" (Walter Brueggemann, *Genesis* [Atlanta: John Knox Press, 1982], p. 337). The frequent weeping, alone, might suggest a softening of this view—perhaps, as Janzen has suggested, a somewhat split personality (see Janzen, prior footnote). In my next chapter I will explore the issue a bit more fully.

he wept on his neck a long while. And Israel said, "I may die now, after seeing your face, for you are still alive" (46:29-30). In fact, it appears that Joseph cares so little for the literal, factual, "truth-content" fulfillment of his dreams that he doesn't even give the second dream a chance to play out its perfection of detail, with the father's bowing down. Rather, Joseph does the bowing, falling on his father's neck. He who had set himself up over his brothers and father and mother falls weeping on the neck of an aged parent. He has done the same with his brothers. His dreams have come true, but more to his concern, his apparent aspirations on behalf of his entire family have come gloriously true. The family reconciliations cause Joseph such pangs of joy as lead to tears. Joseph is extremely pleased. Wouldn't we expect the God who is with Joseph to be similarly—extremely—pleased? This is what blessing looks like.

"And Israel said, 'I may die now, after seeing your face, for you are still alive'" (46:30). Jacob has been experiencing transformation right up to his very old age when he is challenged to let go of a son for the sake of life, for others, for "the little ones." Israel's inward change is indicated by the narrator: it's Israel who said to Joseph, "I can die now, having seen your face." Israel/Jacob is a person who, when very young, took advantage of his blind father's inability to see Jacob's face. Since those dark days, there has been a face-to-face reconciliation with a brother wronged, a face-to-face wrestling match with a man whom he takes for God, and, in his last days, a seeing of his beloved son's face. He who had to learn even in his very old age to relinquish a beloved son has gained back two beloved sons: the son who was lost has been found; the son relinquished has been regained. Whatever their intent, Joseph's tests have worked a kind of magic within himself, with his brothers, and with the old man, his father, Jacob-become-Israel.

Such "magic" has rigor, a painful playing out of choices and consequences over many years' time. Jacob is so struck with emotion when hearing about Joseph that his heart stops beating (45:26). Joseph himself can't stop from weeping—seven times!—with his brothers and with his father. This is a difficult family happiness—equal measures, it would appear, of sorrow and joy. It's not all sweetness and light with the Egyptians, either, who are taxed 20 percent and then must sell their land to Pharaoh—all at

Joseph's insistence. The "little ones" of Joseph's family are provided for, but what of the Egyptians, their "little ones" and their future? And how will the fearful, guilt-ravaged brothers and their lord, Joseph, possibly achieve anything like a family of brothers soon to comprise a nation, let alone a nation of blessing to other nations? This one has presumed to be like God in testing his brothers, to dream for their reorientation of will along with his own. How shall he comport himself with these same brothers and sisters in the real world, the ordinary day-to-day world of getting along with those obsessed with their guilt on the one hand, while faced with his own superiority inherent in forgiving them, on the other? What, finally, will it look like, the blessedness promised through Abraham to all peoples?

REPEATEDLY WE HAVE HEARD THAT GOD WAS WITH
Joseph, yet after providing handsomely for his own
family he forces the Egyptian people to sell all their
land to Pharaoh, and then pay Pharaoh a 20 percent
tax on all produce. In effect, it seems Joseph enslaves
them. Is this how a partner to God is to function in the
everyday world? Other questions remain. What can we
conclude about God's favoritism, about those not chosen for "partnership"? And what is the point of partnership in any case? Is there any happiness in being so
blessed as partner, or in bringing blessing to others?
And finally, in what ways does the ending of this Genesis story suggest recovery of the original loss in Eden
and a discovery of something better than normal?

13

ALL PEOPLES, INCLUDING THE LITTLE ONES OF EGYPT

T HE SPIRIT OF JACOB REVIVES, AFTER HEARING THAT BELOVED SON Joseph is alive, but it's Israel who says, "Let me see him before I die" (45:28). Jacob/Israel, very old now, will once again journey.

Father Israel Journeys to the Son: Third Night Encounter (46:1-27)
Israel *journeys*. The verb used does not suggest what we might expect, that "he arose and set out." This is a verb of wandering, of journeying and migration—as in Abraham's story throughout.[1] Is the state of heart more important in this Genesis story than the place one ends up, than even the land promised? Because God's purposes for global blessing include land for Israel, place is important. But in each of the three major narratives of Genesis, journeying is a literal fact and a possible metaphor: each of the main protagonists undergoes significant reorientation of normal ways of being in the world.

For the third time, Jacob/Israel experiences "visions of the night" (46:2). "Fear not to go down to Egypt," God says to Jacob. "I Myself will go down with you to Egypt and I Myself will surely bring you back up

---

[1]Robert Alter, *Genesis*, note on 46:1.

as well" (46:3, 4). This person who fled in fear as a youth must put aside fear as an old man and journey down to Egypt. God seems to be ever mindful that, for Jacob at least, fear doesn't just go away, ever.

Joseph Provides for His Little Ones—But Egyptians? (46:28–47:31)

Joseph hears that his father is approaching. He harnesses up and rushes out to meet his father, preventing the second dream's predicted bowing by his father as he himself falls on his father's neck. He weeps; the moment lasts (46:29).

Israel says to his son, "I may die now, after seeing your face, for you are still alive" (46:30), whereupon Joseph, so prone to weeping, comes up with a plan to relocate his family in favorable land. The plan is full of cunning. I'll go and tell Pharaoh you're shepherds, he says, then later you say the same thing to him. That way, the Pharaoh will allow you and the family to stay far away, in Goshen, since "every shepherd is abhorrent to Egypt" (46:32-34). Goshen, as Joseph knows, has very good grazing land. And it's up toward Sinai, so this makes it a good point of departure from Egypt at some future date. Is such a departure part of Joseph's calculation? The shrewd manager of human affairs wants his family in Goshen, so he's going to set it up carefully, making sure that Pharaoh will allocate land as Joseph wants that land allocated.

Joseph goes to Pharaoh, and tells him that his brothers are shepherds. The five brothers selected by Joseph—the most presentable?—repeat as Joseph has instructed regarding their "abhorrent" profession. Pharaoh takes it all in, and says, yes, stay way up there in Goshen—and while you're at it, appoint masters from among you for my livestock as well! (47:1-6) Joseph makes things happen for the good of his own family, just as he has for the nation of Egypt and other nations as well. But are the Egyptians all that well off under Joseph's rule?

The narrator brings together Joseph's concerns for his family with Joseph's dealings with the Egyptians, with no break or transition in the text. Is Joseph's cleverness on behalf of his own family being juxtaposed—judged, perhaps—by the narrator?

> And Joseph settled his father and his brothers and gave them a holding
> in the land of Egypt in the best of the land, in the land of Rameses, as

Pharaoh had commanded. And Joseph sustained his father and his brothers and all his father's household with bread, down to the mouths of the little ones. And there was no bread in all the earth, for the famine was very grave, and the land of Egypt and the land of Canaan languished because of the famine. And Joseph collected all the silver to be found in the land of Egypt and in the land of Canaan in return for the provisions they were buying, and Joseph brought the silver to the house of Pharaoh. (47:11-14)

Joseph provides "his father and his brothers and all his father's household with bread, down to the mouths of *the little ones.*" But what of the Egyptians, from whom he is taking silver for the coffers of Pharaoh?

Joseph's attention to his family, all the way down to "the little ones," has precedent. When Judah pleaded with his father Jacob to let go of Benjamin, Judah's own life to be held in pledge, he did so "that we may live and not die, neither we, nor you, nor *our little ones*" (43:8). When Pharaoh finds out that Joseph's brothers are here but his father and family are not here, he offers them all the "fat of the land" and insists that they provide for bringing back the little ones: "Take you from the land of Egypt wagons *for your little ones* and for your wives, and convey your father, and come. . . . The best of all the land of Egypt is yours" (45:19, 20). A bit later "the sons of Israel conveyed Jacob their father and *their little ones* and their wives in the wagons Pharaoh had sent to convey him" (46:5). Joseph has provided "bread, down to *the mouths of the little ones*" of his own family and in nearly his last words of the story, will reassure his brothers with promises of provision for their "little ones." But what of the Egyptians?

The silver runs out, and the people of Egypt plead for bread. In exchange for bread Joseph will accept the people's livestock. Another year of famine, and the people return to Joseph. "We shall not conceal from my lord," the people confess abjectly, "the silver has run out and the animal stocks are my lord's. Nothing is left for our lord but our carcasses and our farmland—take possession of us and our farmland in return for bread, and we with our farmland will be slaves to Pharaoh, and give us seed, that we may live and not die, and that the farmland not turn to desert" (47:18-19). So Joseph takes what remains, "and the land became Pharaoh's" (47:20). And then he moves people "town by

town, from one end of the border of Egypt to the other" (47:21). Later he
acknowledges that "I have taken possession of you this day, with your
farmland, for Pharaoh" (47:23). In exchange, Joseph gives the people of
Egypt seed for planting, but there will be a tax of one-fifth on all future
yields (47:24). What do we make of this seemingly ruthless maneuvering by Joseph, albeit on Pharaoh's behalf? One option is, as many readers suggest, to call it the way it seems: ruthless maneuvering by Joseph
on Pharaoh's behalf.[2] This is the more obvious reading of the account.
But we can also emphasize what the people actually say, how they have
actually fared during this famine and how they might fare in the future,
and what it is that Joseph actually says about the seed, words that echo
prior concern, and anticipate continuing concern, for "the little ones."

The people respond by saying, "You have kept us alive! May we find
favor in the eyes of our lord, in being Pharaoh's slaves" (47:25). Judah
had pleaded with his father for the release of Benjamin "that we may
live, and not die." From the creation on, God is on the side of life over
death. Joseph is preserving life and preventing death. But at what cost
here? Freedom? Freedom, of course, is a notoriously slippery concept.
What has freedom meant for these people? We don't know. Left alone
in their freedom, how would they have managed during this natural
disaster? They would have died—we know that. How will they function in future disasters, without strong managerial help?[3] We can
guess. Well, but couldn't Joseph have just given the seed and worked
out a payment schedule when things finally turned around? Look at
Joseph's key words: "Here is seed for you," he says; "sow the land. And
when the harvests come, you shall give a fifth to Pharaoh and four
parts shall be yours for seeding the field and for your food, for those in
your households and for your little ones" (47:24). Perhaps four parts is

---

[2]Walter Brueggemann expresses this majority sentiment (see *Genesis* [Atlanta: John
Knox Press, 1982], p. 356); see also the more detailed and quite persuasive analysis
by J. Gerald Janzen *(Abraham and All the Families of the Earth: A Commentary on
the Book of Genesis 12-50* [Grand Rapids, Mich.: Eerdmans, 1993], pp. 178–82).

[3]Is it possible, as James Ackerman has suggested to me, that the writer wishes to
make an implicit comparison between the Egyptians' willingness to serve Pharaoh
(with a 20 percent return) over against the Israelites, who will be called upon to
serve God (with a 10 percent return)? In this case, Joseph still does the good that
he can do, given the religious situation in Egypt.

sufficient and even generous: one part for "seeding the field," a second part "for your food," a third part "for those in your households," and a final, fourth part for even "the little ones." In the litany of "little ones" in this narrative, Egypt's children take their place.

This is the fifth mention of the "little ones," the four prior instances and the last one referring to Israel's family future.[4] This time, the words point to Joseph's concern for Egypt's future. Joseph's foresight on behalf of his own family parallels his foresight on behalf of Egypt's people, at least in what the biblical writer catches in terms of phrasing. "And Joseph sustained his father and his brothers and *all his father's household with bread, down to the mouths of the little ones*"; then, almost immediately, sustenance for the Egyptians: "four parts shall be yours for seeding the field and for your food, *for those in your households and for your little ones.*" Households down to the little ones are the concern of Joseph in formulaically similar phrasing both for his own family and for the Egyptians.[5]

Joseph's words reflect not so much the negative of losing one fifth, but the gain, the "four parts" that will be sufficient to avert disaster, including food "for those in your households and for your little ones." In most "developed" countries of the modern era, giving the government from two-fifths to three-fifths, or higher, is the norm. A total tax of 20 percent, which Joseph imposes, might seem like freedom. As Robert Alter suggests, the writer probably marveled at the highly centralized government of Egypt, including its flat tax of 20 percent and tenant-farming.[6] What the account focuses on—which modern sensibilities can easily pass over—is Joseph's faithful management under an apparently benevolent monarch on behalf of a needy and very appreciative people.[7]

---

[4]These are 43:8; 45:19; 46:5; 47:12; and 50:21.

[5]If Joseph has, indeed, caved in to imperial interests as the employee of Pharaoh, and to priestly interests as the husband of an Egyptian priest's daughter (priests keep their land), perhaps his wrong is softened by the narrator's noting of Joseph's words concerning "the little ones." What the text makes clear is Joseph's concern for the future, not only of his own family, but of the Egyptians as well.

[6]See Alter's note on 47:25.

[7]For Nahum Sarna, this account of "tenant farmers . . . has been included here because it provides examples of Joseph's wisdom and leadership capabilities . . . [and emphasizes] the great benefits that Joseph brought to the crown, thus accentuating the base ingratitude of a later Pharaoh 'who did not know Joseph' (Ex 1:8)" (*JPS Torah Commentary: Genesis* [Philadelphia: The Jewish Publication Society, 1989], p. 321).

The biblical writer has made it clear that, through Joseph, the promise to Abraham that "all the nations of the earth will be blessed through your seed" has come true: "all the earth came to Egypt, to Joseph, to get provisions" (41:57). As well, he provides for his own family and the families of Egypt. "Nothing is left for our lord," the people had said, "but our carcasses and our farmland" (47:18). Joseph redeems their "carcasses" along with their farmlands through a process of nationalization. Life is preserved, and the people are grateful. All of Egypt, represented in the elders of various towns, make a procession of hundreds of miles back to Canaan for the burial of Joseph's father. We need to exercise caution in reading back into the situation our modern notions of slavery.[8] Joseph has done what he can—which is a great deal of good—to preserve and extend life, an implicit challenge within the original Genesis mandate to be fruitful and to multiply.

After the land has been taken and given to Pharaoh, and after the family of Israel had become "fruitful" and had "multiplied greatly" (47:27), Joseph and his family are revered more than ever, it appears. Years pass; Joseph's father Israel dies. It is perhaps the best-attended, longest-distance funeral procession of any recorded in the Bible:

> And Joseph went up to bury his father, and all Pharaoh's servants, the elders of his household, and all the elders of the land of Egypt, went up with him, and all the household of Joseph, and his brothers, and his father's household. Only their little ones and their flocks and their cattle they left in the land of Goshen. And chariots and horsemen as well went up with him, and the procession was very great. And they came as far as Goren ha-atad, which is across the Jordan, and there they keened a great and heavy keening, and performed mourning rites for his father seven days. And the Canaanite natives of the land saw the mourning in Goren ha-atad and they said, "This heavy mourning is Egypt's." (50:7-11)

---

[8]Terence Fretheim advises such caution: "The language of 'slavery' appears insufficiently nuanced." Fretheim goes on to explain:"The people become tenant farmers, even though it deprives them of some freedom. . . . [20 percent is] not excessive in that world. They are grateful to Joseph for having saved their lives, and ask for his continuing favor, even as they affirm their status as tenant farmers" (*Genesis,* in *The New Interpreter's Bible,* Vol. 1, ed. Leander E. Keck et al. [Nashville: Abingdon, 1994], p. 654).

What Then Does Perfected Partnership Look Like?

The larger context of the portrait reveals a God-like Joseph. What the text suggests here at the end of Genesis is a near-perfecting of the partnership ideal between God and human, an ideal begun with Abraham and Sarah and carried through the Jacob and Esau narrative to include, now, Joseph, Judah and Jacob-become-Israel. Like Abraham and like Jacob and like Judah, Joseph is being transformed and reoriented over long years of difficulty. In the portrayal of Joseph we have come to a final clarification of what constitutes the moral vision of the Genesis story:

☐ God desires blessing for all nations.

☐ In God's sovereignty (God's power to choose freely and to "make it happen"), God waits for and encourages willing responses from chosen individuals to implement the blessing.

☐ Such willingness requires reorientation from normal but destructive self-aggrandizing ways toward understanding and upholding interests of others.

☐ Blessing for all, God's will, is accomplished.

As a self-promoting, other-belittling person, Joseph sparks jealousy and murderous rage rather than blessing in his own family. With God's assistance, he must learn to see and act as God sees and would act. For example, he comes to understand Pharaoh's divinely sent dreams and to manage things accordingly for the political good of all; and again, he can spurn the advances of another's wife; he can be gracious and conciliatory toward brothers he has alienated.

When Joseph is far enough along in his transformation—when he appears conspicuously as one "in whom is the spirit of God" (41:38), then the partnership ideal is approaching perfection—which is to say, the blessing to all clans of earth promised through Abraham will come true, as it does when "all the earth" comes to Joseph for provisions (41:57). This is reorientation in fairly full bloom, a "coming on board" with God to work as a partner toward the ideal of bringing a blessing to all. Such blessing begins at home—as is always the case in the major narratives of Genesis. Such reorientation from the normal ways of being in the world is political in its broadest effect—and can result, as in Joseph's case, in the shrewdly beneficent politician. Abraham "grew

up" as God's partner when he stopped passing off his wife and became
political in his blessing-bringing (though in comparison to Joseph, on a
much smaller scale). Abraham initiated a legal transfer of land by purchase; and again, he initiated a treaty of land-for-peace with
Abimelech, after noting the increased tensions among their respective
shepherds. Such reorientation requires choosing on behalf of others'
best interests, possibly at the expense of one's own interests. Abraham
pays exorbitantly for the land; Joseph forgoes the perks of power in
leaving his "throne" to go hug his father. The goal of reorientation necessarily includes both personal change and political repercussions. In
the Genesis view, reorientation consists of both "interior" transformation and "exterior" action on behalf of all. God is the initiator and sustainer of, and sovereign partner to, both human transformation and
human blessing.

Here at the close of the Genesis story, Joseph is, fittingly, the most
advanced of all God's partners, the one most able to carry on the mission of provision and blessing. Even the name given Joseph by Pharaoh points to what the biblical writer has been reiterating: "And
Pharaoh called Joseph's name Zaphenath-paneah" (41:45), which
means either "God speaks, he lives" or "Creator of life."[9] Before Pharaoh, Joseph insists—most conspicuously in his dream interpretation—that he is speaking for God, letting it be known, of course, that
God lives. Don't be downcast about your dreams, Joseph advises Pharaoh. "Are not solutions from God? Pray, recount them to me" (40:8).
Zaphenath-paneah, indeed: God speaks, he lives.

God is the "creator of life," who has challenged the human to be fruitful, and multiply—to create life (1:28). Joseph keeps life going, in part
through his Egyptian wife and two sons Manasseh and Ephraim, who
will become tribes of Israel. If not literally "creator of life," however,
Joseph is certainly a sustainer of life *par excellence*. As we have seen, "all
the earth came to Egypt, to Joseph, to get provisions." The narrator lin-
gers on the word "provision" in the immediately following verses:

---

[9]Robert Alter, following Moshe Weinfeld, suggests the former (*Genesis*, p. 241); W. G.
Plaut posits both as possibilities (W. Gunther Plaut, *The Torah: A Modern Commentary* [New York: Jewish Publication Society, Union of American Hebrew Congregations, 1981], p. 267).

And Jacob saw that *there were provisions* in Egypt, and Jacob said to his
sons, "Why are you fearful?" And he said, "Look, I have heard that *there
are provisions* in Egypt. Go down there, and *get us provisions* from there
that we may live and not die." . . . And the sons of Israel came *to buy provisions* among those who came, for there was famine in the land of
Canaan. As for Joseph, he was the regent of the land, *he was the provider*
to all the people of the land. (42:1-6, emphasis mine)

God had proved to be the provider for Abraham, a giver of blessing
that included physical goods, certainly, but more significantly cen-
tered on the miraculous birth of Isaac and the giving back of this relinquished son. And for Jacob, God faithfully supplies all his promises—
promises of provision which Jacob holds God to before agreeing to full
partnership when he finally allows God to be his God, declaring this by
building an altar he calls "God, God of Israel" (33:20). Jacob's is a God
who provided as promised, and now, in the last story of Genesis, as the
partnership is perfected, Joseph "was the provider to all the people of
the land."

There is no hubris, only humble self-assessment and compassion,
in Joseph's very last recorded words in the story: "And so fear not,"
Joseph concludes with his brothers, "I will sustain you and your little ones." Fear not. We know that at the heart of Abraham's fear for
his life and name had been a failure to trust in God's provision for
promised life and name—as was the case for Eve, Adam, Cain,
Lamech and the Babel folks. The resolution to the Abraham and
Sarah narrative came at that point when we—and God!—could take
fullest measure of Abraham's growth: his fear of God, about which
God became finally sure (22:12), a *yere-Elohim* that at its heart evidenced a relinquishing of fearful clutching through trust in *Yahweh-
yireh*, the God-Who-Provides, who sees to it. As God is a provider,
now Joseph provides, encouraging his brothers to "fear not" even as
God had challenged Abraham in their fourth visit. In this way,
Joseph is like God.

When the brothers came back down to Egypt for further provisions,
bringing with them Benjamin and double the amount of silver that
Joseph had put in their sacks, they approached Joseph, as we have
seen, as one would approach God: "They rose [from home] and went

down to Egypt and stood in Joseph's presence" (43:15).[10] The common construction in Hebrew for "stand in God's presence"—and in the presence of royalty as well—is used here.

The writer underscores this God-presence, also, in the scene where Joseph goes out to meet his Egypt-bound father. "And Joseph . . . appeared before him" (46:29), just as "God appeared to Abraham" (12:7; 17:1) and to Isaac (26:2). In the smallest detail, the narrator seems to want to establish the truth of prior insistence, that God is with Joseph. The phrase "appeared before him" is the common construction in Hebrew for God's appearing. Joseph takes the initiative in moving toward his father, even as God has with Joseph's ancestors. In this perfected partnership, Joseph is like God.

The brothers have expressed their concern to the steward about the silver that had been placed in their sacks, and get this response: "All is well with you, do not fear. Your God and the God of your father has placed treasure for you in your bags" (43:23). Spoken lightly? No, this is no fairy-tale explanation.[11] Joseph is like God, unwittingly attested to by the steward and recorded by the biblical writer's unfailingly deft detail of observation. Are we to imagine the possibility that Joseph is acting literally like God? That God, if choosing to do divine magic, would have placed that silver in their sack as part of a divine challenge, for its ultimately good effect? Of course it's possible to read this entire sequence of challenges as God making a good thing out of maliciously intended moves on Joseph's part, but that doesn't fit the larger context very well, the context that includes the gradual reorientation not only of Joseph but also of Abraham and Jacob.

Joseph is so much like God in the perception of his brothers, finally, that Joseph has to insist that he is not the same as God. "Fear

---

[10]They come, also, with many of the same products as accompanied Joseph himself on the first trip down to Egypt (cf. 37:25 with 43:11). Parallels and double-events, double-dreams, abound in this story—all to good point. Here, the idea of restitution is suggested.

[11]"The majordomo dismisses their fears by introducing a kind of fairytale explanation for the silver they found in their bags" (Robert Alter's note on this verse). Perhaps the majordomo is thinking in terms of fairytale, but the reader should recognize the consistent pattern of this writer in ascribing to Joseph Godlike skills and sensitivities and generosity of provision.

not," he says at the end of the story to the brothers about their guilt and fear of reprisals, "for am I instead of God?" (50:19). The story speaks volumes by clothing forgiveness in dramatic dress. Joseph seems to understand how his position as a God-person can be misconstrued, and would stand in the way of true communion with his brothers. Though Pharaoh might see one "in whom is the spirit of God" (41:38), and though his brothers may fear their younger brother as one with superior powers, Joseph himself suffers from no false or arrogant illusion about himself. Furthermore, he understands his own providing and preservation of life to be under the auspices and direction of the great provider on high. To the fearful brothers, in the scene where Joseph finally reveals himself, the younger brother offers this reassurance:

> And now, do not be pained and do not be incensed with yourselves that you sold me down here, because for sustenance God has sent me before you. Two years now there has been famine in the heart of the land, and there are yet five years without plowing and harvest. And God has sent me before you to make you a remnant on earth and to preserve life, for you to be a great surviving group. And so, it is not you who sent me here but God, and he has made me father to Pharaoh and lord to all his house and ruler over all the land of Egypt. (45:5-8)

God is in it all, Joseph assures his brothers; God has made it work for blessing. Does this mean that "the LORD was with Joseph" to such an extent that Joseph is nothing but a transparent medium for God? We could wonder, on one hand, if Joseph isn't a cipher while God is all; on the other hand, we could err by assuming that Joseph is so filled with God's spirit as to be God-in-the-flesh. I think that the biblical writer understands the fine line in all of this by underscoring Joseph's ascent to this fullest realization of partnership in all of Genesis. Joseph knows the "otherness" of God, clearly. To Potiphar's propositioning wife, Joseph asks, "How could I do this great evil and give offense to God?" (39:9). By the time his brothers appear in Egypt, Joseph confesses to a "fear of God"—that which took Abraham so long to appropriate. On the third day after all ten brothers have been put under guard, Joseph had said, "Do this and live, for I fear God" (42:18). Either Joseph is trotting out the piety of civil religion,[12] or he is sincere in reassuring his brothers of the truth of what he has said: "Do this and live." Joseph is too much on the side of life to be mistaken as being glib, I think, in his confession of God-fear.

But in reassuring his brothers, does Joseph engage in exaggeration, emphasizing one side of the coin and not the other? "It is not you who sent me here but God," he reassures his brothers. Was it all God? Was it so simple as God pulling puppet strings? This wouldn't accord with what we've been seeing in the two prior narratives of Genesis. And in this concluding story, we have seen that it's not quite so one-dimensional as Joseph makes it sound in this reassurance to his brothers. Human activity is not all under God's stage-directing and script-writing, at least not in Genesis. The dreams are given to the young Joseph, but the working out of those dreams can be for good or ill, depending on how the parties involved make choices. There is the good bowing that we have seen, versus the bad bowing that would have been more "normal"—that lording-over normally sought by someone in a position of power and particularly with motives for revenge. And clearly the brothers *did* have a role in selling Joseph "down here." Why else would Joseph have engaged in such elaborate testing toward such glorious transformation and reversal of the evil they did in sending him down to Egypt? Or, if in fact Joseph had no such noble intentions, the beneficent results of the testing are nonetheless clear. The whole point relative to the brothers is that they themselves come to realize the depths of their guilt for their self-promoting, Joseph-destroying choices. No, God won't control human choicemaking. Yes, Genesis affirms that God wants to teach humans to make better choices. Yes, God and the human partner can work together to make good things happen out of very bad habits of the heart. Even the brothers of Joseph, and Judah in particular, experience a new clarity of vision and soundness of heart: they are needed for God's desire for blessing. Such partnership is desired by God and, in Genesis at least, is what we can ascribe to God as unchanging. Far from inscrutable, this is the mind of God relative to human attitude and action. God's will, in relation to ordinary persons chosen for extraordinary changes and blessing, is powerfully drama-

---

[12]Walter Brueggemann's view (*Genesis* [Atlanta: John Knox Press, 1982], p. 340).

tized and made known in the way of story, rather than of systematic reflection or scientific analysis. Whatever "consistent" and "systematic" ideas about God that we hope to obtain must arise from and be consonant with this narrative text understood as narrative.

Parental Favoritism Compounded by God's?

Joseph was singled out by God from the start, with the dreams of superiority—just as he had been singled out for special favor by a doting father. What might still bother the reader is a lurking discomfort with this God who favors one over another—especially when the favored one flaunts that favor, or uses natural gifts and talent for self-promotion. God chose Abraham, a talented schemer who pursued a normal course of action in preserving his own life and promoting his own interests at his wife's expense. God chose Jacob, who would not even choose God—Jacob, who used his wily and gifted nature to do what any of us normally do in achieving a sense of self-importance, though not perhaps to the extent of deceiving a parent or cheating a sibling.

God knows a great deal about the innate giftedness of those chosen for partnership—enough, for example, to favor this one over another, even from the womb. But God doesn't seem to be certain about the return of that favor, waiting for twenty-five years with Abraham until finally able to exclaim, "Now I know about you, Abraham. Now I can be sure" (22:12). Can we accept as believable a God whose sovereignty it is *not* to simply rule over all, *not* to follow a divine road-map for all human contingencies and choices? A God who chooses to coax and challenge, rather than coerce? Who has to wait to find out whether the favored ones will come, finally, to favor God and to honor God's goal of having them bring blessedness to others?

Whom God favors, God challenges. From normal darkness of the heart, ordinary people rise to a level of blessedness. Even skeletons in the family closet can issue forth in greatness when God and humans—however unlikely the human actors—become partners. For example, from Tamar's life-preserving harlotry with Judah and from Lot's daughters' life-preserving incest with their father in the cave, come the twin lines of Israel's greatest king, King David. (Ruth, who descends from Moab, son of Lot and his elder daughter, marries Boaz,

who descends from Perez, son of Judah and his daughter-in-law Tamar.
From Boaz and Ruth comes David. See Ruth 4:18-22.) Judah learns,
partially from Tamar. From his life-giving reorientation comes the crucial ingredient in this great family reconciliation. Judah is tested by
Joseph, just as Abraham and Jacob—and Joseph himself, presumably—are tested by God.

Do either Joseph or God know for sure the results of their testing?
Joseph's frequent tears of catharsis suggest not; he has to wait for the
brothers to make their own choices for better or for ill. God's happy
exclamation after the seventh and last test with Abraham, "Now I
know that you fear God!" suggests that God waits for Abraham to make
his own choices for better or for ill. Neither God nor Joseph, in their
respective positions as "lord," choose to lord it over their subjects; each
"lord" respects the choice-making of these subjects. Therein lies the
heart of what makes all of this Genesis drama so riveting. Divine-
human partnership approaches an ideal with Joseph, "in whom the
spirit of God resides"(41:38) and through whom blessing comes to all
(41:57). For both God and Joseph, the results of their respective challenges to Abraham and to the ten brothers are very good indeed.

How does one handle being great, being favored? For Joseph, the
answer includes a lot of hard work, and integrity, and sexual purity,
and mental acuity, and confidence in God, and openness to others.
Joseph becomes the apotheosis of all that God had in mind in choosing
Abraham, Isaac, and Jacob. "And all the earth came to Egypt, to Joseph,
to get provisions, for the famine had grown harsh in all the earth"
(41:57). Joseph, the gifted one, gives. Joseph, the lord, supplies his
subjects over all the earth. Joseph manages things on behalf of others,
and he ministers to Pharaoh as would a "father." Joseph ministers as
well to the soul's need of his own brothers. And this is the one who had
paraded his superiority by needlessly reciting dreams, who had
paraded his moral superiority in telling tales on his brothers, who had
paraded even his garment of favor, wearing it to the grazing fields in
search of his brothers. Joseph had to let go of that garment of favor—to
leave it in Potiphar's wife's hands. He went from being quite normal—
setting out to find his brothers in Shechem wearing his garment of
favor—to being like God. Joseph's character gives the richest meaning

to phrases like "get over it," "get a life," "just do it" and even, "just say no." But he has had to "get down"—to plead with his brothers for his life. He has had to spend time in the various pits that life so predictably provides for any who journey away from the normal choices of self-promotion at the expense of others, toward the "un-normal" choosing on others' behalf, even if at the expense of one's own standing as "lord." Joseph could have clobbered his brothers with his superiority. The brothers are forced down, held under guard three days, but toward an end that finally emerges—hugs and tears of reconciliation and healing. Joseph insists that he will not extract obeisance from his brothers, that he is not in a position to even judge them as guilty. To be favored is to grant favor.

Where's the Happily-Ever-After?

This is a difficult family happiness, I have suggested—equal measures, it would appear, of sorrow and joy. There is a pithy example of this narrative rhythm when Joseph brings his father before Pharaoh. On the one hand, "Jacob blessed Pharaoh" (47:7). These are good words from the one who will father a nation begun way back with Abraham, who was challenged to be blessing to all nations. On the other hand, there is Pharaoh's question and Jacob's answer. "How many are the days of the years of your life?" asks Pharaoh. Jacob gets stuck on "the days," "the years." He answers,

> The days of the years of my sojournings are a hundred and thirty years. Few and evil have been the days of the years of my life, and they have not attained the days of the years of my fathers in the days of sojourning. (47:9)

"And Jacob blessed Pharaoh and went out from Pharaoh's presence" (47:10). Sandwiched between his blessing of a foreign potentate, Jacob offers a realistically poignant response to the question of his age. Jacob has been blessed by God—helped materially, helped in the trip back home from Laban's, helped in facing Esau, helped in finally facing Joseph his lost son. Jacob has been blessed by regaining two sons, one lost and one relinquished. But they have been difficult days, long years. Perhaps God takes Jacob's lament to heart by visiting the now-aged Jacob with a reassuring word, just as God did in the first night vision of the ramp, and the promise with no *ifs*. "And look," God had said so long ago, when Jacob was fleeing for his life, "I am with you and I will guard you wherever you go, and I will bring you back to this land" (28:15). The comfort offered years later is the same: "Fear not to go down to Egypt, for a great nation I will make you there. I Myself will go down with you to Egypt and I Myself will surely bring you back up as well" (46:1-4). Not so with Abraham, who, after God comes to be sure of Abraham's conquering of fear with the fear of God (22:12), experiences a cessation of any recorded divine visits. Grandfather and grandson are two different individuals, and God enters partnership with each respective to the uniqueness of that individual. What unites both is a slow process of transformation, from blessing-thieves to bless- ing-givers. Abraham brings curse to Egypt and to Abimelech's people and, presumably, to his wife Sarah—but ends up bringing blessing through covenant-making, match-making, and a land deal. Jacob has taken his brother's blessing, but years later is able to return it. And, finally, he is able to give blessing to each of his sons (49:1-27) as well as to his grandsons by Joseph.

It has been slow and uneven, this process of transformation for the man now called *Israel*. Happiness seems beside the point. Joy, yes; sorrow, yes. And above all, change into the kind of partner with God who can offer blessing to a Pharaoh. "And Jacob blessed Pharaoh" (47:10). The writer has framed Israel's difficult years with Israel's blessing of Pharaoh and Egypt, just as Israel's blessing of his children— including the mixed-breed sons of Joseph as future tribes of Israel— will help to close out the story of Genesis.

Is the End in the Beginning?
God and Joseph have forged the closest of partnerships. Joseph was willing to change. This is the grand possibility held out by the biblical writer throughout Genesis. Eve and Adam aspired to be like the gods— to have the "name" and perks of God. Joseph, on the other hand, acts like God. Joseph is the grand reversal of his primeval parents, Eve and Adam—and their offspring. Joseph becomes unnatural, moving beyond normal choices to a divine level of providing blessings of all sorts to all kinds of peoples. This was the goal announced by God in changing divine tactics, back with Abraham and Sarah. God will now

work patiently as mentor and as shield for those willing to trust in God's provision, toward the end of finishing with name-making, toward the goal of blessing to all the nations of the world.

Eve and then Adam ascended in their imaginations to the divine. Joseph descended, after youthful braggadocio, into three different kinds of pit. Years went by—it's always a long journey—and he ascended to the heights of greatness with God's spirit, a goodly partner to God.

Like Abraham, Joseph's brothers are forced by famine to go down to Egypt for provisions. God had wanted Abraham to be an instrument of blessing to all peoples. "All the clans of the earth through you shall be blessed," God promised and challenged, in the last word of the first visit (12:3). But in Egypt Abraham brought curse. Joseph completes the story begun with Abraham. He brings blessing not only to Egypt, but to all nations. Such blessing begins at home, with the family of brothers and with their father. Tested by Joseph as if by God, and led by brother Judah, the brothers and even father Jacob—challenged to relinquish a beloved son—have experienced transformation. The conclusion to the narrative of Joseph and his brothers is the conclusion, as well, to Genesis. We come to see much of the mind and ways of God, a significant realization of God's spirit in the God-partners Joseph, Judah and Jacob/Israel.

If great ones were always alert to the needs and gifts of little ones, what would the world feel like? The Joseph narrative, and Genesis as a story, conclude with just such a world. The narrator calls special attention to "the little ones," both of Egypt and in Jacob's now-burgeoning family. This blessedness is made possible through a growing partnership between God and one whom God chooses for the task. Joseph has talent and his father's favor thrust upon him, but greatness is something he must learn, painfully, and be willing to accept. In Joseph we discover a "great one," as judged by standards exquisitely and delightfully dramatized throughout Genesis and focused in its conclusion.

Through the narratives of Genesis, the mind and will of God have become more and more clear. In the character of Joseph we come very close indeed to God's ways. As the narrator repeatedly tells and shows us—and as Egyptians in power affirm—the Lord is with Joseph. He is one "in whom is the spirit of God." By the conclusion to Genesis we have come at last to a rather full portrait of God's spirit and to a playing out of God's will. Joseph is the consummate man of the world, disclosing God's longing for this world.

Remember how Joseph began, however. His normal disposition toward self-promotion was most conspicuous—braggadocio and a tattle-telling diminishment of his brothers. The Babel folk, back at the beginning, were essentially the same, making a name for themselves and thereby extending the primal urge of Eve and Adam to be more than who they were created to be. What's in a name that we are so driven, asks philosopher Kelly James Clark? "We hope to erect a self that cannot be diminished by those who know our name," he answers, " . . . to insure that we have been sized up properly and that we have instilled our worth in the mind of the other person."[13] Such a way of being in the world, claims Clark, is perfectly normal—as the Genesis text supports in each of its major narratives and prologue. Joseph's youthful bragging and tattle-telling can seem innocent enough, if taken in isolation from the rest of the Genesis story or in isolation from its own narrative development. But as Clark understands, self-promotion at the other's expense has many expressions. If "Life is a race with no other good but to be foremost," as Clark asserts, agreeing with political theorist Thomas Hobbes, then it can be a most subtle race we may kid ourselves about running. "Our self-worth is constituted comparatively. . . . We diminish the world to expand our selves."[14] And so it is that Joseph sought to diminish the world of his brothers by telling those dreams and telling those tales of brothers' wrongdoing to his father. Why did he act that way? The answer runs through all of the Genesis story.

But Joseph experiences a reorientation of this fundamental disposition to make a name for himself to a greater degree than any other character in Genesis, as is fitting for the climactic figure of the Genesis story. He becomes a God-partner clothed in a narrative glory commen-

---

[13]Kelly James Clark, *When Faith Is Not Enough* (Grand Rapids, Mich.: Eerdmans, 1997), p. 153.
[14]Ibid.

surate with his lordly garment of Egyptian finery. He walks with God
so intimately that it's as if we see God walking on earth. "Walk with
Me," God had challenged Abraham. It will remain for Israel's family to
continue the dynamics of fruitful partnership by way of a leader,
Moses, and by way of their own participation in the ways of God, ways
which will always have at their heart a blessing for all nations.

The deathly ill Israel, toward the end of Genesis, hears that Joseph
is coming. "And Israel summoned his strength and sat up in bed"
whereupon he immediately recounts his experience at Bethel where
God made promises to provide for the present and future (Genesis
48:2-4). We don't hear of God ever visiting Joseph, or telling Joseph of
the promises to Abraham, to Isaac, and to Jacob. Yet Joseph, on his
own deathbed, repeats the story's kernel, along with final reassur-
ances, to his brothers: "God will surely single you out," says Joseph,
"and take you up from this land to the land He promised to Isaac and
to Jacob" (50:24). Joseph's "trust in these promises—and in the God
who stands behind them—is perhaps the most exemplary in [Genesis],
for in order to trust in God, Joseph must also trust in the 'witness' to
God."[15] Joseph had heard and was faithful to what he had heard. "Abraham had to be hand-led by God both physically and verbally," notes a
student, "but as generations go on, God begins to 'step back' and let the
family pass along the charge to walk in [God's] ways as the nation
emerges."[16] How much more exemplary for the multitudinous people
of Israel in Exodus who would hear the "witness" of this Genesis
story—and for all hearers of the story ever after.

*And how does the Genesis story appear in retrospect from the perspec-
tive of Exodus? Jacob/Israel's family becomes a nation. A major dramatic
event in Exodus is God's gift of the Law and the reasons for its giving. Far
from a mere code of conduct and rules handed down out of the blue, the
Law is given because, as the continuing story demonstrates, without the
gift, normal people die of their own ordinary devices. The story is convincing. "Narrative enhances God's purpose," as Terence Fretheim notes, "that*

---

[15]Thomas Mann, in *The Book of the Torah: The Narrative Integrity of the Pentateuch*
(Atlanta: John Knox Press, 1988), p. 77.
[16]Jill Hohengasser, "Genesis: Learning to Walk Before God," February 28, 2000.

the law is 'for our good always . . .' (Deut. 6:24), that the law always has the best interests of the people at heart. . . . Narrative helps to show that law is fundamentally gift, not burden."[17] At the heart of Exodus is the continuing and expanding role of ordinary people willing to become partners with God, toward the truly good life. Only in that context can the Law be understood as gift, summarized perhaps in the last and most inward of the Law's challenges: do not covet. Do not envy anyone, or anyone's anything; do not strive to be number one, to make a name for yourself through position or possession. Remember, rather, with the help of God, to embrace the other, for the sake of true community—for the sake of family, for the sake of all families.

---

[17]Terence Fretheim, *Exodus* (Louisville: John Knox Press, 1991), p. 203.

CONCLUSION

T HE GENESIS STORY BEGINS WITH A PAGE OF SNAPSHOTS, ITS FIRST eleven chapters. No one is smiling. Despair wears different faces: the marriage of Adam and Eve is an ideal friendship that turns sour, the wife falling under the rule of the husband; Abel is slain by his jealous brother Cain; Lamech boasts about slaying a lad who has merely bruised him; righteous Noah, once off the ark, gets drunk and brings curse through indecent exposure; and the fearful builders of the tower at Babel try to make a name for themselves, bringing upon themselves a state of no-name—a confusion of language and global alienation.

Together, these snapshots offer a family portrait, a collage connected by family resemblance. The dark truth of each character is tied to that of the others by a similarly sinister but ordinary way of being in the world. It's all so human, so perfectly normal, this disposition to promote oneself at the other's expense. What once was—Eden's harmony, intimacy and pleasure—is lost. With unnerving clarity, this preface illustrates the distance between the ideal and its loss.

That distance becomes so great as to affect God, who changes the divine mind about the whole creation effort. By the time of Noah—after the fiasco in Eden with Eve and Adam, and after the fratricide of Cain, and after the savage killing and boasting of Lamech—God has had enough. We read that God is so filled with regret about the whole creation effort, that nothing less than total annihilation of creation will do (6:5-7). Quickly, however, God once again changes the divine mind. Noah's righteousness gives God the idea of a second beginning for the human race, starting with Noah and his family. So most—but not all—will be destroyed by floodwaters (6:17). But things still don't turn out. The last snapshot reveals the scrambling and the sorrow at Babel.

And now it is that God changes direction in dealing with humankind, a near reversal of divine demeanor. Beginning with Abraham, Sarah and Hagar, God will work cooperatively and slowly, over entire lifetimes, with recalcitrant humans. God no longer favors unilateral and devastating measures from on high, as in the Flood devastation or Babel dispersal.

In the image of God: the divine task would seem overwhelming, given the divine power of choice given humankind, an imaging of the divine with which God does not tamper. Beginning with Abraham and Sarah, God is faced with the same human insecurities and self-promotion and destroyed relationships that are captured in the prefatory snapshots. This normal way of being in the world is on full display in the four-generation mayhem that makes up the main body of the Genesis story, from Abraham and Sarah through Isaac, then Jacob, and then Jacob's twelve children, including Joseph. Even at the end, father Jacob, renamed Israel, needs a final and major reorientation; he will need to let go of a beloved son for the sake of the greater family and for life itself. The destroying and dispersing God of the preface is imperial and quick. Beginning with the lifetime of visits with Abraham, God slows down to the human experience of time, to the human need for waking up to oneself and for change.

Such reorientation, in Genesis, is a two-way street. For the major portion of the Genesis story, beginning with Abraham, God is portrayed as tailoring the divine way of responding to wrongheadedness, depending on the individual and his or her distinct manner of self-aggrandizement and deep sorrow. Furthermore, God solicits help from chosen partners-in-the-making toward the goal of global blessing. God wants a return to the ideals of harmony and pleasure and intimacy.

Global blessing may be what God finally wants, but blessing must begin at home. A great deal of divine attention is focused on members of troubled families. God won't enforce the divine will: God waits on human will. Unless select human partners choose well—choose God's will as it works out in their individual cases—God's wishes will not be implemented. There is always the very real possibility, of course, that God's challenge to would-be partners won't be met. What would God do? Choose another partner, presumably, and wait, and work with that one. Exodus, the story following Genesis, reveals the same God, though with a wider lens. The Genesis focus on partnership is expanded and complicated in Exodus; God's need for such partnership appears heightened. Later Hebrew narrative, too, demonstrates what is implied by the Genesis story: God will choose Saul as king for the people of Israel, but Saul doesn't work out; God moves on and replaces that bad choice with a good one, King David. God has real choice. Humans have real choice. Saul chooses poorly, and God moves on to the next possibility.

Genesis represents a world of action in which both God and mortal have real choice, including changes of mind and heart. This is the highest possibility of drama: resolve among clashing human wills is vastly complicated by the need for resolve, also, between human desire and God's desires.

With their normal self-promoting choices, human beings invariably destroy themselves and wreck communities. Only God can help, says the Genesis story. In sovereign greatness, God refuses to force human choice. This God works with and depends on human partners who choose to become reoriented—from making a name for themselves toward the blessing of others. Such transformation is slow and arduous. God waits. Captured in one of the world's best-told stories, this dynamic between God and various individuals leads from the universal chaos of Babel to blessing for all the earth's peoples. It actually happens! This is the Bible story in microcosm, in blueprint form. This is the Genesis story we haven't heard.

God is unchanging in the divine determination to work toward transformation and blessing. But God changes tactics and direction, depending on the individual.

Individual number one: because of her husband Abraham's self-promoting subterfuge, Sarah becomes another man's wife; she must wait years for her double vindication, from an earthly potentate and then immediately from the Most High. With Abraham, God visits seven times over a lifetime of transformation. Hagar is a nameless slavegirl to her owners, Abraham and Sarah. By God, however, Hagar is named—and seen, truly seen. Carefully the text reveals that the outcast Hagar is, for God, part of the story's predominant vision. Hagar is provided for by God, and promised great progeny. The structuring of the text itself provides for Hagar: granted seed through son Ishmael, a nation is built up and recorded as a genealogy that concludes the entire story of Abraham and Sarah. So it is that the original and most essential promise to Abraham is brought full circle. Through Abraham's seed, *all* nations will indeed be blessed.

Individual number two: while sharing common and normal ways of being in the world, Jacob is very different from Abraham, and God responds differently. Jacob and twin Esau have been alienated, separated for years by Jacob's sly self-promotion and Esau's murderous rage: God focuses divine effort on the most troublesome but promising of the twins, the younger. God mysteriously appears in the guise of a nighttime stranger, locked in struggle with Jacob. God wrestles with the one who wrestles away what he can for himself. Jacob is declared a winner. The one who strives with God is blessed, not in spite of striving with God but because of it. This is a special story, as all individuals have their separate stories with God; this is the case of someone called Jacob and renamed Israel after the wrestling match. Jacob's bickering wives—needed as partners to God's enterprise along with Jacob—vie for their husband's favor and seed: God again changes tack by letting Jacob take the lead in dealing with the problem.

Individual number three: in the concluding narrative of the Genesis story we find a final stage of escalating family tangle. Focused in a late-born braggart favored by his father, sibling rivalry among all twelve brothers tears the family apart. Strife leads to a most improbable but totally believable resolve that includes a reluctant and still-favoring father. God again responds with Joseph and the family in a distinctly different style. God backs way off. There are no divine visits with Joseph that we know about, no wrestling matches, no dance of divine promise and corresponding human challenge. Is God behind the arranging of the three descents suffered by Joseph, down into the wilderness pit, down into Egypt, down into the prison-pit? Do these descents allow Joseph clarity of vision and the will to undergo transformation? What the concluding narrative of Genesis dramatizes is Joseph's growth, his rising up as the most God-like character in the Genesis story. Joseph is God's human partner perfected. Joseph accomplishes on earth the blessing for all peoples desired by the Most High, expressed in the cornerstone promise to Abraham that began the Genesis story.

"Minor characters" too are affected by God's presence, though one might argue that, given the story's moral vision of blessing to all peoples, there are no minor characters. Smaller dramatic roles nonetheless point to the new thing God is intending for all peoples. Sarah has her shame removed by an earthly king and heavenly potentate; Hagar comes to be named, seen, and blessed by God; Rachel and Leah discover the possibility of speaking and acting in one voice, rather than vying to "win out"; ultimate rascal Laban is blessed by minor rascal Jacob's work habits; Judah's reorientation moves from self-aggrandizement, at a favored brother's expense, to self-giving on behalf of that brother—which action is undertaken, also, to spare yet another favored brother and still-favoring father.

How God operates through all of this is as varied as are the individuals. How God responds and initiates has a breathtaking range: God can grieve and change the divine mind as in the flood days; or God can change the divine course of action from unilaterally "giving up" on the human scene as in the preface to tailor-made responses that include, always, divine patience, a willingness to wait, and an invitation to "come on board" toward blessing for this family and all families. This is the Genesis story we haven't heard, at least not very well.

Our conventional habits of reading or hearing or studying a text like Genesis in bits and pieces prohibit full understanding and in fact promote misunderstanding. We have looked at contexts, especially those contexts involving repetition. One of the most interesting repetitions in all of Genesis actually holds much of the story together. It occurs with Joseph testing his brothers, an echo of how God tested Abraham—and Jacob. The three major narratives are tied together by this explicit echoing.

How, then, do we avoid misunderstanding? How can we hear better? Let's review, in conclusion, this repetition of testing. Who does it, and to whom, and for what purpose?

At the climactic moment of Andrew Lloyd Webber's popular *Joseph and the Amazing Technicolor Dreamcoat,* the Egyptian lord Joseph, transplanted from Canaan, grants an audience to his ten older brothers. Years before, as we have seen, the brothers had done Joseph terrible wrong, the result of a most normal sibling rivalry. Bowing low, the brothers don't recognize Joseph, who, however, recognizes them. Joseph chooses to remain incognito, figuring that this is his chance. In Webber's version, Joseph wants the brothers to grovel. In a grotesquely fascinating dance, they grovel—to the beat of Webber's musical rock. But Webber almost certainly has it wrong.

It's easy to miss what goes on throughout the Genesis story, including the last narrative about Joseph and his brothers. At the beginning Joseph is seventeen, a perfectly hateful youngster. He's a tattletale and a braggart. His adolescent way of being in the world is so normal as to appear innocent. His father compounds the problem by favoring Joseph. The little kid brother dreams that his older brothers—and father and mother—will some day bow down to him. He prattles on about his two dreams, for no helpful purpose. His family is stunned. Over twenty years later, Joseph has reversed himself from self-promotion and harm toward habits and skills that bring blessing to others. His brothers, driven by famine, are bowing before Joseph. Webber's musical version could seem to have good warrant for its "take" on Joseph's motives. He subjects his brothers, as we have seen, to a series of what can appear at first as capricious and torturous tests. The narrator explains nothing, as is usually the case: what Joseph is doing with his brothers must be figured out by the reader.

How do we proceed in figuring out whether this is testing or teasing? We have looked for contexts, for connections—especially for anything repeated. Joseph has God with him, and we hear a repetition, a very strong echo back to God's testing of Abraham. In Abraham's story, at the climactic moment, God comes up with a test to cap all prior six tests, a seemingly capricious and most torturous challenge: Give me back the son I've given you. Joseph, similarly, comes up with a test that will include, among other good goals, the possibility that his father choose to relinquish a prized son. As the major narratives end, so they began—only now, a fully matured Joseph challenges his brothers and father as God challenged Abraham. The testings devised by both God and Joseph are designed in such a way that those who are tested come to a recognition of an insufficient way of being in the world, toward a reorientation of self-promoting interests. God works with Abraham, won't choose for Abraham, must wait on Abraham, isn't sure about Abraham (22:12, 18). Joseph works with his brothers, won't choose for them, must wait on them, isn't sure about them. Will they change at all, recognizing their life of normalcy and wrong? Will they choose for life, for family, for the future? Only then will Joseph allow himself to be recognized.

The climax of Joseph's story echoes precisely the resolve of Abraham's story. Father Jacob's great challenge, issued from a now-transformed Judah—partner with God—is to relinquish a beloved son. Abraham's last test and greatest challenge, issued him from God, is the relinquishment of his beloved son. Abraham's greatest challenge is tied to his first test, with which the story opens: Abraham is challenged to relinquish his father's house, and his relatives, and his native land. Relinquishment defines the dramatic contours of both stories, but to what point? Abraham has clung to his own life at the expense of his wife's sexual chastity; at the end of his life he learns to relinquish a life dearer even than his own life. Finally, Abraham moves beyond parochial clutching and proves himself a worthy partner to God; he comes to will what God wills. This is what God wants, of course, but won't force. God must do what God can with Abraham—nudge, prod, challenge, promise and wait. God needs Abraham, or someone who will say yes, for implementation of the divine will. Not until the end of many years, the end of the story, is God sure about the one he has chosen for such an arduous and unnatural task: Now I know about you, God says. Now I can make good on promises because you have made good on the challenges (22:12). Now I can count on you as a fit partner to my goal of bringing blessing to all nations (22:18). Only at the end of

Jacob's life, with Joseph "on board" as God's fully cooperating partner, is father Jacob—now renamed Israel—able to offer blessing to a foreign potentate (47:7, 10). God chooses to rely on a chosen few to bring blessing for many; such partnership means painful relinquishment and reorientation of normal ways of being in the world. This is the Genesis story we haven't heard.

Joseph's lordliness is a peculiar thing, resembling as it does God's sovereignty. In this Genesis story, God's majesty is evidenced not in the unfolding of a fully resolved blueprint for the future, but in divine accommodations to feeble but potentially receptive human wills. God's greatness lies in nudgings and proddings—and in the arranging of trying circumstances. So too, the presiding genius of the powerful Joseph. When faced by these brothers who have plotted his diminishment for their own ascendancy, who have torn the family apart and broken a father's heart, Joseph acts with psychological acumen—like God has done with Abraham. What the brothers learn from Joseph's testing is the same complex and demanding lesson that their great-grandfather Abraham learned from God: letting go of the normal and parochial ways of being in the world. The Genesis God, and Joseph, are not inscrutable or capricious. Neither God nor Joseph revel in anything like inscrutable majesties; they are not interested in others groveling before their auspicious power. God and Joseph both want individual reorientation and a measure of reciprocity from those over whom they have power; each desires blessing for all peoples. Herein is a Joseph easily mistaken. Herein is a God we haven't quite recognized. This is the story we haven't heard.

Meanwhile, Joseph has brought blessing to all nations of the earth, completing the story's initial promise to Abraham (41:57; 12:3). All stands or falls on how potential partners choose. Choose what? Without being coerced, they can choose God's vision that all the world's peoples will be blessed (12:3; 22:18). Without that other-directed orientation, nothing personal is worthwhile, nor can anything personal be gained—including "fulfillment." This is the Genesis question: Will the chosen ones accept the painful journey of a lifetime toward relinquishment and reorientation of normal choicemaking? Will they choose transformation in the direction of God's will for reconciliation? This is the question for Joseph and his brothers. If this family can let go of parochial and self-promoting choices toward embrace of the other, with tears and conversation (they do!), and toward blessing of a foreign people (Jacob does!), they will become the "people of Israel," the priests of God to a troubled world as suggested in Exodus. This is the Genesis story we haven't heard, of Abraham, Sarah and Hagar; of Jacob and Esau, Leah and Rachel; and of Joseph and his family. Such hearing illuminates our own journeying, should we say yes on behalf of that which defies our normal way of being in the world, for something far better.

There has emerged for me over many years a story with organic and compelling unity, a story carrying cosmic weight but with a penetrating light into private spaces I had kept hidden even from myself. This is the story I have tried to re-tell, a story that challenges our conventional ideas about God, about human transformation, and about what constitutes the truly good life. Genesis is foundational, the original ethos and the original blessing. It is a story of loss and recovery, of fear and letting go. Reorientation of normal and destructive ways of being in the world is achieved in community, in partnership between divine and human, and in a self-giving consideration of the other. It is the beginning and the end of everything that many of us, believers or otherwise, long to hear.

Selected Bibliography

Ackerman, James S. "Joseph, Judah, and Jacob." In *Literary Interpretations of Biblical Narratives*, Vol. 2, edited by Kenneth R. R. Gros Louis, with James S. Ackerman and Thayer Warshaw. Nashville: Abingdon, 1982.

———. "The Literary Context of the Moses Birth Story." In *Literary Interpretations of Biblical Narratives*, Vol. 1., edited by Kenneth R. R. Gros Louis, with James S. Ackerman and Thayer Warshaw. Nashville: Abingdon, 1974.

Alter, Robert. *The Art of Biblical Narrative*. New York: Basic Books, 1981.

———. *Genesis: Translation and Commentary*. New York: W. W. Norton, 1996.

Auerbach, Erich. *Mimesis: The Representation of Reality in Western Literature*. 1942. Reprint, New York: Doubleday/Anchor, 1953.

Biddle, Mark E. "The 'Endangered Ancestress' and Blessing for the Nations." *Journal of Biblical Literature* 109 (Winter 1990): 599-611.

Bray, Gerald. "The Promises Made to Abraham and the Destiny of Israel." *Scottish Bulletin of Evangelical Theology* 7 (August 1989): 69-87.

Brueggemann, Walter. *Exodus*. In *The New Interpreter's Bible*, Vol. 1, edited by Leander E. Keck et al. Nashville: Abingdon, 1994.

———. "Genesis 17:1-22." *Interpretation* 45 (June 1991): 55-59.

———. *Genesis*. Atlanta: John Knox Press, 1982.

Buber, Martin. "Abraham the Seer." In *On the Bible*. New York: Schocken, 1968.

Calvin, John. *Institutes of the Christian Religion*, translated by Ford Lewis Battles. Philadelphia: Westminster Press, 1960.

Cassuto, U. *A Commentary on the Book of Genesis, Part Two: From Noah to Abraham*, translated by Israel Abrahams. Jerusalem: The Magnes Press, The Hebrew University, 1984.

Chaucer, Geoffrey. "The Franklin's Tale." In *The Canterbury Tales*. New York: Bantam, 1964.

Clark, Kelly James. *When Faith Is Not Enough*. Grand Rapids, Mich.: Eerdmans, 1997.

Coats, George W. *Genesis, with an Introduction to Narrative Literature*. Grand Rapids, Mich.: Eerdmans, 1983.

Dickinson, Emily. *The Complete Poems of Emily Dickinson*, edited by Thomas H. Johnson. 1890. Reprint, Boston: Little, Brown and Company, 1960.

Dods, Marcus. *Genesis Commentary*. In *The Expositor's Bible*, edited by W. Robertson Nicoll. New York: A. C. Armstrong and Son, 1903.

Douglas, J. D., ed. *New Bible Dictionary*. Grand Rapids, Mich.: Eerdmans, 1962.

Dumbrell, William. "The Covenant with Abraham." *The Reformed Theological Review* 38 (May-August 1982): 42-50.

Eliot, T. S. *Four Quartets*. 1943. Reprint, New York: Harcourt Brace & Company, 1971.

Fewell, Dana Nolan. "Divine Calls, Human Responses: Another Look at Abram and Sarai." *Perkins Journal* 41 (October 1988): 13-16.

Fewell, Dana Nolan, and David M. Gunn. *Gender, Power, & Promise: The Subject of the Bible's First Story.* Nashville: Abingdon, 1993.

Fishbane, Michael. *Text and Texture: Close Readings of Selected Biblical Texts.* New York: Schocken, 1979.

Fokkelman, J. P. *Narrative Art in Genesis: Specimens of Stylistic and Structural Analysis.* Assen, The Netherlands: Van Gorcum, 1975.

Fox, Everett. *The Five Books of Moses.* New York: Schocken, 1995.

Francisco, Clyde T. *Genesis.* In *The Broadman Bible Commentary,* Vol. 1, revised. Nashville: Broadman, 1973.

Frei, Hans. *The Eclipse of Biblical Narrative: A Study in Eighteenth and Nineteenth Century Hermeneutics.* New Haven, Conn.: Yale University Press, 1974.

Fretheim, Terence. *Exodus.* Louisville: John Knox Press, 1991.

———. *Genesis.* In *The New Interpreter's Bible,* Vol. 1, edited by Leander E. Keck et al. Nashville: Abingdon, 1994.

Hamilton, Victor P. *The Book of Genesis 1–17.* Grand Rapids, Mich.: Eerdmans, 1990.

Heschel, Abraham Joshua. *God in Search of Man: A Philosophy of Judaism.* Northvale, N.J.: Jason Aronson, 1987.

Hopkins, David. "Between Promise and Fulfillment: Von Rad and the 'Sacrifice of Abraham.' " *Biblische Zeitschrift* 24 (1980): 180-93.

Hunter, Alastair G. "Father Abraham: A Structural and Theological Study of the Yahwist's Presentation of the Abraham Material." *Journal for the Study of the Old Testament* 35 (June 1986): 3-27.

Janzen, Gerald J. *Abraham and All the Families of the Earth: A Commentary on the Book of Genesis 12–50.* Grand Rapids, Mich.: Eerdmans, 1993.

Kidner, Derek. *Genesis: An Introduction and Commentary.* Downers Grove, Ill.: Inter-Varsity Press, 1967.

Kierkegaard, Søren. *Fear and Trembling: The Sickness unto Death,* translated by Walter Lowrie. 1941. Reprint, Princeton, N.J.: Princeton University Press, 1954.

Kikawada, Isaac, and Arthur Quinn. *Before Abraham Was: The Unity of Genesis 1–11.* Nashville: Abingdon, 1985.

Klein, Ralph W. "Call, Covenant, and Community: The Story of Abraham and Sarah." *Currents in Theology and Missions* 1 (1988): 120-27.

Louis, Kenneth R. R. Gros. "Abraham II." In *Literary Interpretations of Biblical Narratives,* Vol. 1. Nashville: Abingdon, 1974.

Mann, Thomas. *The Book of the Torah: The Narrative Integrity of the Pentateuch.* Atlanta: John Knox Press, 1988.

Miscal, Peter D. *The Workings of Old Testament Narrative.* Philadelphia: Fortress, 1983.

Oates, Whitney J. *Basic Writings of St. Augustine.* New York: Random House, 1948.

Plaut, W. Gunther, ed. *The Torah: A Modern Commentary.* New York: Jewish Publication Society (Union of American Hebrew Congregations), 1981.

Polzin, Robert. "The Ancestress of Israel in Danger." *Semeia* 3 (1975): 81-97.

Rad, Gerhard von. *Genesis: A Commentary,* translated by John H. Marks. Philadelphia: Westminster Press, 1961.

Rogers, Martha. "The Call of Abram: A Systems Theory Analysis." *Journal of Psychology and Theology* 9 (1981): 111-43.

Ronning, John. "The Naming of Isaac: The Role of the Wife/Sister Episodes in the Redaction of Genesis." *Westminster Theological Journal* 53 (1991): 1-27.

Roop, Eugene. *Genesis.* Scottsdale, Penn.: Herald, 1987.

Saltzman, Steven. *A Small Glimmer of Light: Reflections on the Book of Genesis.* Hoboken, N.J.: KTAV, 1966.

Sanders, John. *The God Who Risks: A Theology of Providence.* Downers Grove, Ill.: InterVarsity Press, 1998.

Sarna, Nahum. *Understanding Genesis.* New York: McGraw-Hill, 1966.

———. *JPS Torah Commentary: Genesis.* Philadelphia: The Jewish Publication Society, 1989.

Speiser, E. A. *Genesis.* Anchor Bible. New York: Doubleday, 1964.

Sternberg, Meir. *The Poetics of Biblical Narrative: Ideological Literature and the Drama of Reading.* Bloomington, Ind.: Indiana University Press, 1987.

Sutherland, Dixon. "The Organization of the Abraham Promise Narrative." *Zeitschrift für die alttestamentliche Wissenschaft* 95 (1983): 337-43.

Trible, Phyllis. *Texts of Terror: Literary-Feminist Readings of Biblical Narratives.* Philadelphia: Fortress, 1984.

Turner, Laurence A. *Genesis.* Sheffield, England: Sheffield Academic Press, 2000.

Van Seters, John. *Abraham in History and Tradition.* New Haven, Conn.: Yale University Press, 1975.

Vawter, Bruce. *On Genesis: A New Reading.* New York: Doubleday, 1977.

Wenham, Gordon J. "The Story of Abraham." In *Genesis 1-15.* Word Biblical Commentary. Waco, Tex.: Word, 1987.

Westermann, Claus. *Elements of Old Testament Theology,* translated by Douglas W. Stott. Atlanta: John Knox Press, 1982.

———. *Genesis 1-11: A Commentary,* translated by John J. Scullion, S.J. Minneapolis: Augsburg, 1984

———. *Genesis 12-36: A Commentary,* translated by John J. Scullion, S.J. Minneapolis: Augsburg, 1981.

———. *The Promises to the Fathers,* translated by David E. Green. Philadelphia: Fortress, 1980.

Subject Index

For further information related to this book, its themes or its author, Paul Borgman, visit the website < www.gordon.edu/genesis >.